EUROPE AND THE WIDER WORLD

Contributors

*Bernard Waites • Paul Lewis • Alan Sharpe • Ken Ward •
Grahame Thompson*

Edited by Bernard Waites

The Open University and European Association of Distance Teaching
Universities

London and New York

A note for the general reader

Europe and the Wider World forms part of a second level course in the humanities and social sciences. The English language version of the *What is Europe?* course is produced by the Open University in conjunction with the European Association of Distance Teaching Universities. Open University students are provided with supplementary teaching material, including a *Course Guide*, which gives a complete list of all printed and audio-visual components.

What is Europe?

Book 1   *The History of the Idea of Europe*

Book 2   *Aspects of European Cultural Diversity*

Book 3   *European Democratic Culture*

Book 4   *Europe and the Wider World*

First published in 1993 by
The Open University, Walton Hall, Milton Keynes, MK7 6AA

Revised edition first published in 1995 by
The Open University, Walton Hall, Milton Keynes MK7 6AA
                        and
Routledge
11 New Fetter Lane, London EC4P 4EE

Simultaneously published in the USA and Canada by
Routledge
29 West 35th Street, New York, NY 10001

Edited, designed and typeset by the Open University

Printed in the United Kingdom by Bell and Bain Ltd., Glasgow

British Library Cataloguing in Publication Data
A catalogue record for this book is available from the British Library

Library of Congress Cataloguing in Publication Data
A catalogue record for this book has been requested

ISBN 0-415-12420-4
ISBN 0-415-12421-2 (pbk)

The other institutions which participated in the creation of *What is Europe?* were:

Open universiteit,
Valkenburgerweg 167,
PO Box 2960,
6401 DL Heerlen,
The Netherlands

Jysk Åbent Universitet,
Nordre Ringgade 1,
DK – 8000 Århus C,
Denmark

Deutsches Institut für Fernstudien an der Universität Tübingen,
Post Fach 1569,
7400 Tübingen 1,
Germany

Fédération Interuniversitaire
de l'Enseignement à Distance,
l'Université Paris X
200 Avenue de la République,
92001 Nanterre,
France

Contents

NOTE: Where there is no English-language published version, the quotations from German authors that appear in these essays have been translated by Monica Shelley; quotations from other foreign authors have been translated by the author or editor.

General preface to 'What is Europe?'

Kevin Wilson, Chair of the European Association of Distance Teaching Universities (EADTU) Humanities Programme Committee

The four books in the *What is Europe?* series are the product of a collaborative enterprise under the direction of the Humanities Programme Committee of the European Association of Distance Teaching Universities (EADTU). The universities involved in the project are:

- The Open universiteit, The Netherlands

- Jysk Åbent Universitet (the Jutland Open University)

- The Deutsches Institut für Fernstudien an der Universität Tübingen

- The Centre d'Analyse des Savoirs Contemporains at the Université des Sciences Humaines de Strasbourg on behalf of the Fédération Interuniversitaire de l'Enseignement à Distance

- The UK Open University

The Humanities Programme Committee of the EADTU was established in late 1988 with a brief to promote joint course development. The four books in this series were designed as the academic core of its first course which was first presented by the Open University in 1993. For this new edition, the course team have revised and updated the original materials so that they can be made available to students of European Studies at universities and colleges not involved in the EADTU programme in Europe, the United States and beyond.

Starting to plan a course on Europe in the heady year of 1989 was both a challenge and an opportunity. With Europe in a state of flux, we quickly rejected as too narrow the idea of a course focused only on the European Community. We dismissed just as quickly the idea of a European history course, not on grounds of irrelevance, but because numerous such courses were already available. Instead we agreed to write a course on European identity in its various historical, cultural, social, political and economic aspects. This topic was at the centre of the debate on Europe, called for a wide-ranging approach across academic boundaries and stood to benefit from the different national perspectives that could be harnessed to the project.

The course has four objectives:

1 To provide a context for the understanding of contemporary European developments through a consideration of the history of the idea of Europe.

2 To consider aspects of European cultural diversity through investigations into language, education, mass-media and everyday culture.

3 To examine the theory, function and practice of democracy as, arguably, fundamental components of European culture.

5

4   To locate Europe as a political and economic entity in a context of global change.

These objectives – and the European nature of the course – are reflected in the titles and provenance of the respective books:

1   *The History of the Idea of Europe* is a Dutch–Danish collaboration.

2   *Aspects of European Cultural Diversity* emanates from Germany, though one of the authors is British.

3   *European Democratic Culture* is a French product, though there are Italian, German and British, as well as French, contributors to the book.

4   *Europe and the Wider World* comes from the UK.

We have framed the title of the series as a question – *What is Europe?* – yet we are under no illusion that there is a simple, straightforward answer, or even a series of agreed definitions that satisfy. Nor are we making the assumption that Europe is stamped with a unique identity, or that it has a manifest destiny, or that a singular meaning is revealed in its history.

We follow in the footsteps of Hugh Seton-Watson, who tells us that 'the word "Europe" has been used and misused, interpreted and misinterpreted in as many different meanings as almost any word in any language. There have been and are many Europes…'[1] The question, then, is a provocative device to set you thinking, and to prompt further questions. Instead of rushing into definitions we have approached the topic from a number of points of view and from the standpoint of various methodologies, raising questions as we go about how 'Europe' has been conceptualized, organized, structured and utilized, both in the past and in the present. The contributors to this series do not have any particular axes to grind. The essays are not propaganda pieces for a 'European spirit', cultural unity, a single market, political union, or any other European project. On the contrary, they are scholarly explorations designed to enhance our understanding of the many facets of European identity.

So, the essays cover a wide canvas. They deal with various ideas of Europe in the past and present; with different aspects of everyday life and associated tensions making for cultural uniformity or accentuating cultural difference; with a political culture founded on public opinion, law and democracy; and with Europe's relationship with the United States, Russia and the developing countries and with its place in the world economy.

The series as a whole presents Europe as a work in progress rather than a finished product, a construction yard rather than a museum. As a project Europe can never be completed. It will always need to be re-made, emancipated from the past, re-invented.

[1] SETON-WATSON, H. (1985) 'What is Europe, where is Europe?: from mystique to politique', *Encounter*, July/August, vol. LX, No. 2, p. 9.

Introduction to Book 4

The essays in this volume have been specially written for the course *What is Europe?* which the UK Open University prepared in collaboration with a number of European distance-teaching universities. The selection of essay themes was governed by the overall needs of the course and was not intended to be comprehensive. Rather, the aim was to highlight certain historical and contemporary features of European relationships with the wider world at a time when the political, economic and cultural identity of 'Europe' was undergoing revolutionary transformation with the completion of the Single Market (and the prospect of monetary union) in the European Community, and the collapse of Soviet hegemony and communist power in eastern and central Europe.

'The Plum-pudding in danger; – or – State Epicures taking un Petit Souper' by James Gillray, 1805. One of Gillray's most brilliant political satires, showing Napoleon and Pitt dividing the world between them (illustration: Mansell Collection).

The contents of the essays can be briefly described: Bernard Waites provides a historically wide-ranging essay entitled 'Europe and the Third World' which analyses European imperial and colonial expansion into what we now call the 'underdeveloped' world in terms suggested by 'dependency' and 'world system' theorists. He is generally sceptical as to whether the exploitation of resources in the colonial 'periphery' contributed significantly to Europe's own development and, though he acknowledges that European colonialism distorted economic growth in the Third World, argues that it cannot be considered a major cause of present-day global inequality. His conclusion is that the political impact of the European presence in the underdeveloped world – manifested, for example, in the sovereign state borders of contemporary Africa and the Middle East – has been more consequential than the economic.

Paul Lewis's essay entitled 'Europe and Russia' has been placed next in this volume because it, too, is historically wide-ranging. There is an acknowledged ambiguity in his title because Russia is European in culture, in its Orthodox Christian tradition, and in the ethnic ties of its people with other Slavs, but as a state, it has been periodically cut off from the mainstream of European development by Tatar conquest, the patrimonialism of the tsars, the persistence of serfdom, and revolutionary upheaval. Throughout most of its history, Russia has been an imperial power on the eastern borders of Europe, ruling large minorities of non-Russians and intervening with military force when its imperial interests were threatened. Thus, there were broad parallels between the Soviet Union's intervention in Hungary in 1956 and in Czechoslovakia in 1968, and tsarist Russia's march into Hungary in 1849 (when it helped crush the democratic revolution). With the accession of Mikhail Gorbachev in 1985, public pronouncements indicated a desire on the Soviet leadership's part to enter (or re-enter) the 'Common European House'. Lewis discusses what this meant in greater detail, but we could think of it as an attempt to realign (declining) international power with cultural identity, or in other words bring the Soviet Union's stance in international relations into accord with Russia's cultural traditions as a European nation. How far this realignment will proceed is one of the great imponderables of contemporary European politics. The essential prerequisites for the incorporation of Russia in a trading bloc of politically congenial European states are a viable 'mixed' economy and democratic development under the rule of law. Governments of the leading industrial nations can do something to facilitate the process; students of contemporary Europe can only wait and see.

Our third essay, by Alan Sharp and Ken Ward, is almost wholly concerned with relations between the United States and Europe during the period of global 'bipolarity', when the continent was divided politically, economically and ideologically, and the two great flanking powers enjoyed a preponderant role in their respective spheres. Just how we should characterize the United States' relations with western Europe during this period is a matter of considerable interest, and Sharp and Ward stress the ambiguities and multiple layers of the relationship, analysing the cultural dimensions of American influence, as well as the political and economic. Despite the presence of American forces, the United States' preponderance did not rest upon the threat of force and, as Gaullist France demonstrated,

European states could follow independent foreign (and supposedly independent defence) policies without fear of sanction. Particularly in the late 1940s and 1950s, American influence in western Europe stemmed from economic and industrial strength and its willingness to finance European economic recovery through the Marshall Plan. The relative decline of the American economy, and the integration of western Europe into a single trading bloc which excludes (or threatens to exclude) US agricultural exports, have sapped the basis of American influence and weakened enthusiasm for maintaining expensive military commitments in Europe. Whether the exacerbation of trading disputes will precipitate a complete withdrawal from Europe is another issue for whose resolution we will have to wait and see.

The final essay by Grahame Thompson entitled 'Europe and the global economy' analyses the economic integration of western Europe up to the completion of the Single Market and the Maastricht treaty on European Union – whose future is even now undecided. Questions raised by Thompson are why economic integration was so much more successful in western than in central and eastern Europe and what trading patterns and international institutions will emerge in the economic vacuum created in the former Soviet bloc by the collapse of the Council for Mutual Economic Aid (Comecon). But he is more concerned to locate the EC in an emergent 'globalizing economy', which increasingly determines economic decision-making in the individual economies that constitute it. 'Globalization' – as he demonstrates – is not leading to a simple integration of the world's different economic regions. The underdeveloped world is being increasingly marginalized in terms of world trade and foreign investment, while the advanced industrial nations are clustering in three trading blocs (western Europe, North America and the Pacific Rim) of roughly equal size and economic strength. Whether this triadic division can avoid the type of economic whirlwind which swept round the world in 1931, when world trade collapsed and foreign investment (wherever located) was repatriated on a massive scale, is the final issue Thompson addresses. He is cautiously optimistic. Knowing the terrible consequences of the economic crisis of the 1930s for Europe and the wider world, so must we be.

These essays are, as far as possible, written in non-technical language. Though they are supported in the Open University course by documentary sources and commentaries, they are nevertheless self-standing and comprehensible to the lay reader. We hope they will reach an audience outside the student body for whom they are primarily intended.

Essay 1
Europe and the Third World

Prepared for the Course Team by Bernard Waites
Lecturer in European Humanities Studies, The Open
University

Introduction

The term the 'Third World' was coined in 1952 when the French demographer, Alfred Sauvy, used it to refer to the 'underdeveloped' countries outside the orbits of the two superpowers, the USA and the USSR. The historical context which gave the expression meaning was the Cold War, which polarized the globe between two hostile 'worlds' based on incompatible economic systems, capitalism and socialism. In this situation, Sauvy argued, the existence of a 'third' world of poor neutral states was in danger of being forgotten. Like the 'third estate' in pre-revolutionary France, the Third World was unrepresented in international fora and now wished to stand up for itself (see Lacoste, 1980, pp. 10–18).

In subsequent years, the Third World did become an organized body in international relations in the form of the Movement of Non-aligned States, whose origins go back to the efforts of Nehru of India, Sukarno of Indonesia and Nasser of Egypt to negotiate an independent political path for the 'emergent' nations between the Cold War power blocs. The struggle against European colonialism had been a common experience of this first generation of 'non-aligned' leaders and, as decolonization swept through Asia and Africa in the 1950s and 1960s, so newly-independent countries were recruited to the non-aligned with the same ideological solidarity. The Movement was not formally constituted until the third non-aligned summit at Lusaka in 1970, by when the original concern with East–West conflict had shifted towards the threats posed by 'imperialism, colonialism and neocolonialism' (to quote the conference *Declaration*), and the unresolved crisis of white domination in southern Africa. Since then, the Non-aligned Movement has put forward a common programme of demands for more equitable exchange between the industrialized and less developed countries in its campaign for a New International Economic Order, launched at Algiers in 1973 (Lyon, 1984, pp. 229–36; Mortimer, 1980). Unfortunately, both the unity of economic interests and political solidarity of the non-aligned have proved fragile, and the Movement has been quite ineffectual in the face of international conflicts within the Third World, such as the Iran–Iraq war of 1980–1989.

Forty years on, there is no sign of Sauvy's coinage passing into disuse – in the English-speaking world at least – even though the international context which originally made it meaningful has been transformed by the end of the Cold War and the 'liberalization' of formerly socialist economies throughout the world (including communist China's). Furthermore, though it may have been valid in the early 1950s to think of the 'underdeveloped' societies as constituting a single bloc with a common range of economic problems, this is no longer satisfactory. Four decades of development have resulted in the marked differentiation of the 'less developed countries'. The world demand for oil, and the quadrupling of its price by the OPEC cartel in 1973, transformed a handful of desert sheikdoms into the world's richest societies in terms of per capita GNP. A group of newly industrializing countries, of which the economies of the Pacific Rim are the most successful, has emerged to compete with the established industrial powers in international markets for consumer and capital goods. At the same time, the poorest societies of sub-Saharan Africa and south Asia have had their developmental problems exacerbated by the rising cost of energy imports, adverse movements in the terms of trade for their major exports, unmanageable demographic growth and (in much of Africa) ecological deterioration and persistent drought. In many, per capita GNP has declined since 1970. Summing up the growth trends, one economist has written:

> The most significant development since 1945 is *not* a widening of the average gap between Third-World and OECD countries. Some widening seems to have occurred, but more significant is the sharp pulling apart of growth rates *within* the Third World itself.
>
> *(Reynolds, 1985, p. 392)*

Despite these developmental changes, humanity remains divided by gross disparities between the material well-being of most people in the 'developed world' of Europe, North America and Japan, and the mass poverty which persists in Asia, Africa and Latin America. Of course, the poor are still with us in Europe, and a less developed country such as India can now boast a substantial stratum of the urban and rural population who have benefited from the economic growth in the subcontinent since 1947. But an estimated 50 per cent of India's rural population (still the overwhelming majority) have incomes around or below a level barely sufficient to secure the minimum of food required to sustain the human body. In the subcontinent as a whole, between 250 and 300 million people are chronically undernourished. According to World Bank estimates, throughout the developing countries around a third of the population (about 730 million people) suffer undernourishment; maybe as many as 40 million die each year from hunger and hunger-related diseases. (Raychaudhuri, 1985, p. 801; Drèze and Sen, 1989, pp. 35–6)

The 'Third World' is indefensible as a term of analysis (and with the disappearance of the 'Second' socialist world, it is frankly illogical), but it still performs a useful function because it has lodged in the public consciousness as a metaphor for humanity's 'have nots', and as a constant reminder of the gross inequalities between major regions of the world. The Brandt Report popularized another metaphor, North–South, and outlined the contours of global inequality at the end of the 1970s:

- The North, including eastern Europe, had a quarter of the world's population and four-fifths of its income.

- The South, including China, had three billion people – three quarters of the world's population – but lived on one fifth of the world's income.

- Over 90 per cent of the world's manufacturing industry lay in the North which dominated the world's economic system and monopolized its technology through multinational corporations.

(Brandt, 1980, p. 32)

These contours have not changed fundamentally since Brandt, save perhaps through the decline in real incomes in what was formerly the Soviet bloc. The 'poverty curtain' has turned out to be more permanently divisive of humanity than the 'Iron Curtain'.

Today's stark inequalities between the world's richest and poorest regions are not, as far as we know, the continuation in the present of economic disparities stretching back into the distant past. According to the economic historian Paul Bairoch, there were no such things as strikingly rich and strikingly poor states in the pre-industrial world. Around 1700, the per capita income gap between the poorest and the richest country was, he claims, certainly smaller than a ratio of 1.0 to 2.0, and probably in the order of only 1.0 to 1.5. Bairoch asserts that Europe (inclusive of Russia) did not then have a particularly privileged position in terms of its average standard of life which was, if anything, slightly lower than that of the 'rest of the world'. This was due to the relatively high level achieved by the Chinese civilization (whose average living standard throughout the millenium before *circa* 1700 was certainly ahead of the most advanced in Europe) and the importance of this society in the 'rest of the world' and also to the low level achieved by Russia which represented a significant proportion of Europe (Bairoch, 1986, p. 194). It must be said that not all scholars endorse these speculations, and many stress the economic advances, relative to other civilizations, made by Europe in the early modern period as a result of climatic, geographic and ecological advantages (see Jones, 1981). But whether we attribute the 'miracle' of European development primarily to causes operative since the eighteenth-century industrial revolution or to much longer-run factors preceding it, does not alter the fact that widening global economic inequality is a major theme of modern history. How it related to the expansion of Europe, and of the capitalist 'world system' of which Europe was the core, is one of the questions we shall address in this essay. Were the economic development of Europe and the impoverishment of the Third World interdependent parts of a single process of global change? Is it true – as Franz Fanon claimed (1967, p. 81) – that, since its development has required the spoliation of the non-European world, 'Europe is literally the creation of the Third World'?

An allied theme of modern history has been the unification of the globe in a society of sovereign states, a process resulting from the dominance (in some cases permanent, in others temporary) of Europeans over non-European peoples. A glance at the political map of the contemporary world shows how the European presence has been imprinted on the frontiers of Africa, the Americas, the Middle East, South-east Asia and Oceania. There are, of course, states of ancient origin, with a history of unbroken independence, and which conform politically to an indigenous tradition (examples are China, Japan and Iran). But these are a minority amongst the states represented at the United Nations.[1] The majority are modern political structures imposed by Europeans on native communities and have only become self-governing since 1945.

This essay will provide a schematic, historical analysis of the relations between Europe and the extra-European periphery within the twin contexts of global economic inequality, and global disparities in political power. The colonial and imperial relationships between *western* Europe and the wider world since the late fifteenth century, and the course and consequences of decolonization, form the substance of the discussion. For reasons of space, the expansion of Russia into central Asia – which certainly falls under the rubric of Europe and the Third World – will not be considered.

Before proceeding, however, we must consider some of the issues and controversies in development economics – whose modern form dates from around the time people started to talk of a Third World – since they have been important in conceptualizing the past and present relationships between the metropolitan economies of Europe and the dependent economies in the extra-European periphery. One key debate has revolved around the question as to whether the international exchange of manufactured for primary goods (which long typified trading relationships between Europe and the 'Third World') can be said to be 'unequal'. In classical economics (including classical Marxism) products exchange at equal values, and the international division of labour offers a benign environment for countries to specialize in forms of production where they enjoy a 'comparative advantage'. This theory was challenged from the early 1950s by a group of Latin American economists led by the former Argentine finance minister Raúl Prebisch. It is no accident that so much of the literature on economic 'underdevelopment' should have been written by Latin Americans, since their own societies had enjoyed political independence from the 1820s (and been insulated from further European imperialism by the Monroe Doctrine[2]) yet failed to 'take-off' into sustained economic growth before the 1950s. They had not been isolated from world markets; on the contrary, around 1900 a very high proportion of the GDP of countries such as Argentina and Chile had been exported, with their agricultural and mineral products (beef, wheat, copper, etc.) being traded for manufactured imports from the industrialized economies. According to Prebisch, this pattern of exchange had generated structural inequality because the prices of primary exports had declined relative to manufactured imports. The essence of his argument was that the greater productivity gains of manufacturing had led to higher wages for better-organized European (and American) workers as compared with the labour force in the export sector of the underdeveloped regions, and this disparity was reflected in

---

[1]   The UN came into effect on 24 October 1945 when the original 50 member states ratified its Charter. By early 1992, membership had grown to 159 states, but we must expect this number to increase during the life of the course. The membership is listed in the current edition of *Whitaker's Almanack*.

[2]   The Monroe Doctrine – enunciated in 1823 by US President James Monroe – embodied the principle 'that the American continents…are henceforth not to be considered as subjects for future colonization by any European power'.

prices. The validity of this argument is much disputed, and there is no convincing evidence of a long-term deterioration in the terms of trade for primary products between *circa* 1850 and 1929. It is, nevertheless, true that primary producers in the Third World experienced very adverse relative price movements during the world trade recessions of the 1930s and the early 1980s. World prices for their agricultural and mineral products plummeted and, while workers in industrialized economies maintained their nominal wages, primary producers' incomes in under-developed regions were slashed.

Prebisch was largely responsible for persuading the United Nations to convene its first Conference on Trade and Development held at Geneva in 1964, when the Third World (with which Latin Americans were now beginning to identify them-selves) first presented its collective demands to the industrialized economies. Its objectives were the improvement and stabilization of primary product prices, ac-cess for its own manufactures to their markets, and greater financial flows from the rich to the poor. Within Latin America itself, Prebisch's advocacy led to pol-icies of import substitution industrialization which were imitated in many other parts of the developing world.

The indifferent success of these policies encouraged a more radical critique of 'de-pendency' by a younger generation of scholars, of whom André Gunder Frank is the best known. It is misleading to speak – as many do – of 'dependency' *theory* since this somewhat amorphous concept has provided a perspective on economic relations between the metropolitan and peripheral economies rather than a precise theory. A leading target for the *dependistas* has been the model of economic de-velopment put forward by W. W. Rostow, which envisages a transition from 'tra-ditional society' to self-sustained growth taking place through clearly defined stages (Rostow, 1956, 1960). The assumption of the model was that the 'under-developed' societies were in something akin to a 'traditional' state and would rep-licate the transition provided certain conditions were met during the critical 'take-off' stage (chiefly an increase in the rate of investment and improvements in labour productivity which promote rapid technical changes in production, and hence further productivity increases and further investment). Frank forcibly re-jected the idea that 'underdeveloped' societies resembled pre-industrial Europe. He viewed 'underdevelopment' not as original or traditional, but as a state of affairs resulting from the world-wide expansion of the capitalist system from the six-teenth century when the European powers first created satellite economies in Latin America and the Caribbean, using slave or otherwise unfree labour to extract min-eral wealth and grow plantation crops. Since manufacturing was largely forbidden in European colonies under the mercantilist system (see below, p. 19), the surplus value created in them was not invested in productive enterprises, but either repatri-ated or used to support the parasitic life-style of a colonial élite. According to Frank, this pattern of metropolitan powers pumping surplus value out of their sat-ellites persisted after former colonies won their independence and was essential to the development of capitalism on a world scale (Frank, 1973, pp. 94–5). In other words, the 'underdevelopment' of the poor has been a necessary condition for the 'development' of the rich, and it is – we must conclude – only by severing relationships with the capitalist world market that balanced, autonomous growth becomes possible on the periphery.

The perspective provided by the concept of 'dependency' has underpinned an historical account of global inequality and remains hugely influential within the Third World to this day. But numerous critics have pointed to its imprecision and to Frank's cavalier disregard for the discontinuities in centre–periphery relations. The historical record does not show that economic growth was consistently retarded in the Third World by the great expansion of world trade after 1850, and recent events would appear to have refuted the more pessimistic prognoses of the *dependistas*, for the fact is that rapid industrialization has taken place in peripheral countries such as South Korea and Mexico. If the 'dependency' perspective is so questionable, why introduce it here? Partly because it has figured so prominently in debates on the Third World that to ignore it would be a disservice to readers. More important, knowledge progresses by conjecture and refutation and, as a crude hypothesis, 'dependency' remains a useful point of departure for historical analysis.

The European encompassment of the world after 1450

In 1522, a single vessel belonging to the expedition begun three years earlier under Ferdinand Magellan returned to Cadiz, having completed the first circumnavigation of the world. It was more than an extraordinary feat of seamanship; when the Spanish crossed the Pacific and reached the Moluccas they encountered the forces of Portugal already ensconced in the Far East. Both Iberian powers had papal authority to claim title to any non-Christian lands their expeditions encountered, claims they enforced with remarkable energy and effect. So their meeting was token of a political encirclement of the world by Christian powers whose rival imperialisms were, in the following centuries, to draw distant parts of the globe into the European states system.

Why should it have fallen to Europeans – more particularly western Europeans – to encompass the world in this way? When the process began with Portuguese and Spanish maritime expansion along the African littoral and out into the Atlantic, western Europe had no obvious technological or military-political advantages over other centres of advanced civilization, nor was it motivated by any exceptional moral cohesion. The world's most populous, economically developed and highly centralized state was the Chinese empire, and it might have seemed a more likely sponsor of global encirclement. Fifteenth-century Chinese merchants participated in long-distance trade which fostered impressive shipbuilding and maritime skills. Somewhat earlier than the Portuguese exploration of the African Atlantic coast, Chinese fleets – with larger vessels than the Iberians – pushed out into the Indian Ocean, reaching the Persian Gulf and the East African coast. But this Chinese expansion was cut short by imperial edict, when the empire had to concentrate its forces on a renewed Mongol threat from the north. Henceforth, the construction of ocean-going vessels was forbidden and long-distance trade frowned upon. One might argue that the size, political and cultural unity, technological accomplishments, and (by comparison with Europe) centralized authority of the Empire became obstacles to its territorial expansion. They enabled the Empire to retreat into self-sufficiency and cultivate its own sense of moral and political superiority to the outside world.

The roots of Chinese stasis are, in a negative way, indicative of the sources of European dynamism: the distinctive feature of western Europe was its combination of political fragmentation with some measure of economic unity. Because of the absence of centralized political authority there arose a competitive system of states whose endemic conflicts encouraged technical improvements in weaponry, warships and (since wars had to be financed) the machinery of taxation and credit. But while political power was dispersed amongst individual states, their economies tended to interlock: Europe's varied climate favoured regional specialization and a variety of agricultural products, and geography facilitated international exchange. Thus, apart from the luxury trade in spices and silks through the Levant, fifteenth-century Europe had developed a relatively unified market for long-distance trade in certain bulk goods (grains, timber, woollen cloths, wine) and had a system of mercantile credit which cut across political divisions and was not controlled by any one state. Autonomous economic activity of this kind and on this scale did not flourish in other regions of advanced civilization, chiefly because they were empires in which political power subordinated economic development (see Kennedy, 1989, pp. 20–30).

European encirclement did not necessarily entail the subjugation of native institutions and European dominion in their stead. Indeed, a broad distinction can be made between European contacts with Asia – where the indigenous land powers could resist European domination until the eighteenth century – and the dominion established over biologically-defenceless societies in Latin America, whose acquisition was Europe's first and most spectacular colonial achievement. This land empire was seized by small groups of lesser Castilian gentry, fired with crusading zeal from the Reconquest of Spain from the Moors (only completed in 1492 with the capture of Granada) and acclimatized to the winning of wealth by the waging of war. The persistence of the empire, and its institutional character, were due to the Spanish state's determination to keep the process of colonization under its control: Spanish America was denied colonial assemblies (such as developed in English North America) and government and jurisdiction remained functions of the royal bureaucracy.

During the 'second conquest' – when lands were settled, cities built, the native population forced into patterns determined for it by the Spaniards – the institutions and ways of life of Castile were transplanted to the Americas (Elliot, 1963, p. 55). During the Reconquest of Castile, urban corporations had been the principal agencies for land settlement. This pattern was repeated in the New World where the towns became the centres of a colonist population with the style of life of Castilian aristocrats who were parasitic on the countryside and could only survive by exploiting native labour in the fields and mines. From the traditions of the Reconquest, they reasoned that conquest in a 'just war' entitled them to enslave the native population. This conflicted with the Catholic sensitivities of Spanish monarchs who, technically, held the new territories as a papal fief and were, therefore, obliged to Christianize their new subjects. Enslavement of the Indians was prohibited by a decree of 1500, but since it excluded those who attacked Spaniards or who practised barbarous customs, there were many exceptions. In the first decades of settlement, the natives were more usually compelled to labour through the institution of the *encomienda* – under which temporary, non-hereditary grants of lordship over specified groups of Indians were vested in individual Spaniards who were obliged to civilize and Christianize them, and in return received labour services or tributes.

The intervention of the Mendicant Orders, and the determination of the absolutist state to resist a reversal to feudalism in its overseas empire, limited native enslavement and halted the rise of a transatlantic, slave-owning aristocracy. The Indians most eloquent champion was Bartolomé de las Casas who challenged the Aristotelian doctrines of natural slavery espoused by some Churchmen and whose advocacy led to a remarkable stirring of public conscience inside Spain. The debate turned not on the rights and wrongs of slavery as such – which was still quite common in Christendom, particularly around the Mediterranean – but on the duties of a Christian monarch towards subjects ignorant of the Faith through no fault of their own. The latter sentiments prevailed: a royal decree of 1549 forbad the use of forced labour in the mines of Mexico and Peru, where the typical silver miner was a capitalist and an employer of native labour, skilled and unskilled, on a fairly large scale (Parry, 1949, p. 73). The Crown repeatedly insisted that Indian complaints of forced labour should be freely heard before the ten courts of appeal established in the Indies in the sixteenth century, at which the judges were always peninsular Spaniards and school-trained lawyers. As the rights of individuals to compel the natives to work were curtailed, so the role of the *encomienda* in the economy declined. In its stead, a new system of state labour was introduced, under which the Indians received wages (at prescribed rates) for work exercised under official supervision.

This could not meet the needs of labour-intensive plantation agriculture, especially sugar cultivation; consequently the importation of negro slaves from the African Guinea coast quickened after about 1545. (Few had any moral and legal scruples about enslaving negroes because, unlike the Amerindians, they had been the subjects of barbarous African kings and not of the king of Spain.) This was the origin of a notorious triangle of commerce and exploitation linking Europe, west Africa and the plantation economies of the Caribbean, Brazil and the slave-owning states of Anglophone America. By 1600 an estimated 275,000 west African slaves had been *landed* overseas, chiefly in Spanish America (many died *en route*). The seventeenth-century figure for total overseas landings is thought to have been about 1.34 million; the figures for the eighteenth and nineteenth centuries seem to have been about 6.05 million and 1.9 million respectively. (These figures are from Curtin, 1969, who stresses the many imperfections of the data on which they are based.) Initially, the trade with Spanish America was carried on through Portuguese intermediaries who had established footholds on the Gold Coast, although as with all other goods sent to Spanish America, slaves had to be shipped through Seville whose merchant guild had a trade monopoly. During the seventeenth century the Dutch captured the Guinea trade from the Portuguese (though these continued to ship slaves from Angola to Brazil). Subsequently the British and French contested Dutch supremacy with, in terms of trade alone, victory going to Britain. By the end of the eighteenth century, British ships were carrying nearly half the slaves taken to the Americas.

Apart from semi-tropical plantation produce, the most important exports from the New World were precious metals, particularly the silver from the legendary Potosí mine, which flowed via Spain into the wider European economy. Its economic significance has been much debated: although it must have inflated the money supply to some degree, and fuelled the secular rise in prices from the later sixteenth century, its inflationary impact was almost certainly less than was once thought. The inflow of silver may have had the advantage of easing a shortage of specie in Europe, the result in part of the luxury trade with Asia where there was no market for European manufactures generally inferior to local products. The oriental powers were not yet in a position to have trade forced upon them and their silks, calicoes, porcelain and spices had to be purchased with silver.

The origins of the 'modern world system'?

Before we consider Europe's impact on Asia during the 'Vasco da Gama era', it is worth pausing to analyse early modern colonialism within the context of the development of capitalism and global economic inequality. Whether there were long-term economic advantages for any individual state in colonial empire as such is clearly debatable: witness the case of Spain, the most extensive and powerful imperial state during most of the early modern era, yet in serious economic decline from the seventeenth century and one of Europe's most backward economies until well into the twentieth century. The Spanish case is particularly problematic for those wanting to link colonial exploitation to the 'primitive accumulation of capital' and 'The Genesis of the Industrial Capitalist', and Spain is significantly absent from the chapter in *Das Kapital* where Marx posited this relationship (Marx, 1867; 1976 edn, Chap. 31). The Spanish 'exception' demonstrates that there was no necessary connection between colonial exploitation and economic development. Nevertheless, it is undeniable that western Europe as a whole gained extraordinary advantages in the prelude to modern economic growth through the conquest of the New World. Most basic was the huge addition to its physical resource base in terms of fisheries, sub-tropical plantation lands, timber forests, prairies and granaries.

> An unparalleled share of the earth's biological resources was acquired
> for [Europe], on a scale that was unprecedented and is unrepeatable.
> *(Jones, 1981, p. 82)*

Their full exploitation awaited the nineteenth century, but long before then the new acres available to Europeans were biologically colonized with horses, cattle and sheep, sugar, rice and cotton.

As I have indicated, Marx argued that mercantilism, or the system whereby European powers tried to monopolize colonial commerce and retain captive markets for their budding manufactures, led to the accumulation and concentration of capital in privileged chartered companies, as well as the 'hot-house' growth of credit institutions. Looted treasure supplemented the sources of commercial and industrial capital. The commercial-and-imperial preeminence which Britain secured during the eighteenth century was, for Marx, the explanation for her early industrialization. In summary:

> In the period of manufacture [i.e. pre-industrial capitalism]...
> commercial supremacy produces industrial predominance. Hence the
> preponderant role played by the colonial system at that time.
> *(Marx, 1867; 1976 edn, p. 918)*

Marx's views did not explicitly relate the development of capitalism to increasing global inequality but in recent years a number of *Marxisant* scholars have made this link the keystone of an overarching analysis of world economic history. The most influential is Immanuel Wallerstein who has, to date, published three out of a projected four volumes tracing the development of the 'capitalist world system'. Wallerstein argues that, apart from the now defunct 'minisystems' of hunter-gatherers, the only kind of social system is a 'world-system', characterized by a division of labour over a large geographic area, such that the various regions in it depend upon economic exchange with others for the smooth and continuous provisioning of their needs. Where such a system coincides with a polity which can pump revenue from the whole – as in early-modern China – then we can designate it a 'world empire'. A 'world economic system', by contrast, can contain many polities, no one of which subjugates the whole, and he has argued that between 1450 and 1640 such a system came into being with the origins of modern capitalism. It must be said that in this analysis 'world' is a term of art applied either to a political or economic entity extending over a large area; no one would deny that before the later nineteenth century vast tracts of the world were scarcely touched by international exchange. As Wallerstein defines it, a 'world economy' is constituted by an international division of labour and production for sale and profit on a unified market. In his view, what happened in Europe from the sixteenth to the eighteenth centuries was that over an area going from Poland in the north-east westwards and southwards throughout Europe and including large parts of the western hemisphere as well, there grew up such an economy, based on the exchange of agricultural products (Wallerstein, 1974; 1979, p. 16). Regional specialization occurred as different areas concentrated on different crops and by about 1640 three structural positions had stabilized: the core, the periphery and the semi-periphery. Production for the world market in each zone was characterized by a particular mode of labour control: at the core, free wage labour, at the periphery coerced labour, and in the semi-periphery share-cropping. By reason of its geography and ecology, sixteenth-century north-west Europe was better situated than other parts of the continent to diversify its agricultural specialization, and add to it certain industries such as textiles, shipbuilding and metal wares. Consequently, north-west Europe emerged as the core of this 'world economy', specializing in agricultural production at high skill levels, which favoured tenancy and wage labour. Eastern Europe and the western hemisphere became peripheral areas specializing in exports of grains, bullion, wood, cotton, sugar – all of which favoured the use of slavery and coerced cash-crop labour. Mediterranean Europe emerged as the semiperipheral area specializing in high-cost products and credit and specie transactions; as a consequence in the agricultural arena sharecropping became the mode of labour control and there was little export to other areas.

The novel features of this analysis, which distance it from 'classical Marxism', are that it interprets capitalism as the creation of world inequality, and dispenses with the linear 'progression' of modes of exploitation from slavery through serfdom to free, waged labour. In Wallerstein's view, the re-introduction of serfdom in eastern Europe and the adoption of plantation slavery in the Americas were as integral to the development of capitalism as the growth of free labour at the core. Moreover, he insists that surplus value was not just appropriated by owners of productive resources from labourers, but by core areas from the whole world-economy. Because – Wallerstein's claims – 'strong states' (strong, that is, both internationally and with respect to their own societies) developed in north-west Europe, the 'core' was able to enforce 'unequal exchange' on the weak states on the periphery.

Wallerstein's and Frank's views of global economic change in the early modern period broadly coincide: for both the development of western Europe and the underdevelopment of the 'periphery' were complementary processes. Both regard highly profitable trade in colonial products, slaves and bullion as a source of 'primitive' capital accumulation and a necessary, but not sufficient condition for the industrial revolution that began in Britain in the late eighteenth century (Frank, 1978, Chap. 7). Isolated parts of this argument are unchallengable: the prosperity of individual European cities (such as Bristol, Bordeaux, Nantes) *was* built on trade both in slaves and the produce of slave plantations and some of this commercial wealth did flow, via country banks, into manufacturing enterprises. The demographic effects on certain African coastal regions of enslaving millions of the able-bodied were appalling: vast areas were depopulated. But though all would assent to certain features of the thesis, the significance of the extra-European periphery for European economic development is very debatable. In this argument, we must judge 'significance' by measurement and the admittedly meagre statistical sources available to us scarcely confirm 'world systems' theory.

As one critic has pointed out, intercontinental trade with the extra-European periphery formed only a small proportion of the international trade of the European powers, which was predominantly amongst themselves. If we include the slave states of North America in the extra-European periphery, then by the late eighteenth century it received about 20 per cent of western Europe's exports and supplied about 25 per cent of its imports.

> *A fortiori*, the importance of such trade must have been far less as we go back in time... Throughout the mercantile era Europeans sold and purchased far more merchandise from each other than they did from other continents'.
>
> *(O'Brien, 1982, p. 4)*

Moreover, external trade formed only a small share of economic activity: the ratio of domestic exports to gross national product in the Netherlands and Britain, the leading maritime powers in the late eighteenth century, was only about 10 per cent (of which less than half was destined for the periphery). Total imports were per-haps 10 to 15 per cent of GNP, again with smaller proportions purchased from the periphery. But did this small volume of trade with the periphery make a dispro-portionate contribution to capital formation in the 'run up' to industrialization? Even on the most favourable assumptions, and even with respect to Britain, which was the pre-eminent colonial and industrializing power by 1800, it seems most un-likely: O'Brien has calculated that commerce with the periphery generated a flow of funds sufficient, or potentially available, to finance about 15 per cent of gross investment expenditures undertaken during the Industrial Revolution (ibid., p. 7). Although it is true that the produce of slave labour enabled Europe to vary its diet, supplement its manufacturing raw materials (notably with cotton) and increase its bullion supply, it cannot be econometrically demonstrated that these were more than marginal advantages in the advent of industrialization, which economic his-torians now insist proceeded on a very broad front. The conclusion seems inescap-able that as long as oceanic trade remained as a tiny proportion of total economic activity it could not propel Europe towards an industrial society. Certainly, contact with western Europe promoted underdevelopment in southern America, Asia and Africa but it does not follow that the gains which accrued to Europe did much to push its economies onto paths of sustained industrialization after 1750.

Europe and Asia in the first imperial age

No Asian state was seized by the type of coup that Cortés and Pizarro executed, and the European powers generally required the cooperation of native princes to establish their Asian footholds. The first to do so were the Portuguese who, after reaching India in 1498, created a chain of maritime forts and entrepôts which, at its greatest extent, stretched from the east African coast to Macao in southern China, and included bases in the Indonesian archipelago. This *Estado da India* rested upon the superiority of Portuguese naval gunnery over local warships and never became a body of lands and peoples effectively controlled by a metropolitan authority. Its chief rationale was control of the lucrative, long-haul spice trade, which was made a royal monopoly. Although the Portuguese had pretensions to tax and regulate indigenous shipping in the Arabian sea, the Indian Ocean and straits of Malacca, it is not now thought that their impact on regional trade was very great. The global significance of the *Estado* was twofold: first, it enabled western, Atlantic Europe to establish direct contact with the vast Asian maritime economy. Hitherto, trade with east Asia had been a monopoly of Venice and un-dertaken through Arab intermediaries. The Portuguese began a shift of commercial power away from the Mediterranean, first to the west and then the north-west. Secondly, the Portuguese introduced European sea-power into Asian waters, which was to be the main instrument of western dominance until the twentieth century and the means by which China and Japan were effectively insulated from the wider world until the nineteenth century (Panikkar, 1953, p. 13). Though they were to be eclipsed by the Dutch and British in Asia, the Portuguese hung on to their imperial outposts longer than any other power. Goa, seized in 1510, was not overrun by independent India until 1961.

The Portuguese position in the far east was first challenged by the western expansion of Spain across the Pacific: in 1565, a squadron from South America seized the Philippines and subsequently Manila became the entrepôt of trade between Mexico and China. When Portuguese–Spanish rivalry was ended by their dynastic union, the principal European contestant to Iberian power in the East became the Protestant Dutch, who dominated Europe's carrying trade and were the leading naval power in the seventeenth century. In 1595, during their rebellion against the Habsburgs, Lisbon – hitherto the monopoly entrepôt for the long-haul spice trade – was closed to their ships. The Dutch broke into the trade with superior vessels that carried cargoes to Europe more cheaply than the Portuguese who, when they attempted to expel the interlopers by force, were defeated in Javanese waters in 1601. The Dutch extended their war of rebellion to Brazil and Africa, as well as the East Indies, seizing Portuguese forts and founding their own mercantile empire. Competition between the Dutch and Portuguese, and amongst the Dutch themselves, led local sultans to drive up prices and harbour dues; in order to create a single buyer, the Dutch founded in 1602 the Dutch East India Company. This was both a permanent commercial organization, with a trade monopoly from the Cape of Good Hope to Magellan's Strait, and an agent of the imperialising state, empowered to make war, conclude treaties, establish colonies, construct forts and coin money. In return, the Dutch States-General exacted customs dues and retained the right of financial and general supervision of the Company's affairs. The Company did not immediately effect a transformation of commercial relationships between Europe and south-east Asia; as with the Portuguese, initial advances depended on negotiation with native princes and exploiting their internecine quarrels. However, the Dutch were ruthless in destroying their European rivals: the English East India Company was excluded from Indonesia and the Moluccas, the Portuguese driven from Malacca and Ceylon. Moreover, unlike the Portuguese, the Dutch aimed to control not just the long-haul trade between Europe and Asia, but to canalize the far greater inter-Asian trade through their entrepôts. This required a type of political supremacy over Asian societies which no Europeans had hitherto established: between 1640 and 1700 the Dutch moved from being one amongst several powers in the Indonesian archipelago to the dominant power, although they always preferred to rule indirectly through the local polities. Native commerce was ruined by the Dutch success in imposing monopoly contracts for selling spices on local princes; the pattern of Javanese agriculture was distorted, and its population impoverished by the enforced growing of market crops for which the Dutch were monopoly buyers. By 1690, they could fix the price of cloves and nutmegs (but not pepper which had many more sources of supply) in Europe and Asia.

The Dutch grip on the archipelago was one reason why the activities of the 'late comers' to the East, the British and the French, were concentrated on the Indian subcontinent. But other reasons were the declining importance of spices for Europe as a result of agricultural improvements which allowed more livestock to be kept over the winter, and the growing market for high-quality Indian textiles. Between 1612 and 1616, the Mughal authorities granted merchants of the English East India Company rights of residence and trade in Surat, although there was no question of founding a fortified entrepôt since the British were there under the protection of a mighty Asiatic empire on whose favour they long depended. During the seventeenth century, minor territorial acquisitions were made (initially outside the Mughal dominion) by Britain and France as part of a commercial penetration tolerated by local states.

Up to 1740, Europe's political and military influence in India was negligible. What transformed this situation was the decay of the Mughal Empire and the intrusion of the Anglo-French struggle for commercial and colonial supremacy into the subcontinent. Mughal decline led the Hindu princes of the Maratha confederacy to establish themselves as a *de facto* independent power; elsewhere imperial provincial officials were tempted to make their offices hereditary and set themselves up as autonomous war-lords. This situation jeopardized European interests in the ports but was also an opportunity for the companies to intervene on behalf of princes promising the most liberal rewards or the greatest concessions. Initially, France appeared the more likely successor to Mughal authority than Britain: from 1742, its ambitious Governor in Pondicherry, Dupleix, laid the foundations for French political preponderance in the south east, becoming a vassal of the Mughal emperor and driving the British from Madras. When challenged by a local *nabob* to hand over the town, his small force of French troops defeated a much larger Indian army – a landmark in the history of the subcontinent. British naval superiority during the Seven Years' War checked French ambitions – decisively, as it turned out, although they were renewed during the maritime war of 1778–1783 (when a French fleet harassed the British in Indian waters) and during the Napoleonic wars.

The first step towards the acquisition of a huge British imperium in Asia was taken when the East India Company received the *diwani* (or revenue collecting authority) of Bombay in 1765 from the Mughal emperor – which put the Company in the novel and highly ambiguous position of administering a large and prosperous part of eastern India. The impulse behind this move to direct rule arose on 'the turbulent frontier', for the British government had no wish to involve itself in a land empire in Asia – and besides had scarcely any control over the Company at this time – while the Company's Court of Directors were too distant to influence events. Company officials on the spot, many of whom were trading privately on their own account, and the 'free' merchants operating under the Company's wing were anxious to secure a peaceful hinterland for their operations. Undoubtedly, too, they expected to exploit office for personal gain, for Mughal officials made their own fortunes by extortion from peasants and traders, and bribery was an established part of the Europeans' relationship with officialdom. The first decades of Company rule were notorious for these abuses. Its representatives in the villages forced the peasants to sell their cloth and other produce at artificially low prices and compelled native traders to buy them dear (Panikkar, 1953, p. 101).

The repercussions of 'the rape of Bengal' on the British polity itself forced the state into the closer regulation of the Company and obliged it to acknowledge ultimate responsibility for Company rule. Some of the wealth acquired by the abuse of office in India flowed back into the already corrupt stream of British politics. Indian affairs became an important issue in the complex struggles between the parliamentary cliques and the royal executive. Warren Hastings (Governor General of Bengal between 1772 and 1785) was impeached for corruption, and the demand for greater parliamentary control of the Company was met by the Government of India Act of 1784. This stiffened ministerial control of the Company through appointees to the Court of Directors. At the same time, the first steps were taken to establish a properly trained, salaried and pensioned élite of officials to govern British India.

We should not pre-date the moment when British subcontinental paramountcy was achieved; Maratha power was not destroyed until 1818 and the frontier of direct British rule continued to advance in a series of 'small wars' until the great revolt of 1857 deflected the British into the preservation of client princes and compelled the state to wind up the vestiges of Company rule. Nor should we exaggerate the transformation effected by British dominion. Indeed, in its first decades it resembled previous Asiatic conquests more than modern European colonialism. The Company's purpose was to wring a surplus from the revenue system sufficient to finance its annual purchases of Indian goods and the growing tea trade with China (for which the chief item of exchange was opium). Otherwise, it preserved the forms of Mughal rule, using Persian in official correspondence and the law courts, and forbidding Christian missions to enter British-controlled territory until 1813. Initially, therefore, the new rulers accommodated themselves to the culture and customs of their subjects. Though the cultural forms of British rule later changed markedly – particularly after the regular steamer service through the Suez Canal led to an influx of wives and fiancées – British rule basically conserved indigenous social and economic institutions and always depended on native collaborators. We should not imagine that the tiny numbers of 'covenanted' Indian Civil Servants (only 1300 in 1900 when the total population approached two hundred million) ever constituted a ruling class in themselves. The British were only able to establish themselves in India because they found a set of collaborators with a self-interest in welcoming them; the subsequent history of their rule can be charted as a continuous search for new collaborators as the usefulness or goodwill of one set after another was dissipated.

Our task here is to place the British Raj within the context of global inequality and to do that we must speculate a little about India's potential economic fate had British rule not been imposed. Was it the case that British rule led to the 'underdevelopment' of a region otherwise capable of modernizing through its own resources, as was Japan? The classical economists did not think so: for them the traditional Asian political economy (or 'Oriental despotism') was history's stagnant backwater, incapable of progressing to a higher social form through its own efforts. Its salient characteristics were believed to be an unchanging and self-sufficient village community at the base, the absence of private ownership of land, and the appropriation of the surplus by the central governing power which used some of this wealth to maintain public irrigation works, but otherwise flaunted it in ostentatious consumption. From the perspective afforded by 'Oriental despotism', British rule had the progressive functions of 'annihilating… old Asiatic society, and the laying of the material foundations of western society in Asia' (Marx, 1853).

'Oriental despotism' now appears as part of a larger discourse which opposed Europe's progress to the Orient's decadence and European rationality to Oriental mysticism: a form of knowledge (Orientalism) which embodied and expressed Europe's power over the East, and helped define Europe as the point from which the flow of history was determined and interpreted (Said, 1978). Few now regard 'Oriental despotism' as a useful framework of historical enquiry. But many are equally sceptical of the thesis advanced by the first generation of Indian nationalist historians that eighteenth-century India was both a great agricultural and a great manufacturing power, and that the imposition of British rule brought 'de-industrialization' of the local textile industry and general economic stagnation. One scholar surveying the mid-eighteenth century Indian economy concludes that it is inappropriate to describe it as 'backward' or even 'stagnant'. Although agricultural technology was primitive compared with western Europe and China, yields were quite high because of the availability of very fertile land.

> More important, there was a large [indigenous] commercialized sector
> with a highly sophisticated market and credit structure, manned by a
> skilful and, in many instances, very wealthy commercial class.
> *(Raychaudhuri, in Kumar (ed.), 1983, p. 32)*

Native bankers and merchants participated in local, regional and inter-Asian trade. In early eighteenth-century Surat, two thirds of the ships engaged in the 'country' trade were owned by non-Europeans (Brown, 1985, p. 13). Though it is true that the subcontinent did not have a fully integrated economy, there was nevertheless considerable mobility of goods, a common price level and long-distance discounting of bills of exchange. What we might call proto-industrial capitalism had emerged in several handicraft trades, most notably textiles where a 'putting out' system linked merchant capitalist, middlemen and village-based weavers, but also shipbuilding where artisans had set themselves up as capitalist entrepreneurs hiring waged labour. These dynamic elements notwithstanding, there is 'little to support the thesis that we have here the anticipation of an industrial revolution, later frustrated by colonial rule' (Raychaudhuri, in Kumar (ed.), 1983, p. 27). Though there are no precise data, commerce and manufacturing can only have accounted for a small proportion of total economic activity. The poverty of the rural masses and the absence of an agrarian revolution restricted the domestic market and the surplus available for investment. Furthermore, India's comparative advantage in textiles was due only to the manual dexterity and cheap labour of her spinners and weavers. Technological advances made centuries earlier in China had simply been ignored, and consequently the Indian industry was highly vulnerable to the quantum technological leap made in Lancashire. (Nevertheless, Indian weavers continued to be competitive in local markets for poorer quality cloths.) Finally, the system of hereditary occupational castes was a major barrier to individual social mobility and inimical to the culture of capitalism, while by encouraging the docility of the peasantry it made societal change through revolutionary upheaval rather unlikely. To summarize, while Indian society was not static, and did have its own resources for development and change, it did not have the potential for 'modernization from above' that was to be shown by Meiji Japan. (For an explicit comparison of Japan and India, see Moore, 1967, Chapters 5 & 6.)

The opening of China

The British position in India had geopolitical consequences going far beyond the subcontinent. The most crucial was the fact that commercial interests in India created a wedge with which China was forcibly opened to British (and other western) traders. We cannot pursue this complex story in any detail here; the essential points are that by the early nineteenth century a mass market had developed in Britain for tea, of which China was then the only source of supply, whose export through Canton was until 1833 a monopoly of the East India Company. There was no reciprocal market in China for British goods, and the Company had originally paid for its tea purchases in bullion, derived from the profits of inter-Asian trade. The increasing British demand for tea led to a search for Indian goods with which to redress the trade imbalance between Britain and China, and the product for which there were many Chinese consumers proved to be opium whose cultivation was a Company monopoly in India, and whose consumption, sale and import were illegal in China. By 1836, total annual opium imports were worth 18 million US dollars – it was the nineteenth-century world's single most valuable commodity trade (Wakeman, in Fairbank (ed.), 1978, p. 172).

In 1840, friction between imperial officials trying to enforce the edicts banning opium and western traders in Canton culminated in the first 'Opium War', in which small Anglo-Indian forces demonstrated Chinese vulnerability to modern armaments and technology. Under the Treaty of Nanjing, August 1842, Hong Kong was ceded to Britain (in perpetuity according to the English version), four new 'treaty ports' were thrown open to foreign trade and a large indemnity was imposed. The question of opium was left unanswered and Hong Kong subsequently became a centre of the commerce. Between 1857 and 1860, two further military assaults were made on China (although on these occasions Britain acted in conjunction with France) and their upshot was the opening of ten more 'treaty ports', the payment of indemnities to Britain and France and the enforced reception of ambassadors at Beijing.

The Chinese empire had for centuries been at the centre of its own international system in which the emperor was considered a universal monarch and relations with neighbouring states (such as Korea and the Annamite empire in what is now Vietnam) were tributary in form. International diplomacy, as practised by the European powers, was unknown to Chinese scholar-officials, though they had developed subtle techniques for managing the 'barbarians' on China's inner Asian frontier – techniques with which they unsuccessfully confronted the maritime intruders on the south coast. Western intervention shattered China's ancient international system; the celestial empire was forced to enter the diplomatic community created by Europeans, and the colonial powers expanded into her erstwhile tributary states. French troops first landed in Vietnam in 1858, partly to protect Catholic missionaries, and by 1867 the whole province of Cochin-China around Saigon had been forcibly ceded. In subsequent decades, the French were drawn north into Tonkin by the prospect of commercial access to southern China, where they 'envisaged an enormous market that would enable them to win their own "India" and set themselves up besides England as an Asian Great power'

(Albertini, 1982, p. 195). When China decided to resist French encroachments on suzerain territory, her forces were defeated by France in 1883 and 1884 and the French protectorate of Annam recognized.

Western and Japanese intervention gravely weakened the imperial Chinese polity and, although it was to the advantage of foreign intruders to preserve the Ch'ing dynasty, their actions hastened its collapse in 1911. The West's impact on the economy and society of China outside the treaty port zones was far less dramatic. The long-established patterns of trade and handicraft production within China proved remarkably impervious to foreign stimuli; according to one estimate, as late as the 1930s, small-scale handloom weavers still accounted for about two-thirds of Chinese cloth production, and factory-made imports never satisfied more than a quarter of China's total demand for cloth (Murphey, 1977, pp. 119–21). Even within the enclave economies of the 'treaty ports', Chinese merchants re-tained control of the import–export trade. Foreign firms who imported into China did so only on order from Chinese buyers, and were in effect commission agents. They could not operate in China without their *compradors* – contractual em-ployees who handled the Chinese side of the foreign firms' business and bridged the cultural, linguistic and institutional gap between East and West. Many *com-pradors* became investors in enterprises within the 'treaty port' zones and a modernizing element within China's commercial class; by the late 1890s, about 40 per cent of the stock of western firms in shipping, cotton spinning and banking was Chinese owned. Foreign investment went almost entirely into the infrastruc-ture of the 'treaty ports' and indirectly benefited Chinese entrepreneurs who began to compete in factory-based manufacturing within the concessionary territories. By the close of the 'treaty port' system in the 1930s, foreign firms were left with less than one-third of China's total modern manufacturing output. In stressing the sys-tem's marginal impact on China's economy, we must not minimize it altogether: the Chinese state lost control of key instruments of economic policy because its external tariff regime was imposed by foreign powers, and foreigners within con-cessionary territories were exempted from Chinese taxation. Modern mining and railways, together with the largest insurance and financial institutions were predominantly owned by foreigners, and they used their privileged legal and fiscal status, and diplomatic pressure to maintain their position at Chinese expense (Murphey, 1977, p. 126). These manifestations of economic imperialism notwith-standing, recent scholarship has tended to play down Chinese 'dependency' during the 'treaty port' era and to stress a rate of industrial growth in coastal China almost as rapid as that achieved in Japan (see, especially, Gray, 1990, p. 152).

Contemporary China has an ambiguous relationship with the 'Third World', with which it has identified itself since the Sino-Soviet split became public in 1961. With so many Third World countries it shares the fundamental problem of an im-balance between explosive demographic growth and exiguous material and econ-omic resources, and its long-term history reveals a reversal of its position as a civilization of (comparative) mass prosperity. But explanation for this reversal must be sought within a Chinese economy which, though highly productive and relatively commercialized, lost the power to increase production in proportion to population growth, and so stagnated in what economists call a 'high-level equilibrium trap'. Neither western intervention nor the expansion of a capitalist world-economy played a significant part in this long-term decline.

Industrial capitalism and the 'imperialism of free trade'

During the nineteenth and early twentieth centuries, European states and states created by Europeans (notably the USA) came both to monopolize the productive resources of the world and to control it politically. To adopt Wallerstein's terminology, the European world economy expanded to engross the whole of the globe, with Africa being absorbed into the periphery from about 1880. The present-day structure of global inequality took shape: while average real incomes in the developed countries increased by 260 per cent in the course of the nineteenth century, they declined in the future Third World. The critical decades were 1830–1860 when the productivity gains of western industrialization were felt on a global scale: in 1800, Third World countries accounted for approximately two-thirds of world manufacturing production; by 1860, they accounted for about one-third of global production and, by 1913, for less than one-tenth. Some 'de-industrialization' resulted from the influx of European machine-produced products, particularly textiles, but its extent is a matter of debate: Chinese weavers remained fully competitive with European factories. Around 1900, the Third World's share of 'modern industry' was tiny (perhaps 1 to 2 per cent) and heavily concentrated in Latin America where political independence had stimulated local economic growth, at least to some degree (Bairoch, 1982 and 1986).

The concentration of political power in the 'North' was nearly as striking: in 1800, the proportion of the world's land surface actually occupied by Europeans, whether still under direct European control as colonies or as one-time colonies, was 35 per cent; by 1878, this had risen to 67 per cent and by 1914 to 84.4 per cent (Fieldhouse, 1973, p. 3). The very word 'colony' – which originally meant a settlement of immigrants hived off from their parent country – now came to mean primarily the rule by 'white men' over 'non-white' Asians and Africans (Watson, in Bull and Watson (eds), 1984, p. 30). This rule was at is apogee in 1939 when the total population of the colonial dependencies was about 645 million people. Most were subjects of the British empire and well over half lived in the Indian subcontinent. This preponderance notwithstanding, the colonial commitments of other European powers were huge: the Netherlands, with a home population of less than nine million, had an East Indian empire of nearly 70 million; Belgium, again with a population of less than nine million, had a Congolese empire of 14 million.

What were the causal connections between economic expansion and political domination? In his seminal study, the liberal economist J. A. Hobson advanced the theory of imperialism as a syndrome whereby surplus capital, unable to find a satisfactory rate of return in the metropolis, was placed outside the area of existing metropolitan control and then a policy of political expansion was fomented to incorporate the new areas (Hobson, 1902). The theory's signal weakness is the poor 'fit' between the geographic location of European foreign investment and the actual areas of European political expansion, which took place principally in Africa – the least important of the overseas recipients of European finance between 1875 and 1914. Despite this weakness, the theory influenced Lenin considerably when he redefined imperialism as the 'latest' (subsequently amended to 'highest') stage in the development of capitalism. He equated imperialism with the separation on a vast scale of money capital from industrial or productive capital, the 'domination of finance capital', and the 'crystallization of a small number of financially "powerful" states from among all the rest'. Whereas the domination of industrial capital had promoted free competition at home and abroad and the export of goods, the domination of finance capital promoted monopolies, tariffs and the export of capital. In so redefining imperialism, Lenin did not entirely detach the term from its original meaning of the power of command exercised by one country over another. Rather, he argued that political subordination was a requirement of capitalism at its highest stage. He contrasted the years 1840–1860, 'when free competition in Great Britain was at its zenith... and the leading British bourgeois politicians were opposed to colonial policy', with the transition, after 1880, to the stage of monopoly capitalism which 'beyond doubt... is bound up with the intensification of the struggle for the partition of the world' (Lenin, 1947 edn, pp. 73–4, 95–6).

As this quotation makes clear, Lenin – like Hobson – identified imperialism with a distinct break in world economic history when Britain's monopoly position as the sole industrial power gave way to economic and political competition amongst the developed states. This periodization is implausible in the light of the continuities in both British and French overseas expansion: in the fifty years before 1865 the British empire expanded by an average of *circa* 100,000 square miles per annum, which was not far below the rate of expansion in the subsequent half century. France's empire in north Africa dates to the invasion of Algeria in 1830, and in south-east Asia to the late 1850s. But there are more interesting objections to Lenin's concept of imperialism which arise from world history *since* 1945. Decolonization occurred during a period of sustained export-led growth in the capitalist economies, while world trading arrangements were simultaneously being liberalized. If the concept was to remain relevant to the post-colonial world it had to be fully detached both from the formal political control of one state over another, and from such instruments as tariffs and cartels which were evidently not essential features of 'high' capitalism. Moreover, the concept would have to accommodate the type of hegemony exercised by the United States in post-war international affairs, for here was a power which (despite its occupation of the Philippines between 1898 and 1945) had normally opposed formal empire. Furthermore, although the United States had traditionally been a protectionist state, after the Second World War it took the lead in sponsoring trade liberalization.

There had not been a political movement of comparable force in international trade since the middle of the nineteenth century, when Britain had systematically dismantled her tariffs, and yet dominated the global economy in a way which had no parallel until American hegemony after 1945. In 1953 two non-Marxist historians, Jack Gallagher and Ronald Robinson, took up the challenge of reinterpreting the past in the light of the present when they radically reassessed British 'imperialism', which hitherto had been exclusively identified with formal empire. They argued that legalistic criteria were quite inadequate to conceptualize the way Britain's industrialization caused a continuous, ever-extending and intensifying development of overseas regions. Instead, they defined imperialism as 'a sufficient political function of this process of integrating new regions into the expanding economy…' It was not a necessary function since whether or not imperialist phenomena showed themselves was determined not only by the economic expansion of the metropolis, but equally by the political and social organization of the regions brought into the orbit of the expansive society. They coined the phrase 'the imperialism of free trade' to characterize Britain's policy of recognizing newly-independent governments (notably in Latin America), signing commercial treaties with them, and using the consular service to promote British economic interests. They claimed:

> In both the formal and informal dependencies in the mid-Victorian age there was much effort to open the continental interiors and to extend the British influence inland from the ports and develop the hinterlands. The general strategy of this development was to convert these areas into complementary satellite economies, which would provide raw materials and food for Great Britain, and also provide widening markets for its manufactures.
>
> *(Gallagher and Robinson, 1953, reprinted in Shaw (ed.), 1970, pp. 142–163)*

Gallagher and Robinson did not discuss whether the 'informal empire of free trade' led to the 'underdevelopment' of the satellite economies, but otherwise their theses anticipated and complemented the 'dependency' perspective. Frank, for example, has argued that

> The development of industrial capitalism increasingly opened Latin America to free trade, and transformed the economic, political and social structure of the continent to suit the new metropolitan needs and local bourgeois convenience.
>
> *(Quoted in Platt, 1980, p. 115)*

Gallagher and Robinson were right to reject legalistic criteria of imperialism and to emphasize the continuity of British expansion, but most of their substantive claims with respect to British economic interests and political power in Latin America were either greatly exaggerated or simply wrong, as indeed are many of the historical arguments of the dependency theorists. It is true that Britain supported the insurgent Latin American states during the 1820s in the expectation of commercial advantages, but for the first half century of their independence these expectations must have been gravely disappointed. Although Britain was by far the largest exporter to Latin America, the region took a very modest share of the total value of British exports: a mere five-and-a-half per cent went to eight leading Latin American countries in the decade 1851–1860 (Platt, 1980. p. 116). Compared with Europe, North America, the British colonies of settlement and

India, Latin American markets were trifling (as indeed were other areas of supposed 'informal empire' such as Turkey and China). A fundamental reason for their limited commercial importance was that they exported very little and so had no basis for reciprocal trade. Far from being tied to the international economy through export-orientated monoculture, they were, up to the late 1880s, largely inward-looking societies that sustained themselves almost entirely on domestic demand and production. To illustrate: the total value of Argentine exports to Britain in 1883 was less than a million pounds sterling.

It is true that foreign (largely British) capital flowed into Latin America from about 1860 in order to finance railway development; as early as 1873, British companies controlled almost three-quarters of the Argentine railway network (Davis and Huttenback, 1986, p. 50). When such an overwhelming proportion of a country's vital means of communication is foreign-owned then we might appear to have unassailable evidence for 'economic imperialism'. I would nevertheless argue that it makes no sense to characterize economic relationships between two or more independent states as 'imperialist' unless they are constrained by non-market forces for the more or less exclusive benefit of the richer. Such constraints were rarely evident in South America. With respect to the most important regional economy (which Lenin considered a 'semi-colony') one historian writes: 'The British Government has never had the power to oblige Argentina to pay a debt, to pay a dividend, or to export or import any commodity whatever' (Ferns, 1960, p. 488). On the other side, the attitude of Argentine governments towards the railway companies was rarely compliant; disputes between them illustrate the limitations of any pressure that the companies could bring to bear, and underline the ultimate sovereignty of the state.

> Despite an appearance of strength, and the vital position occupied by the foreign companies in the economy, there was little that the railways could do when Argentine opinion favoured a specific course, no matter how inimical to the interests of the foreign-owned railways.
>
> *(Lewis, in Platt (ed.), 1977, p. 405)*

Foreign investment was attracted to Latin America simply by the prospect of a higher rate of return than could be obtained in Europe. The investment was not one-sidedly beneficial, and its initial purpose was the integration of national markets in South America, not the promotion of their export sectors. It is useful to recall that before 1914 the United States was massively indebted to foreign investors for the financing of its industrialization, because its example suggests that large-scale foreign investment was compatible both with local entrepreneurial control and broad-based economic growth. The reasons for the extreme specialization of the Argentine and other South American economies on agricultural exports lay, first, in the very advantageous terms of trade which food producers enjoyed from about 1896 to 1929 and, secondly, in such obstacles to industrial growth as the shortages of skilled labour and key raw materials.

Europe and Africa

The debate begun by Hobson was sparked off by the 'scramble' for Africa, for it was this most flagrant demonstration of European power over the wider world since the conquest of Latin America which persuaded contemporaries that 'imperialism' was a qualitatively new phase in European expansion. The 'scramble' remains the best context in which to analyse a concept which, ever since it entered the Marxist lexicon, has been essentially contested, although I have no illusions of synthesizing a consensus from the vast historiography of nineteenth-century imperialism here. For our purposes it is sufficient to distinguish between (a) a 'Eurocentric' paradigm, which interprets imperialism as a distinct phase in international and social politics that was intimately related to the management of uneven economic growth by conservative élites, and (b) a 'peripheralist' paradigm, which locates the origins of imperial expansion at the points of contact between western and traditional societies and emphasizes its continuity throughout the nineteenth century. The first paradigm continues to find neo-Marxist theses fruitful, and is most clearly delineated in the work of Hans-Ulrich Wehler (see Wehler, 1970b, for a convenient statement of his theory of 'social imperialism'). The second is resolutely sceptical of economic explanations of empire-building and is ably represented by D. K. Fieldhouse (see Fieldhouse, 1973). Inevitably, to oppose paradigms in this way glosses over a variety of interpretations and implies they are incommensurate; whereas, I would argue, Wehler's theory addresses the intentions and expectations of the 'New Imperialists' and the 'peripheralist' theory accounts for processes which occurred irrespective of intentions.

Before 1879, Europe's political presence in Africa was concentrated in three areas: Algeria, where the French army had been extending the occupation begun in 1830; Egypt, where the French and British exercised an informal imperialism over the Khedive's administration; and south Africa, where the British occupied the Cape as a Crown Colony, and claimed suzerainty over the independent Boer Republics of the Orange Free State and the Transvaal. Only in South Africa was there a dynamic frontier of white settlement, and the extension of Boer grazing areas brought periodic conflicts with African states. Elsewhere, the European presence was mainly restricted to coastal enclaves; the Portuguese had shadowy claims over the interior in Angola and Mozambique, but as with all the other European possessions (except Senegal) their rule did not penetrate more than a few dozen miles inland. For some years, the British and French had considered relinquishing their west African colonies because their interests there were so trivial. North of the Equator, Islam was the truly revolutionary factor in Africa's politics. The degeneration of the nominally-Turkish administrations in Egypt and Tunisia resulted chiefly from their indebtedness to European bondholders, to whom the state revenues had been mortgaged, and in its turn caused a profound Muslim reaction against foreign interests. Meanwhile, in the Sudan and the Sahel region, warrior theocracies were arising from one of the periodic revivals of Islamic puritanism.

By 1900, European governments were claiming sovereignty over all but six of some forty political units into which they had by then divided the continent, and of the six exceptions, only two (Ethiopia and Liberia) were still independent states in 1914. The established colonial powers hugely extended their empires: between 1884 and 1900, France acquired 3.6 million square miles and 37 million people; British acquisitions in Africa were somewhat less extensive but more populous. These powers had African interests which predated the 'scramble' and their actions were to some extent determined by existing imperial commitments; thus, France was drawn into the occupation of Tunisia by the need to protect its stake in Algeria, and British expansion up the Nile and into east Africa was much influenced by its perennial strategic concern for the defence of India. The really novel feature of the partition of Africa was the part played by European powers with no colonial tradition whatsoever: Leopold II of Belgium led the way when, in his personal capacity, he claimed the Congo basin for the Association Internationale du Congo (AIC); he was followed by Willhelmine Germany, which acquired a considerable land empire in south-west Africa, the Cameroons and Tanganyika, and Italy which established colonies in Somaliland, Eritrea and Libya.

Explaining the partition is bedevilled by the fact that there was no single process but a concatenation of events driven forward by unrelated regional crises within the continent. Leopold's original project was for a trading monopoly in the Congo – which the explorer Henry Stanley was despatched to negotiate with local chiefs in 1879 – and it would have remained a commercial venture had not France (in 1882) ratified the treaties her own explorer, Brazza, made with incomprehending chiefs, treaties by which she claimed territory on the northern bank of the Congo. What gave a great international impetus to this local competition was its coincidence with the breakdown of French and British Dual Control in Egypt and Britain's military occupation in 1882. France had strong historical and cultural links with Egypt, and a French engineer and French capital had built the Suez canal: resentment of exclusion from Egypt was a running sore in Franco-British relations for the rest of the century. To embarrass Britain, and as part of a strategy to reverse that exclusion, France supported Leopold's project to transform his Association into a political entity (making a deal by which she secured the reversion of the Free State should the resources of the AIC prove inadequate for its development). To counter the threat of British traders being excluded from the Congo by a protectionist regime, Britain backed Portugal's ancient – and quite unenforced – title to the estuary, with the proviso that the Portuguese guarantee free trade.

At this point, Bismarck was induced to make a bid for a formal German empire in Africa and the Pacific. Wehler has demonstrated that this was much more than a diplomatic move in the European balance of power. Rather, Bismarck felt impelled towards imperial expansion by an economic crisis of industrial overproduction and a social crisis of political alienation in the German working class, which was flocking to the outlawed SPD (Sozialdemokratische Partei Deutschlands). He was aware, too, that the era of international free trade was drawing to a close and feared that unless Germany acted immediately the imperialism of other powers would exclude her burgeoning economy from the world's less developed regions (Wehler, in Sheehan, ed., 1976). In May and July 1884, he seized the opportunity provided by Franco-British differences to proclaim German protectorates in areas of south-west and west Africa where Hanseatic traders were operating, while in the interim demanding an international conference to settle the Congo's future. Britain's acquiescence in Germany's claims was the price paid for German neutrality in the Egyptian dispute. (Meanwhile, a parallel sequence of events was leading to the disruption of the old *modus vivendi* of native states, Arab slave traders and European merchants on the east coast. Here, a leading actor was Carl Peters, representing the German Colonial Society, who on his own initiative secured protectorates where sovereign authority was later vested in the German East African Company.)

Contrary to myth, the Berlin Congo Conference (1884–85) did not deal formally with questions of sovereignty, and since the declared aim of the Berlin Act – to establish free trade zones in the Congo and the Niger – was soon nullified by the establishment of protectionist regimes, the whole affair would seem in retrospect pointless. However, Leopold's skilful diplomacy prior to the Conference brought international recognition of the Congo Free State, which was indispensable for the foreign investment he required to exploit its resources, and thus indirectly the Conference gave an international sanction to the partition. Moreover, by making 'effective occupation' the prerequisite for international recognition, the Berlin Act accelerated the process whereby paper claims became real annexations: expansionists 'on the spot' took this as a signal to by-pass native intermediaries and penetrate more deeply into the interior. The powers had hoped to wash their hands of direct state involvement in Africa and delegated to the various chartered companies the tasks of translating the cartography of partition into effective occupation and making the colonies pay. But in hoping to discard national commitments in this way, the diplomats 'had reckoned with an Africa without Africans' (Gallagher and Robinson, 1962, p. 36). In French west Africa, where the military were a particularly important element in the colonial presence, the movement into the interior brought European imperialists into conflict with Islamic states whose authority and coherence rested on the *jihad* (holy war) and for whom collaboration with the unbeliever was impossible. The French colonial commanders, acting more or less independently of the responsible Ministry, were drawn into a war of pacification which eventually resulted in the subjugation of the western Sudan and the consolidation of a block of territory running continuously from Algeria to the Congo.

The partition of Africa was a complex series of events which cannot be reduced to a single, or even neat set of causes, and what should be most emphasized is the political agency of Africans themselves. Everywhere, initial occupation was facilitated by indigenous conflicts: the aggressive expansion of warrior polities which preceded the European partition meant that there was no shortage of aggrieved African peoples to whom the Europeans could turn for allies and collaborators. Commercial motives were locally important in, for example, French expansion from Senegal, and commercial penetration in west Africa in the pre-partition period may well have provided a precondition for colonial take-over because it upset existing power structures within native states. Nowhere, however, was trade of sufficient volume to make it an overriding determinant of national colonial policy. Corporate economic interests of a different sort were clearly involved in the

Congo and Zambezia since the leading actors were capitalist corporations (such as the British South Africa Company) whose purpose was to exploit the mineral and other natural resources of the newly-acquired regions. It was to these corporations that their administration was initially entrusted and around 1900 it must have seemed self-evident that formal annexations were made for their benefit (as Hobson argued). With respect to Leopold II there can be no doubt he was in for loot. However, Cecil Rhodes – who floated the BSAC – was a complex visionary who was prepared to *jeopardize* economic interests for the political project of establishing a 'civilizing' British African empire from the Cape to Cairo (Fieldhouse, 1973, pp. 350–51). Men such as Rhodes and Peters are best described as 'sub-imperialists', usually acting without the authority of the metropolitan power, whose behaviour was conditioned by later nineteenth-century notions of racial destiny and biological-cum-cultural superiority.

The colonization of Africa was not caused by the varieties of racism which had taken root in the nineteenth-century anthropological and evolutionary sciences, but racism rationalized the expansion of European power and helped fashion a 'colonial mentality' for the continent's new rulers. By the 1890s 'scientific' racism had gained further credibility from the migration of the Darwinian concepts of 'natural selection' and the 'survival of the fittest' into the language of international politics. Within the colonies, heightened racial consciousness was manifested in stricter taboos on miscegenation and the introduction of an often mandatory colour bar tightly controlling social relations between the colonized and the colonials.

Racism did not altogether displace an older humanitarian tradition. A frequently forgotten aspect of the Berlin Conference was its formulation of an humanitarian framework for European relations with African societies: throughout its deliberations all expressed a desire to protect them from expropriation, to guarantee the possession of land, to stamp out tribal warfare and slavery. A direct line of descent runs from the conference to the Trusteeship System of the United Nations (Louis, 1971, p. 219). This amnesia about a vital aspect of the conference's deliberations is understandable given that its chief beneficiary flouted every humanitarian precept imaginable. Since indigenous society in the Congo was not monetized and wage labour was unknown, Leopold's Free State could only realize its commercial potential by coercing Africans into gathering wild rubber and ivory (which were decreed state monopoly products) and working as porters and labourers. Belgium accepted no constitutional responsibility for the State until 1908 and so there were no metropolitan subventions for the development of an economic infrastructure. Consequently, Leopold was obliged to hand over vast tracts of territory to concessionary companies who were supposed to bring in development capital. These 'mini-states' – of which the Anglo-Belgian India Rubber Company was the most notorious – actually invested minimal sums and ruled atrociously. Agricultural peoples of the riverside were forced into the forest at gunpoint to gather and hunt; punishments for the recalcitrant were whippings and maimings. Leaving aside these physical atrocities, forced rubber collection accentuated the natural disasters of famine and sickness which everywhere accompanied the precolonial opening of the continent and its later subjugation to colonial authority. The Congolese forest population may have been reduced by half between 1880 and 1920.

Although the suppression of the slave trade and domestic slavery was universally cited as legitimizing European intervention in Africa, colonial rule, in its initial phase, often substituted one form of forced labour for another. In the Sudan, the French set up 'freedom villages' with the ostensibly humanitarian purpose of accommodating slaves escaping to their lines; the real motive was to create pools of forced labour at the disposal of the army command. Official reports described them as inhabited by 'Gangs of wretched men dying of hunger ... yet ... forced to provide all the forced labour for the [local command] post...' (Cited in Suret-Canale, 1971, p. 64.). The French Congo witnessed all the malpractices of the Free State and they were not temporary features of the period of conquest: when André Gide travelled in the colony in the later 1920s he saw gangs of tribesmen, tethered by the neck, compelled to build roads; thousands of forced labourers died on the railway linking Brazzaville to the coast, which was not completed until 1934.

Another, less onerous form of forced labour, was the compulsory growing of cash crops, such as cotton, which the Germans attempted to introduce into east Africa. Here, the inefficient and frequently brutal way that forced labour was organized provoked the Maji-Maji rebellion of 1905 when for three months the Germans lost control of much of Tanganyika. The rebels killed the few Europeans and all their non-European agents, and burned the cotton crops. The Germans recovered the territory with savage 'scorched earth' tactics: 75,000 Africans are thought to have died in the war and the subsequent famine. Almost simultaneously, the Herero rebellion in German south-west Africa was being repressed with exemplary 'frightfulness': the tribespeople were driven into the desert and, in a notorious proclamation, all setting foot on German territory were threatened with extermination. Some have seen a continuity between these dreadful events and the genocidal violence of National Socialism (for example, Wehler, 1970b, p. 132). Possibly, but it must be said that wherever indigenous societies rose up against the consolidation of colonial rule, European powers crushed rebellion with unwarranted savagery. In this respect, German actions can be compared to the atrocities committed by the British after the Indian mutiny (1857–58) and the French after the Algerian uprising of 1871. As Albertini comments, 'The repression [of the Algerian uprising] was extraordinarily gruesome and bore all the earmarks of racist revenge' (1982, p. 259).

Who profited from modern colonialism?

It might appear incontestable that modern colonialism secured the political conditions for the expansion of capitalism and the enrichment of 'core' states at the expense of 'peripheral' regions; the pillage economy of the Congo could be cited as an extreme form of this process. Rather surprisingly, however, the profit-and-loss account of colonialism has shown that its economic benefits to the imperial powers were normally outweighed by unavoidable defence costs. Whoever profited from colonialism, it was not the state, and it is hard to show that the metropolitan economies grew more rapidly because of their imperial connections.

(Indeed, in Britain's case the tendency of her manufacturers to 'shelter' in imperial markets may have delayed the modernization required to compete with Germany and America.) Some time ago Henri Brunschwig demonstrated that, in the period 1871 to 1914, the French colonies did not pay: neither as sources of raw materials nor as markets for French products did they bring significant economic advantages. Colonial trade was a small proportion of total French commerce, never accounting for as much as ten per cent of total imports before 1914 or as much as 11 per cent of French exports. Despite a tariff regime favourable to French exporters, the trade of foreign countries generally benefited more than French trade from France's colonial expansion. French investors had few illusions about the profitability of French colonial investment, and most of their foreign investments were made in Russia, South America and British South Africa. Individuals and companies did, of course, benefit from commercial ventures in the French empire, ventures which would not have been viable without France's political domination, but private profit was achieved only at considerable public expense. By 1910, disillusionment with colonialism was widespread and the Minister for the Colonies was repeatedly asserting that the period of colonial expansion had now ended (Brunschwig, 1966, pp. 87–95, p. 146). It is true that the economic importance of the colonies increased during the inter-war depression when, in response to the collapse of world trade, protectionist barriers and the system of imperial preference were strengthened. The colonies became major suppliers to France of tropical products such as ground-nuts, bananas, cocoa and coffee, and colonial markets took a proportionally larger share of French exports (about 25 per cent by 1938) although absolute values did not rise greatly. In 1938, the 'franc area' accounted for 82 per cent of the exports and 69 per cent of imports of French West Africa; for Madagascar the proportion of both imports and exports was about 75 per cent (Deschamps, in Duignan and Gann (eds), 1970, p. 241). However, there was a hidden cost to this economic assimilation to the metropolitan economy in that the French consumer paid above world prices for colonial produce. Private and public investment in the colonies remained at a very low level and it would seem unlikely that, even in the circumstances of the inter-war depression, their economic advantage outweighed their disadvantages.

The costs and benefits of Britain's imperialism have been scrutinized even more closely than France's by two American scholars and their conclusions indicate no less emphatically that the debit side of the balance sheet outweighed the credit (Davis and Huttenback, 1986). Britain was more reliant on imperial sources for imports of raw materials and foodstuffs (by 1914, 25 per cent were colonial produce) and the Empire was a more important market which received about a third of British exports. However, unlike France, Britain traded freely with the whole world and expected its dependent colonies to do the same. Its colonial officials did not regard it as part of their remit to give exceptional support to British traders and businessmen; the watchword was 'a fair field and no favours'. Most, if not all the economic advantages from imperial trade could have been gained had Britain not had political control of vast regions of the world. As has been long appreciated, the argument that political control was necessary for the security of surplus capital invested abroad is fatally flawed by the fact that foreign countries and the self-governing dominions were much preferred fields of investment. Between

1865 and 1914, only 11 per cent of the private and public capital raised on the London money market for overseas investment went to the dependent colonies and India. The costs of defending the Empire were greater than is generally appreciated, chiefly because they were unequally distributed between Britain and the 'white' dominions, which by 1870 had responsible government and were in no sense objects of British exploitation. (They could and did impose tariffs on British goods, for example.) Whereas Britain was the most highly-taxed nation in the world around 1900 – with per capita defence expenditures significantly greater than other developed countries – the dominions taxed themselves very lightly and looked to the imperial exchequer to fund their strategic defence. Certainly, individual investors gained from the Empire, as did Indian Civil Servants whose large salaries were raised from local taxes and mostly remitted home, but equally certainly the British as a whole did not (ibid, p. 305). Modern research has vindicated the 'Little Englanders', such as Richard Cobden, who, in the 1850s, believed that Britain's best future lay in international free trade, withdrawal from empire, a minimum military establishment and settlement of disputes by arbitration (O'Brien, 1988).

A global analysis of the contribution of modern colonialism to western development made by Paul Bairoch exposes many of the myths surrounding the role of colonial exploitation to the economic success story of the West. Up to about 1950, the developed world was basically self-sufficient in industrial raw materials. With respect to energy sources, for example, more were produced than consumed in the developed countries and up to the Second World War their energy exports to the Third World slightly exceeded their imports from the Third World. Western dependency on Third World oil has, of course, reversed this situation, but it is of comparatively recent origin. Conversely, industrial raw materials represented only a small fraction of Third World exports throughout the nineteenth century and well into the twentieth. Textile fibres and raw rubber together accounted for about 14 per cent of Third World exports in 1830, 18 per cent in 1936–38. Minerals (excluding precious metals) and energy sources constituted only 4 per cent of Third World exports in 1911–13, and though with the expansion of oil this grew appreciably, it had still only reached 16 per cent in 1936–38. Bairoch's figures confirm the relative unimportance of the Third World in international trade: as far as Europe was concerned, between 1800 and 1938, only 18 per cent of total exports were destined for Third World countries (although for exported manufactured goods the proportion was significantly higher). More than four fifths of the developed world's international trade took place between developed countries. Since on average, exports accounted for some 8 to 9 per cent of the total production of the developed countries, exports to the Third World represented on average about 1.5 per cent of the developed world's total production. Britain was quite exceptional in that, over this period, some 40 per cent of its exports were to the Third World, and for one industry – cotton textiles – the proportion was 67 per cent (Bairoch, 1980, pp. 37–8).

The economic and social legacy of colonialism in the Third World

If colonialism brought, at best, marginal economic benefits for Europe, what were its consequences for the economies and social structures of the colonies? It is a question we must pose in pursuit of our theme of global inequality, even if space permits only the sketchiest of answers. In answering, one ought to distinguish between Asia (where decolonization began in 1947 with Britain's withdrawal from India) and Black Africa, where decolonization occurred later and was preceded by a policy of investment and development. But, leaving aside such nuances, three broad analytic frameworks present themselves. They do not represent mutually exclusive truths and are suggested as a means for organizing an unavoidably ragged discussion.

The first framework emphasizes the negative consequences of colonialism for the colonized: the over-specialization in one or a few cash crops or other primary products (such as copper) for export earnings; the neglect of food production; 'de-industrialization' of handicrafts; the fact that large-scale capital units tended to be confined to mining and processing primary products, and were foreign-owned. In this perspective, colonialism was one source of present-day impoverishment. Jean Suret-Canale has analysed the colonial economy of French tropical Africa from this perspective, arguing that, through the coercive mechanisms of poll-taxes and statutory labour days, the traditional equilibrium between society and nature was destroyed. Peasants were compelled to furnish a surplus of export products, as well as provide for their own subsistence, and because the new demands had to be satisfied with unchanged techniques, the margin of subsistence became painfully narrow:

> ... reserves kept back for traditional feasts or bad years disappeared. Malnutrition became a permanent feature. Any natural or economic catastrophe, such as a bad harvest or falling prices naturally resulted in famine... .
>
> *(Suret-Canale, 1971, p. 297)*

According to other analysts, the centralizing tendencies of colonial administrations in sub-Saharan Africa are implicated in the present inability of African societies to cope with natural disasters:

> A most discernible change in the agrarian basis of African societies occurred during colonialism, which fundamentally altered the relationship of rural Africans to one another and their environments. In colonial areas, control over essential elements of agricultural production was centralized by force and coercion. This centralization was of immediate and dramatic consequence for society's ability to respond to drought, because complex social relations based on local environmental requisites were radically altered. The centralizing thrust of colonialism alienated societies from their environments, upsetting traditional, localized patterns of coping with uncertainties.
>
> *(Glantz (ed.), 1987, p. 440)*

An alternative framework, while not necessarily denying the negative features of colonialism, insists that it had compensatory, 'modernizing' consequences. Rudolf von Albertini, for example, concludes his comprehensive history of the colonial empires thus:

> ...I remain committed to the view that the colonial period was a period of modernization for the colonized. The imposition of peace... the creation of larger territorial units, establishment of modern administrations and communications systems, and economic development were a part of this modernization, as were expansion of education and health services. The conserving of old ruling structures notwithstanding, foreign rule in the end was destabilizing and launched social changes that characterized the western way to modernization as the ideal way.
>
> *(Albertini, 1982, p. 514)*

The most important of these changes was the introduction of western property law, above all the law pertaining to the ownership of land (ibid., p. 499). Even if we reject the 'modernization' framework, we would agree that it was with respect to land ownership that the colonial presence impinged most on the lives of the peasant producers of Africa and Asia.

A third, intermediate framework insists upon the limited impact of colonialism on native institutions and the preservation of indigenous social patterns and traditional economic roles under the carapace of colonial administration. This framework has emerged from the analysis of the economic consequences of colonialism for British Black Africa and may have particular applicability to these territories, where the practice of indirect rule designedly minimized the disintegrative effects of western penetration. The central thrust of the argument is that, under colonialism, neither political nor economic forces proved sufficiently strong to change the essential character of African societies, except possibly in parts of south Africa. Very few Africans became capitalists in a European sense of depending exclusively on their ownership of the means of production to extract surplus value from others. Nor did most Africans become proletarians entirely dependent on selling their labour. Most remained in some sense peasants with the option of moving out of wage labour into rural self-sufficiency. Although foreign capitalism and fiscal demands compelled or persuaded the majority of Africans to become linked with the international economy as producers of cash crops, or small entrepreneurs, or paid employees, very few adopted any of these roles so exclusively as to sever their ties with their indigenous social and economic background.

> In short, colonial rule had a limited impact on African society and economy, sufficient to enable western capitalism to deepen its operations, insufficient to carry through a complete transformation or to make Africa entirely dependent on international capitalism.
>
> *(Fieldhouse, 1986, p. 31)*

This intermediate framework may prove the most useful in assessing the consequences of colonialism on the Indian subcontinent, by far the most populous area subjected to long-term European rule. Many of the economic and social indices are witness to gross under-investment in productive industry and social overhead

41

capital, and (*pace* Albertini) demonstrate that the 'modernizing' aspects of British rule were confined to the highest level of administration, and the building of the railway network and other communications facilities. In 1947, 88 per cent of the population was illiterate and only a fifth of children were receiving primary education. Vital statistics do not indicate any amelioration in health until the last decade of British rule, when the improvements were modest: the expectation of life for a male infant in 1941 was just over 32 years, and for a 10-year-old boy just over 41years. India had been, of course, the *locus classicus* of de-industrialization: British rule had indirectly destroyed India's trade in manufactured exports, and so reversed the historic trading relationship between Europe and Asia. Indian handloom textiles were all but eliminated from international markets and the subcontinent became a major importer of Lancashire cloths. Around 13 million yards of cotton cloth were imported in 1820; by about 1890 this had grown to 2050 million. In time, India developed her own mechanized textile industry, but Britain's free trade policy meant that until the First World War India was denied the tariff protection available to independent states. British imports entered India duty free, and when a small tariff was required for revenue purposes Lancashire pressure led to the imposition of a corresponding excise duty on Indian products to prevent them gaining a competitive advantage.

> This undoubtedly handicapped industrial development... If India had enjoyed protection there is no doubt that its textile industry would have started earlier and grown faster.
>
> *(Maddison, 1971, p. 56)*

Although factory-based, mechanized production began as early as the 1850s, its direct impact was minimal. At independence, the manufacturing sector was grossly frail, entirely dependent for its capital goods and replacement parts on imports, and lacking a technical cadre.

As we have noted, the colonial presence generally made its deepest social impact by introducing the western concept of individual proprietorship of land, and this was true of the subcontinent. In pre-colonial Hindu society, different social groups were customarily recognized as having an interest in land without any individual having an exclusive property right. In order to secure their revenues, which were largely derived from land taxes, the British 'settled' property rights on individuals and groups who accounted for only about 4 per cent of the agricultural population. In Bengal and adjacent territories, hereditary land titles were vested in *zamindars* – tax collectors of the old Mughal empire – in the hope that they would prove both improving landlords and a political prop of the raj. Elsewhere land titles were vested in *ryots* – peasant proprietors, although mostly belonging to the traditionally dominant castes. The great mass of the population now had to compete for the right to use land in a market where proprietary rights had been immensely strengthened. Furthermore, to meet British demands for revenue payments in cash, they had to sell part of their produce to near-monopsonistic buyers and rely on usurious money-lenders for credit. These factors greatly exacerbated mass rural impoverishment, and the recurrent famines of the 1860s and 1890s reinforced a cycle of misery by driving marginal holders to sell their land in unfavourable circumstances, and augmenting the resources of money-lenders (Raychaudhuri, 1985, p. 806).

One reason for the limited impact of western colonialism on the subcontinent's economy and society was that Europeans never settled there in any significant numbers. We can usefully contrast this situation with the Maghreb where customary rights were disrupted in the interests of European agricultural colonization. In the highland areas of pre-colonial Maghreb, where sedentary agriculture was concentrated, the private family property rights of Berber peasants were well-established, but villages were recognized as having a communal right to pasture lands. In the lowland areas, the dominant groups were nomadic tribal pastoralists to whom the private ownership of land was quite alien, though their collective grazing rights were recognized by Muslim law. European agricultural settlement necessitated the expropriation of the tribes and the placing of prohibitions on common lands. But it also required the 'forced individualization of property rights': a law of 1873 broke up collectively-owned land into individual plots which became private property and could be 'mobilized' under the provision of French law.

> The idea was to Gallicize all the land. If only a single collective holder
> desired it, the collective ownership of an entire holding could be
> nullified. The result was a veritable plundering of tribal properties...
> [as] the natives began to sell their land... .
>
> *(Albertini, p. 268)*

The French never realized their ideal of a European peasantry in the Maghreb, for there were only 30,000 non-Muslim farmers in 1955 (although they were responsible for one-third of agricultural output) and nearly all were expropriated after independence. But the colonial experience had changed agrarian society beyond recognition: the settlers had revolutionized agricultural methods and transformed the face of countryside by introducing vineyards and extending citrus fruit and cereal production. The French land laws had encouraged the concentration of Muslim landed property (often in the hands of wealthy townsmen) and greatly contributed to the growth of a rural proletariat that comprised about one-fifth of the agricultural labour force in 1955. By the end of the period of colonial development, the structure of Muslim rural society was extremely inegalitarian, although not solely because of socio-legal changes – for the population explosion exacerbated the problem of the impoverished landless labourer (Amin, 1970, Chap. 2, especially pp. 84–5).

Would the Maghreb's agricultural development have been any more 'balanced' had the colonial regime not been imposed? It is a difficult question which ties in with the larger problem of whether colonialism accelerated or retarded economic and social modernization. Comparison with Ethiopia, which resisted colonization until 1935, and where feudal relations and chattel slavery persisted well into the twentieth century, suggests that a similar social stasis might well have prevailed in the interior of the Maghreb without the shock of colonial rule. Samir Amin – his sympathy for North African nationalism notwithstanding – stresses the conservative effects in the pre-colonial Maghreb of social fissures between settled Berber agriculture in the highlands, the nomadic Arab or arabized zones, and the coastal cities which were divorced from the hinterland and whose closest links were with distant commercial centres such as Cairo. As a consequence,

Traditional Maghreb society on the eve of the French conquest was not united or integrated into the organic whole. It was composed of three different and relatively isolated worlds...[which] entertained very tenuous relations with another...

(Amin, 1970, p. 77, pp. 94–5)

Until the arrival of the French, central government was too weak to integrate these disparate communities and the creation of national units must be looked upon as an accomplishment of colonialism (ibid.).

The most tangible legacy of European colonialism in the Third World is the western city. Two illustrated here were founded by the great European chartered trading companies: Jakarta (formerly known as Batavia) founded in the 1620s by the Dutch East India Company (and modelled on Amsterdam), and Calcutta (see page 46), founded in the 1690s by the English East India Company.

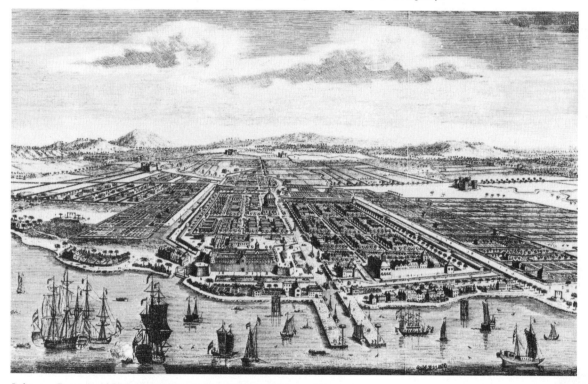

Jakarta, Batavia, 1754 (illustration: Mary Evans Picture Library).

Jakarta,
Indonesia,
1952
(illustration:
Popperfoto).

Jakarta,
Indonesia,
1966
(illustration:
Popperfoto).

Calcutta, India circa 1749 (illustration: Mary Evans Picture Library).

A Calcutta Street, 1953 (illustration: Hulton Deutsch Picture Collection).

The political legacy of colonialism in the Third World

We can be crisper and more emphatic in summarizing the political legacy of colonialism: it is evident in the persistence of the former colonies as territorial units, in their central institutions, and their induction into the international society of 'sovereign' states. The colonial regimes brought sharply defined frontiers to regions where they had never existed and they often divided tribal polities or artificially confined nomadic peoples. Nevertheless, the legitimacy of these territorial arrangements has been a keystone of the post-colonial order, above all in Africa where

> With amazing speed, a veritable African international public law for the
> preservation of colonial partition boundaries sprang up with
> independence, quickly enshrined in the 1963 Charter of the Organization
> of African Unity
>
> *(Young, in Gifford and Louis, 1988, p. 24)*

The new African states have generally been weak, fissiparous and crisis-ridden, yet paradoxically have maintained their territorial integrity. The explanation for this must be sought partly in the stance adopted by educated native élites during the anti-colonial struggle. They regarded the territory of the colonial state as the unit of self-determination and mimicked its monolithic character with a unitary vision of nationalism. When power was transferred, many of the new rulers were nationalists without nations; the colonial regimes had restricted the voluntary associations which constitute a national 'civil society' and foster a community of national sentiment. The new leaders sought legitimation and security through sanctifying their territory as embodying nationality. Since independence, many have imitated colonial autocracy by instituting a single party which claims to incorporate the popular will of the new nation and is thus entitled to unencumbered exercise of national sovereignty. In addition to these internal forces holding the former colonial territories together, international factors have played a part in their preservation. During the Congolese crisis of the early 1960s, for example, the United States and the Soviet Union were, for different reasons, both committed to the maintenance of the Congo as a single state, and the United Nations, the United States and to some extent Belgium play 'supervisory' roles in preserving the territory through its post-colonial crisis (ibid.).

The chief institutional legacy of the colonial powers took the form of unified administrative and judicial systems and general taxation, though they had also (usually late in the day) created representative bodies as part of the continuous search for collaborators amongst local élites. These institutions were part of the patrimony of independence and their inheritance afforded a strong degree of continuity between the colonial and post-colonial regimes. The African states have frequently witnessed the new rulers 'coming into their own' in the worst possible sense: all too often they have succeeded 'to the inflated salaries and living standards and, above all, to the vast and virtually untrammelled political power of the former colonial administrators...' (Oliver and Fage, 1975, p. 267). On the other hand, the political institutions of contemporary India are witness to a more

47

democratically constructive continuity between the colonial and independent regimes. In the decades before 1947, in response to organized Indian political opinion, the British had been forced to concede fiscal autonomy to the government of India, to devolve power to elected representative governments in the provinces and begin the 'Indianization' of the Civil Service. When independent India's constitution was drawn up, it embodied many of these institutional reforms: about 250 of its articles were taken virtually unchanged from the 1935 Government of India Act, which had been passed by the British parliament (Brown, 1985, p. 343).

Let us finally note in this section that, when colonial regimes were imposed on Asia and Africa, the pretensions of the European powers to absolute sovereignty and juridical equality (which were unique to their international society) were at their apogee. The colonial empires transmitted these characteristics of the state's personality to non-European parts of the globe, first, by endowing their own colonial administrations with vicarious sovereignty and untrammelled powers and, secondly, by bequeathing them to successor regimes. It is as sovereign, juridically equal states that the 'emergent nations' have joined the United Nations, other international agencies and (in the case of Britain's ex-colonies) the Commonwealth. In the French Community, the transition from a relationship of colonial dependency to equality between sovereign states was more protracted because, when negotiating independence with their former colonies, the French have taken it as axiomatic that the counterpart to independence was interdependence and close cooperation, that decolonization should preserve rather than destroy *'une presence française'*. But the French attempt to create a political community of Francophone African states in which responsibility for all matters of common concern lay with a single representative authority failed. For different reasons, Guinea, the Ivory Coast and Mali would settle for nothing less than complete sovereignty, and such interdependence as exists between France and her former colonies rests upon bilateral treaties of cooperation signed by independent sovereign states (Panter-Brick, in Gifford and Louis (eds), 1988, pp. 73–4, *passim*). In post-colonial Africa, tendencies to federalism or the pooling of sovereignty in regional groupings have been extremely weak and the new states have imitated 'old' Europe in their political egoism.

Decolonization

Colonial rule collapsed in two phases: between 1947 and 1954, the European powers either quit or were driven from their Asian empires; between 1957 and 1964 power was transferred in virtually all African colonies save the Portuguese. For the international society of states this has resulted in the displacement of a 'European' by a global world order. Not the least of its consequences has been the disrepute into which imperialism, and its associated racist syndrome of rule, have fallen. Before the break-up of the colonial empires, 'white' sovereign states outnumbered 'non-white' states and international relations accommodated themselves to the notions of white supremacy, which infected the political culture of even the liberal powers. A telling illustration of this was provided by the negotiations over the League of Nations Covenant in 1919: the Japanese delegates proposed that the clause in the Covenant affirming religious equality should be broadened to embrace racial equality. Prime Minister Hughes of Australia – which restricted immigration to 'whites only' – pronounced the theory of racial equality nonsense. President Wilson of the USA – where the southern states had disenfranchised blacks and legalized segregation – deemed that the Japanese motion failed for want of unanimous support. The contrast with the United Nations Charter – drawn up after a war against racism in Europe – is instructive: this declared the respect for and observance of human rights and freedoms, without distinction as to race, sex, language and religion, a principle of international society and recognized self-government as the ultimate objective of colonial territories (Vincent in Bull and Watson (eds), 1984, p. 252). The altered international regime is evident in the disposition of former colonies after the two world wars: in 1919, Germany's colonies and Turkey's *vilayats* (imperial provinces) in the Middle East were the victors' spoils; after 1945 Italy's possessions were treated very differently: Libya became independent in 1951, Eritrea was attached to Ethiopia, and Italian Somaliland returned to Italy in order to be prepared for independence within a strict ten-year deadline. The UN's Trusteeship Council (unlike the League's Mandates Commission) included representatives of anti-colonial Third World states, and increasingly saw its role as speeding the process of decolonization. The General Assembly provided a further anti-colonial forum, especially after the admission of Ghana (formerly the Gold Coast), the first Black African colony to gain independence.

Decolonization had different chronologies and modalities according to the strength of indigenous political movements, the colonial setting (in which the presence or absence of a 'white' settler community was a major variable), and the domestic political circumstances of the colonial power. Older accounts, which traced a continuous process of decline from the Wilsonian concept of trusteeship and the League of Nations mandate system, are unsatisfactory because they disguise the revival of the political project of colonialism, especially during and immediately after the Second World War when Britain, France and the Netherlands came to regard their colonial empires as indispensable for their own economic reconstruction. In south-east Asia, Algeria and Portuguese Africa decolonization was a prolonged internal war between the colonial state and revolutionary peasant nationalism, but elsewhere in Africa it took the form of a swift, unexpected, and peaceful transfer of power to successor élites. In these latter circumstances, nationalism was a consequence and not a cause of decolonization.

Asian decolonization

The political antecedents of Asian decolonization were several decades in advance of Black Africa's: modern political nationalism in India originated before the turn of the century and in French Indo-China during the 1900s. The emergence of Japan was inspirational for Asian nationalists generally and the Chinese Kuomintang a political 'model' for many. The Indian National Congress staged its first campaign of mass civil disobedience between 1920 and 1923. In 1930, Vietnamese nationalists attempted a revolutionary coup in Tonkin. During the

Depression, the peasant colonial economy in Indo-China was hit hard by falling prices which created a receptive social base for communist agitation. Three communist groups united under Nguyen Ai Quoc's (later known as Ho Chi Minh) leadership in 1930, and attempted a peasant rising in Annam, during which land was divided amongst the peasants, people's courts set up, and collaborators liquidated. The French used their Foreign Legion and aircraft to suppress the rebellion. In Indonesia, the Dutch faced a rather more diverse set of challenges to their rule: a mass religious movement, Sarekat Islam, competed with the secular revolutionary parties, chief among which were the Communists (who attempted a poorly managed coup in 1927) and the Partindo of Achmed Sukarno, founded in 1932. The three colonial powers all responded to nationalist challenges with armed force, the gaoling of nationalist leaders, and the execution of insurgents, but only Britain matched repression with significant concessions to nationalism. Political reform in 1919 promised Indians a share in provincial government and set up a Legislative Assembly in New Delhi; the 1935 Government of India Act gave complete control of provincial government to elected Indians and clearly implied a future progress to dominion status for a federation of the provinces and princely states. After the elections of 1937, Congress was the governing party in seven out of eleven provinces. It is worth noting that the Governor-General of Indonesia in the early 1930s was anticipating another three hundred years 'before the Dutch Indies may perhaps be ready for some kind of autonomy' (quoted in Albertini, 1982, p. 188).

Why should the UK – and not France and the Netherlands – have been prepared to make far-reaching concessions to nationalism? Britain had, it is true, an experience of decolonization with the Dominions who achieved full political sovereignty but maintained constitutional and sentimental ties within the Commonwealth. Decolonization, with dominion status as its goal, was thus recognized as a lawful pursuit. However, we must dismiss the old 'Empire-to-Commonwealth' mythology that portrayed decolonization as the graduation of new nations under Britain's benign political tutelage as one more instance of the national talent for self-congratulation. Self-interest and the realities of the colonial situation were rather more evident than altruism. In Indo-China and Indonesia, the European and Eurasian communities were powerful brakes on liberal policies; indeed, the colonial minority in Cochin (which was represented in the French Assembly) came to enjoy a degree of economic and political power which justified comparing it with Algeria's *pieds-noirs*. No such community existed in India which had fewer European administrators than Indo-China, though its population was far greater. Moreover, Congress nationalism was successful in winning the support of landowners, business people and professionals – whose moderation balanced the 'extremism' of its socialist left wing – with whom the British considered they could negotiate a settlement which would preserve their essential interests. Finally, the economic foundations of British rule were undermined in the late 1920s and 1930s by the collapse of India's foreign currency earnings from her export of primary produce. The military expense of governing India was rising and the revenue base contracting. Britain benefited most from an 'open' Indian economy which could receive British manufactured goods and export raw materials and whose currency was closely tied to sterling. But during the Depression there were strong pressures, from both the Government of India and Indian business élites, toward a 'closed' economy, which would protect native industry and control currency movements, and from which Britain would benefit much less. The option of an amicable transfer of power looked increasingly attractive (Tomlinson, 1979).

The upheavals of war overwhelmed European imperialism in Asia, even where the colonial powers were not actually defeated on the ground. Anger with the way India declared war without any popular consultation fired the 'Quit India' movement, the most massive challenge to British power since 1857, and its repression was a serious bone of contention with American public opinion. 'Diehard' imperialists were increasingly isolated within the British political class, and most accepted that the real issue was not whether Britain should quit India, but to whom power should be transferred. Even on this issue, British influence was eroded by the growth of the Muslim League and the degeneration of the subcontinent's communal politics into mass violence. East and south of India, the prestige of the European empires was shattered irreparably when they succumbed to small Japanese armies in 1942. The Japanese were widely welcomed as liberators in British and Dutch territories which they initially administered with a light touch that allowed local political activity to flourish. The consequences of these defeats for Allied diplomacy and post-war global politics were enormous:

> Empires *per se* were deplorable enough in many Americans' eyes; yet here was something even worse: an Empire [the British] that could not even protect its peoples, win their active allegiance, or put up a stern resistance to the common foe.
>
> *(Thorne, 1978, p. 207)*

Hitherto, the United States had shown little concern with south-east Asia, but from this point it saw itself as obliged to take a strategic interest in the region.

The connection between the Japanese occupation of Indonesia, and the post-war nationalist struggle against Dutch attempts to restore their authority, was particularly direct. Japan's projected Greater East Asia Co-Prosperity Sphere, though conceived as an instrument of Japanese hegemony, played a vital role in generating Asian consciousness which, after 1945, could not be forced back into colonial containers. The Japanese encouraged the formation of para-military youth organizations which heightened the political and racial consciousness of the generation of young adults facing the post-war world. For the first time, Indonesian nationalism became a majority sentiment amongst the urban political classes who seized upon it as a point of anchorage in a world in flux. With the deterioration of Japan's military position in 1944, local nationalists, led by Sukarno, were promoted as political barriers against the returning colonial powers. In the hiatus provided by Japanese defeat, they established a republic centred on Jakarta in Java. It was in a weak position: popular support was limited to the urban Javanese and the republic could easily be detached from its food supplies. In Sumatra and the other islands, the traditional allies of colonialism were initially prepared to collaborate with Dutch attempts to reshape Indonesian politics in a new federation (in which Dutch authority would be paramount). The key to the republic's final success in the post-war struggle was the growing involvement of the United States in south-east Asia. The Truman administration was dismayed by the squandering of Dutch resources on colonialist 'police actions' and regarded anti-communist nationalism as the appropriate ideology for emergent nations in the Cold War. After the Javanese nationalists had ruthlessly put down a communist rebellion in the republic, the Americans were convinced it was an acceptable successor regime and persuaded the Dutch to cooperate through the United Nations Good Offices Committee in a settlement highly favourable to unitary republicanism (though the Dutch hung on to western New Guinea until the early 1960s).

In Indo-China, the situation was significantly different because the Japanese preferred to retain the Vichy authorities so long as Japan's regional paramountcy and occupation rights were recognized. The local population experienced the war through its economic disruptions: the cessation of intra-regional grain shipments and the military requisitioning of grain caused a severe famine in Indo-China in 1944 (just as they had in Bengal in the previous year). The political grouping best placed to capitalize on popular discontent with the grain requisitions and repressions of the Franco-Japanese regime was the Viet Minh (or League for the Independence of Vietnam), an alliance of communists and nationalists formed after the Central Committee of the Indo-Chinese Party had taken refuge in China in 1941. The Viet Minh offered the only effective resistance to the Franco-Japanese condominium, and for this reason its military arm, under Vo Nguyen Giap, was aided from 1944 by the Americans. In March 1945, the Japanese displaced the Vichy French Governor (who had been making overtures to the Gaullists) and announced Vietnamese independence under the puppet Emperor Bao-dai. However, his conservative regime was allowed little effective power and had little hope of winning popular support amidst conditions of famine and chaos. The chief beneficiaries of the caesura in colonial rule were the Viet Minh. At the conclusion of the war in August 1945, the Japanese in Vietnam did not intervene when Ho Chi Minh proclaimed independence in Hanoi – with some expectation of being recognized by the Allies – and Bao-dai abdicated.

South of the 16th parallel, the Japanese surrendered to British forces who helped restore a French military presence in Saigon; but the Allied occupying power north of this line was Nationalist China, a fact that delayed the reimposition of colonial rule – although it did not exclude an agreed devolution of power to a Viet Minh regime which would have acknowledged French interests. In March 1946, a preliminary Franco-Vietnamese accord was signed which recognized Vietnam as a Free State with its own parliament, army and finances. It was left to a later conference to determine the exact status of Vietnam as a member of the proposed Indo-China Federation and the French Union, and a referendum was to be held to decide whether Cochin would adhere to the new republic. The Viet Minh were confident they would win a fairly-conducted ballot and Ho, and other leaders, went to Fontainebleau in June in the expectation of finding powerful supporters for an independent Vietnam amongst the Socialist and Communist Parties (both participants in government at that time). In this they seriously underestimated the strength of the 'stubborn colonial consensus' running from the Socialists to the right wing, which regarded the maintenance of 'overseas France' as the prerequisite for the restoration of national greatness (Smith, 1978, p. 80). With respect to

Indo-China, the consensual ambition was to construct a federation under French supervision which would secure the Laotian and Cambodian monarchies in power, leave pro-French, socially conservative groups in local control of Cochin, and confine the Viet Minh to Tonkin. The political communities of Indo-China would have had far more autonomy than before the war, and when coupled with the many progressive articles of the newly-constituted French Union (outlawing forced labour, for example), the federation represented a real liberalization of French colonial thinking.

This ambition now seems quite unreal in the light of France's own economic weakness. However, it foundered not so much on French incapacity as on the nationalist determination to unify the three Kys (or provinces) in an independent Vietnam, and the promotion by the French administration in Saigon of political separatism in Cochin, where Viet Minh guerillas were liquidating 'collaborators' and many had good reason to fear a Viet Minh victory. Cochin was the rice bowl of Indo-China and the French expected the Hanoi regime to collapse without access to its resources. (In fact, the Viet Minh cajoled and coerced the Tonkinois into producing sufficient to feed both the civilian population and the militias.) Under the agreement with Hanoi, French forces began to return to the north where they clashed intermittently with local defence groups and tried to reassert French control over the customs in the port of Haiphong. In November, local commanders demonstrated French firmness in dealing with Hanoi's truculent insistence on real independence by ordering the shelling of the port, killing about six thousand people. This was the real beginning of a war that did not end for the French until the Geneva agreement of July 1954.

We cannot recapitulate its course here. The principal point to note is that, what began as a war of colonial restoration, was transformed into a conflict in which France was cast in the role of defending the 'Free World' against international communism. Before the defeat at Dien Bien Phu, France had lost all 'colonialist' interest in the war's outcome because it had conceded to its nationalist collaborators in the south a political autonomy which vitiated its own position. The event which transformed the struggle, and led France to continue the fighting, was the communist victory in China. In 1950, Beijing and Moscow recognized the Viet Minh regime and China started to supply it with arms. This persuaded the United States that the 'Free World's' frontier lay in Vietnam; consequently, America stepped up its financial support for the French war effort, assuming two-thirds of its costs by late 1953. France's political ascendancy in Vietnam was increasingly undermined as anti-communist nationalists looked to the USA as their chief Western ally and mentor.

African decolonization

The Second World War had quite a different impact on Africa. There was certainly a radicalization of indigenous politics, particularly in the economically-advanced regions of British west Africa, but the war strengthened economic ties with the metropoles and initiated – or greatly accelerated – purposive colonial 'development' on the part of Britain and France. After the fall of France and Italy's declaration of war, the continent acquired a critical strategic significance, which had diverse repercussions on colonial polities and economies: the Gaullists launched their struggle against Vichy in the French African Empire; African human and material resources were drawn on by the Allies; industrial production increased in Britain's Black African colonies to meet the needs of the Middle East theatre.

Awareness of this strategic significance reinforced the determination to maintain imperial ties. This was strikingly evident in the declaratory principle of the African Conference, which the Free French convened in February 1944:

> The purposes of the civilizing work which France has accomplished in her colonies exclude any idea of autonomy, any possibility of evolution outside the French imperial *bloc*; the eventual establishment – at however remote a date – of 'self-governments' in the colonies must be ruled out.
>
> *(Cited in Grimal, 1978, p. 172)*

The constitutional position of the Black African territories in the post-war French Union reflected the dual desire to match African political aspirations with a degree of liberalization, and simultaneously to bind the territories into greater France. The metropolitan franchise was extended to large numbers of Black Africans, whose elected national deputies normally sat in the French Assembly as members of a metropolitan party (mostly in the SFIO, the French Socialist Party). However, this political assimilation of French Black Africa was half-hearted, for the territories were under-represented in proportion to their population and not given the administrative status of *départements*. Furthermore, although many Africans were added to the electoral rolls for the territorial assemblies, all legislative powers were reserved to the National Assembly in Paris, and the influence African politicians could bring to bear on colonial administrations still dominated by the French was limited. With hindsight, it seems clear that the post-war settlement was an unstable compromise between integration and autonomy, and exposed on the one hand to those pressing for full assimilation with metropolitan France and on the other hand to those demanding greater self-government. This instability was doubtless less evident in the later 1940s when nearly all Black African leaders, whether from the traditional chiefs (*Chefferie*) or from the educated (*evolué*) élite, retained a strong political attachment to France.

After 1945, official circles in the metropolitan states regarded the Black African colonies as essential to the reconstruction of their own devastated economies. An important restraint on European recovery was the shortage of dollars with which to finance capital imports, and the colonies acquired a novel value because of their dollar-earning capacities in the world market where commodities such as copper, palm-oil and ground-nuts were in short supply. Administrative controls were instituted to retain hard currency earnings in sterling and franc balances, while colonial produce was purchased in bulk through marketing boards to keep down prices in the metropoles, and restrictions placed on the export to the colonies of manufactures that might earn hard currency elsewhere. All in all, the metropolitan states squeezed and exploited their colonies in Africa in ways never seen before (Fieldhouse, 1986, p. 6). The positive side of this reinvigorated colonial relationship was an unprecedented level of state investment by the colonial powers, although in Britain's case the amount extracted between 1945 and 1951 appears to have exceeded public investment under the Colonial Development and Welfare Acts by an order of three to one. The French state invested on a far greater scale than the British, and was rewarded by a huge increase in exports from France to the colonies and of colonial imports into France. Though this brought undoubted advantages to France during the period of acute dollar shortages, the economic benefits for the metropolis after about 1952 are much more debatable. The colonies were mostly supplying tropical produce no longer in short supply at uncompetitive prices, so the metropolitan consumer was not advantaged, while as markets they were valuable chiefly to the least modern French industries, such as textiles. By the mid-1950s, many were objecting to the considerable sums allocated to African aid and development as diverting investment from metropolitan France; rapid industrial growth in the Netherlands after the severance of colonial commitments in Indonesia was regarded as an object lesson in enlightened self-interest. A new, anti-colonialism of the Right was emerging in French public opinion.

The decolonization of Africa presents an historical 'mirror image' of the partition of the continent: there were unrelated crises north and south of the Sahara, and the unexpected momentum acquired by the decolonization of Black Africa was like the 'scramble' in reverse. Unlike the partition, however, African decolonization had major political repercussions within Europe: Portugal's colonial wars sapped the manpower and economic resources of the authoritarian Salazarist–Caetano regime and finally led to its overthrow in 1974; the revolutionary junta of left-wing army officers granted immediate independence to Portuguese Guinea and quickly sought accommodations with nationalists in Mozambique and Angola.

In France, the incapacity of the 'parliamentary' Fourth Republic, when confronted with the Algerian insurrection that began in November 1954, had also proved fatal. Chronic ministerial instability and chronic deadlock in the French Chamber when major constitutional and colonial issues were debated clearly contributed to this incapacity, but it stemmed fundamentally from the European society France had implanted in Algeria. Constitutionally, Algeria was four departments of France and, in 1954, home to about a million non-Muslim French citizens who had long and effectively opposed the political enfranchisement of the majority of Muslim *sujets*. This society was largely made up of 'poor whites', imbued with a racist disdain for the Muslims (*sales ratons* – 'filthy rats' –was a commonplace epithet) and fearful that the Europeans' jobs and status would not survive democratic reform. French Algeria was represented in French political life, both formally through its deputies and informally through the Press, and had many sympathisers in the army's officer corps. (The political and constitutional ties of Kenyan and Rhodesian white settlers with Britain were by comparison tenuous.) On 13 May 1958 the European population of Algiers demonstrated against any negotiation with the National Liberation Front (FLN) and sacked the Residency of the Governor-General. Sympathetic army officers helped form a Committee of Public Safety, which in turn demanded of President Coty that he create a government of public safety, 'capable of preserving Algeria as an integral part of the mother country'. The insurrectionists also made a veiled demand for de Gaulle's return to power and on 15 May General Salan, the Commander-in-Chief in Algeria, voiced the cry '*Vive de Gaulle*!'. Both the threat and reality of military intervention in metropolitan politics persuaded de Gaulle to declare his willingness to return to office, but his price was the sweeping away of the political system of the Fourth Republic. A genuine fear of a military coup and even civil war drove the politicians to agree to a de Gaulle government with power to rule by decree for six months, and the authority to seek a mandate for a new constitution. The historic irony of these astonishing events is well known: the insurrection of French Algeria brought into being a presidential regime whose head had the constitutional power to impose a negotiated settlement and the strength of will to break *pied-noir* resistance. The reverberations of the Algerian crisis throughout metropolitan society reached a climax in April 1961, when France was threatened by a military *putsch*, led by generals opposed to peace talks with the FLN. In the wake of its failure, irreconcilable army officers (with the support of right-wing politicians such as Georges Bidault) spearheaded the terrorist campaign of the OAS – the Secret Army Organization, whose murderous activities did as much as anything else to persuade French public opinion of the advisability of precipitate withdrawal from Algeria (see Horne, 1977, for the fullest account in English of the Algerian war).

The Algerian revolution was extraordinarily important in creating a new political consciousness of the Third World, both within Europe's intelligentsia and throughout the wider world. The writings of its best known spokesman, Frantz Fanon, articulated a demand for the restitution of the wealth plundered by Europe from the colonized world, and for an egalitarian world economy, which anticipated the call of the Non-aligned Movement for a New International Economic Order (see above, p. 11). They also gave a new twist to the history of the idea of Europe by demonising the humanist and universalist ideology of 'Man' which had been a basic element of post-Enlightenment political culture. Fanon concluded *The Wretched of the Earth* with a call to

> Leave this Europe where they are never done talking of Man, yet
> murder men everywhere they find them…
>
> *(Fanon, 1967)*

The book can be taken, in a number of ways, as a kind of epitaph to the 'European' history of the world, for it proclaimed both the end of Europe's colonial domination of the wider world, and the end of Europe as a source for the revolutionary emancipation of humankind. Ironically, Fanon's writings had their greatest influence within Europe itself: they persuaded Jean-Paul Sartre – and others on the non-communist Left – that the revolutionary agent in world history was no longer the proletariat of the developed world, but the dispossessed peasantry of the Third World.

Though the Algerian revolution was inspirational for other African independence movements, it is hard to fit into any 'pattern' of African decolonization. It was exceptionally sanguinary – the loss of life amongst Muslims has never been exactly computed, but Algerian sources claim one million war dead – and much of the violence was internecine. During the 'settling of scores' after independence tens of thousands of the ex-colonial regime's native functionaries were liquidated. Whereas France maintained close ties with most of its former colonies, official relations with independent Algeria were icy until the mid-1970s. It is true that there was no immediate economic break, for France provided a high level of aid as its price for the continued exploitation of the Saharan oil wells and for the freedom to transfer funds. But the socialist regime of Ben Bella initiated an economic rupture by expropriating French agricultural holdings and nationalizing oil and gas properties; his successor, Boumedienne, completed it by taking over a majority holding in all companies and nationalizing foreign trade. The economic tie with France which independent Algeria found impossible to sever was the provision of immigrant labourers whose remittances have been crucial in sustaining its development programme. The break with France at a cultural level has been equally sharp; whereas nearly all the former French colonies have identified with the grouping of French-using states, known as *la Francophonie*, Algeria has not done so, and now gives equal importance to the teaching of English.

Decolonization in the British and French empires south of the Sahara was comparatively bloodless and not, on the whole, the work of the freedom fighters. In 1938, British officialdom stated for the first time that leading the peoples to independence was the ultimate goal of its rule in Black Africa, but considered this would take 'generations, or even centuries' (Wilson, 1977, p. 290). Yet as early as 1947 the strategists in the Colonial Office were planning to dismantle the colonies, or at least those without a significant settler presence. Given the considerable economic advantages Britain was now deriving from them, and the absence as yet of any broad-based independence movement, this sudden contraction of the time-scale for self-government is rather baffling. What explains it? That there was a Labour administration with anti-colonialist sympathies was of some significance, and Britain's humiliating dependence on the United States was still more important in drumming home the message that the age of empire was ending. But more immediately relevant was the recognition on the part of key permanent officials that the traditional tribal institutions of indirect rule were incapable of providing the structures needed to oversee rapid development. The native chiefs were too compromised to be agents of national unification, and the colonial administrations were ordered in 1947 to replace indirect rule through the chiefs with elected local councils. This initial democratization of colonial government largely created African nationalism as a popular movement, for it obliged the tiny, educated nationalist élites to turn to the organization of mass political parties. The Accra riots on the Gold Coast, in 1948, accelerated the process of keeping ahead of African politicization in order to make it more manageable: plans for self-government were brought forward and, after the overwhelming success of Kwame Nkrumah's party in the 1951 elections, he was released from gaol and made leader of government business in the legislative assembly – a kind of prime minister to the Governor's constitutional monarch (Robinson, in Morris-Jones and Fischer (eds), 1980). This arrangement functioned well, and the economic conditions for full independence also appeared particularly propitious on the Gold Coast: it was the most prosperous area of Black Africa whose development as a whole was rapid during the 1950s (in comparison both with the past and Asia). The granting of full independence in 1957 had a 'domino' effect on the other territories of British West Africa, and because two of them (Togoland and the British Cameroons) were trusteeships linked to adjacent French territories, France was obliged to offer full independence to French Togo and the French Cameroons.

A stark contrast is often made between Britain's voluntary withdrawal from empire and France's fighting retreat, but the speed and smoothness with which France decolonized her Black African empire between 1956 and 1961 quite belie this stereotype. Negotiated withdrawal was eased by the escalating cost of economic aid to French Black Africa and the growing consensus that the modernization of France demanded the concentration of her economic and political efforts on Europe. (Indeed, it is noteworthy that the negotiations which culminated in the Treaty of Rome coincided with the first phase in the movement to independence.) Withdrawal was initiated by the much denigrated politicians of the Fourth Republic: Edgar Faure oversaw the granting of independence to Morocco and Tunisia in 1955. A year later the government of Guy Mollet responded to the growing demand in Black Africa, if not for independence at least for greater autonomy, with the '*loi cadre*' (outline law), which the Ivory Coast politician Félix Houphouet-Boigny (who was in Mollet's cabinet) was instrumental in drafting. The law introduced a universal franchise and a single college for all elections and granted legislative powers in matters of local concern to the territorial assemblies which were now responsible for electing executive ministerial councils. Though the governors were to chair these councils, real authority would lie with the vice-presidents who were also leaders of the majority parties in the assemblies. By reserving certain powers to the metropolitan assembly and delegating the rest to the ministerial councils, this law weakened the federal administrative units of French west Africa and equatorial Africa. Black African leaders, such as Léopold Senghor of Senegal and Sekou Touré of Guinea, suspected France of deliberately 'Balkanizing' her African territories into such weak units that they would be unable to break their economic and political ties with the metropolis. Both advocated a union of territories more firmly independent of France. De Gaulle's return to power created a new situation. In the constitutional referendum of September 1958, de Gaulle held out two options to French African colonies: political autonomy within the framework of the French Community or immediate independence. Community status for the colonies would allow for eventual independence with no time limit specified. With the exception of Guinea, where Sekou Touré secured a vote for immediate independence, all the colonies elected to stay with the French Community, although not for long. Even before the institutions of the Community had been set up, individual African states (beginning with the short-lived Mali federation) began to demand full independence and, by the end of 1960, all had achieved it.

Though the African states acceded to juridical independence, their economic, military and cultural ties with France remained far stronger than those linking Britain to her former colonies, and it was for this reason that the debate over 'neo-colonialism' was much livelier in the French-speaking world. Apart from Guinea, whence France withdrew all aid immediately after the 1958 referendum, French economic institutions and administrative personnel exercised a preponderant influence over the former colonies for at least a decade after formal independence (Coquery-Vidrovitch, in Gifford and Louis (eds), 1988, pp. 105–34). French experts prepared all the first national development plans, and many of the later ones. The monetary and banking links between the CFA (French-African Community) Franc Zone and Paris were exceptionally strong (much more so than comparable ties in the Sterling area): the value and exchange rate of the African franc were pegged directly to the metropolitan franc, the two currencies were fully convertible, and two issuing banks in former French Africa were in fact branches of the Bank of France, which held their reserves and foreign-currency holdings. The Bank of France imposed financial rectitude by forbidding the African issuing banks any deficit, while French government subsidies covered the budgetary and balance-of-payments deficits run up by the new states. Though these arrangements smack of 'neocolonialist' control, they secured a stable and convertible currency for small, economically fragile states – which was a major advantage in attracting foreign investment. The currency tie reinforced the former colonies' commercial dependence on France, which remained their single most important supplier and market (one-third of their exports went to France in 1978 and France supplied forty per cent of their imports).

These economic links were complemented by France's occasional military interventions on behalf of sympathetic regimes (as in Senegal in 1970 when the Senghor regime was discreetly protected by the French army) and by the vigorous promotion of the French language, education and culture. Secondary and higher education were, up to the 1970s, closely modelled on French syllabuses and methods, and university staff were mostly French nationals, funded by France. Partly because of the assimilationist tradition in French colonialism, the cultural impact of France on individual Africans, whether educated intellectuals or recruits to the French forces, was much greater than Britain's. Post-independence regimes in Francophone Africa displayed – even flaunted – French cultural influences in ways that had no parallels in the formerly British territories.

Since the early 1970s France has become more detached from its former colonies: with the revision of the cooperation agreements it relinquished its economic privileges but also reduced its financial aid, and its influence has waned with the 'Africanization' of the civil service, the teaching professions and private sector management. Economic withdrawal has been, in fact, speedier and more complete than the political and cultural retreat. As a market and source of supply, French-speaking Africa is now quite insignificant for the French economy. Although France remains an important market and supplier for the former colonies, the bilateral relationship is no longer the predominant external factor in determining their economic fortunes. It has been displaced by multilateral relationships with the international economy which are typical of the asymmetrical bonds between rich and poor, North and South. The origins of this growing multilateralism can be traced back to the formation of the European Community and the securing by France of preferential access to the entire Common Market for the produce of the states within the French Union, which have reciprocated by lowering barriers to EC trade and investment and granting establishment rights to all EC firms. The purpose of the French policy was to make the original Common Market six share

The apogee (or nadir) of French cultural influence in Africa: the coronation of Jean Bedel Bokassa as Emperor of the Central African Empire in a regalia modelled on that of Napoleon Bonaparte. Bokassa was a former paratroop sergeant; he maintained his French citizenship and told an interviewer at the time: 'Like Napoleon, I am proud of being a French soldier. I am Emperor by will of my people, but I will also remain a Frenchman as long as I live …' (The Guardian, *5 December 1977; illustration: Popperfoto*).

the burden as well as the benefits of the colonial pact, and in this it has succeeded: the EC took over many of France's developmental obligations to its former colonies and nearly all the aid provided under the European Fund for Overseas Development has been for the benefit of former French territories.

The Francophone African states are amongst the world's poorest countries and those in the Sahel region face catastrophe. Would their level of development and prospects have been any different if the French presence had been exerted in another fashion? Have the specific forms of the transfer of power modified in any fundamental way the unfolding of economic processes in French-speaking Africa? In a searching analysis, Catherine Coquery-Vidrovitch responds negatively to both these questions:

> In the economic field, there has been nothing to distinguish the
> operation of French interests in Africa from any interests originating in
> the developed world. ...French or not, domination of the South by the
> North would have expressed itself in more or less the same way and in
> the same channels, it would have exploited the same collusion of
> national governments reflecting the interests of factions (rather than
> classes), which would probably have led to the same mistakes.
>
> *(Ibid., p. 130)*

Many of the problems facing the Francophone states are common to other parts of Black Africa, and – as is the case elsewhere – inherent difficulties of climate, ecology and overpopulation have been exacerbated by misguided policies and the abuse of state power.

Notoriously, Black African political independence has not fulfilled the expectations placed upon it in terms of economic well-being, and the confident predictions of sustained development made by many development economists and the nationalists in the 1950s and 1960s have been falsified by the decline in real per capita incomes in many states since the later 1970s. Explaining this situation, and assessing the extent to which the colonial past and post-colonial 'dependency' have contributed to it, is controversial. The once commonly heard argument that 'neocolonial' economic dependency was the intended result of decolonization, and that the colonial powers withdrew when they were confident that their economic interests would remain intact in the states they had created, has not been demonstrated by the historical record. Economic calculations do not appear to have weighed heavily in the decisions to withdraw, and business interests appear to have had little influence one way or another. Moreover, it is rather implausible to attribute (as Amin has done) 'blocked' development to neocolonialism, when economic growth in most of Black Africa was in fact positive until the mid-1970s, and regression has occurred since the marked decline of the economic interests of ex-colonial powers in the region.

This is far from asserting that there are no 'external' causes to Africa's current crisis. African governments are powerless before the declining terms of trade for primary agricultural products, protectionism on the part of industrialized countries, commodity price fluctuations in the international market, and the burden of debt-servicing – which all weigh on peasant producers. But 'internal' causes are scarcely less important. African societies have been betrayed by their states, so many of whom are guilty of 'autocratic economic management, one-party rule, hypertrophied bureaucracy, and clientelism – the whole bringing with it decisions and practices that defy any good economic sense' (Coquery-Vidrovitch, in Gifford and Lewis (eds), 1988, p. 133). The region's chronic political instability has disrupted the customary ways of coping with long-term drought and ecological deterioration, impeded economic development, and is the cause of the high incidence of refugees: although sub-Saharan Africa has only about 10 per cent of the world's population, it now accounts for approximately a quarter of the world's refugees. Underlying the dismal economic record since the 1970s are the disastrous agrarian policies (some of them initiated by colonial administrations) pursued by African governments as part of the programme of import-substituting industrialization. These policies have resulted in very disadvantageous internal terms of trade for peasant farmers who are still the great majority of the population. Prices for agricultural cash crops have been kept artificially low in relation to locally manufactured consumables. To raise food prices would inflame the underemployed urban working class on whose support political leadership must rely. Agrarian policies are administered through parastatal agencies, which are notoriously corrupt, maladministered and (since they operate with the police power of the state) oppressive. Farmers have no incentive to produce for off-farm sale nor to raise their productivity; agrarian stagnation or contraction has occurred while population has soared (Lofchie, in Glantz (ed.), 1987, pp. 85–109). Nor can we be hopeful about the future: further famine is anticipated, chiefly because ongoing civil wars in the Sudan, Ethiopia, Liberia and Eritrea have exacerbated the effects of drought.

Western aid to the Third World

Since the emergence in the 1950s and 1960s of the new nations of the Third World, economic 'aid' – or official development assistance – has been an important, though controversial link between them and Europe. Aid covers a spectrum of activities resulting in the transfer of resources on concessional terms, and mostly takes the form of 'soft' loans (i.e. at an interest level below market rates). It is provided through two types of agency: the development ministries of the individual states which channel bilateral aid to Third World countries, often those with whom they have constitutional or historic links (thus about one-third of French aid is directed to the Départements et Territoires d'Outre Mer and is akin to regional assistance within a European country); and international sources of multilateral aid such as the International Development Association (IDA), which is the soft loan 'window' of the World Bank. Bilateral aid still accounts for most development assistance and the most important donor is now Japan. However, the proportion of multilateral aid has been growing for some time and this trend will probably continue. In a western European context, the trend is manifested in the increasing share of development assistance channelled through the European Development Fund (EDF), the main instrument of the European Community's aid programme. The origins of this concerted policy towards the developing countries lay in the first Lomé Convention of 1975 by which a group of African, Caribbean and Pacific countries (all ex-colonies) negotiated associate status – entailing trade advantages and contractual development assistance – with the EC. It is a matter of debate whether concerted 'European' aid is more advantageous for developing countries than bilateral aid. Non-associated states have lost out to a degree because the Lomé signatories have received a 'disproportionate' share of EC aid. Moreover, the effectiveness of the EDF and other agencies has been called into question because their lending criteria seemingly reflect internal political, rather than developmental considerations. We must note that subsequent Lomé conventions curtailed development aid in real terms (Cassen *et al.*, 1986, p. 272). Although our focus is western Europe, it is worth recalling that the erstwhile Soviet bloc was a significant source of aid which, by the later 1980s, was heavily concentrated on Cuba, Mongolia and Vietnam.

Aid has many critics: some decry it as a 'massive' handout from the rich to the poor (but 'profligate') nations. Neo-liberals object in principle to the governmental allocation of resources and argue that aid goes to statist regimes which obstruct market-based growth. Critics on the Left condemn 'aid' as a misnomer for neocolonialist policies of the donor national governments. According to them, aid represents a one-sided political bargain between the rich, advanced economies, with surplus capital and technology that they are prepared to put to use in the developing countries, and poor countries whose resources the rich want to obtain or control:

> All too often [the poor countries] are obliged to settle for aid on the
> terms which the donors offer… the long-term effects [of aid] are usually
> to tie the economy of the donor still more closely into the system of the
> donor… the more a country takes in aid the greater the restraints upon
> its real economic independence or its chances of achieving such a state.
> *(Arnold, 1979, p. 8)*

On the other hand, humanitarians applaud the principle of aid, but condemn the niggardly percentage of the rich countries' national products devoted to it.

Amongst the western European states, we can discern a variety of motives for providing development assistance. National interest is certainly one of them: donors support countries with which they have, or hope to have, strong economic, political and cultural ties, and for this reason Britain and France have directed much of their aid towards their former colonies and sought to gain commercially thereby. Britain has tried to increase domestic employment by tying aid to the purchase of British-made goods. For France, cultural objectives (not least the promotion of the French language) have been particularly important: about one-third of the aid going to Francophone Africa has been devoted to education. But it is difficult to discern 'national interest' in the aid programmes of the Nordic countries, the Netherlands or Federal Germany (as it was) which, in terms of the percentage of their GNPs devoted to overseas development assistance, have all been generous donors. For these states, humanitarian motives have almost invariably been in the ascendant. The Nordic donors have for many years devoted the bulk of their aid to the relief of poverty in the poorest countries.

Despite the element of national interest in some donors' policies, the critique of aid as a lubricant of neocolonialism is not credible. An examination of the aid record shows that it has promoted autonomous development in Asia and Latin American countries and enabled some, which started in the low-income group, to rise to the middle-income category. South Korea is the most spectacular example, but Brazil, Columbia and Thailand have made remarkable progress (Cassen *et al.*, 1986, p. 14). In newly-independent Bangladesh, aid served the basic functions of ensuring survival and holding a society together, and also contributed significantly to economic reconstruction and population resettlement. In India, both food and financial aid, though modest in relation to the whole economy, have at critical times eased savings and foreign-exchange constraints and permitted faster growth than would otherwise have been possible. Aid has also been a factor in Asia's 'green revolution'.

Transactions between developing countries and development agencies have, certainly, infringed on the recipient's national autonomy, but this has been most evident in the negotiation of structural adjustment loans from the World Bank, a multilateral agency. The Bank has required borrowers to agree to a stabilization programme drawn up by the International Monetary Fund (not itself an aid agency) as a condition for a loan, and recipients have had to acquiesce in procedures that could be considered infringements of national sovereignty. The IMF espouses monetary stability and has imposed deflationary measures and the restriction of government spending as loan conditions. During 1982–84 nearly sixty indebted counties (most of them 'middle-income') were engaged in stabilization programmes supported by the IMF's conditional resources. There is a similarity with the way the nineteenth-century imperialist powers regulated the state revenues of insolvent Turkey, Egypt and China, but no exact parallel: the IMF has imposed deflationary measures on developed countries (such as the UK in the late-1970s) and developing countries alike, and it acts self-consciously in the interest of the stability of the world capitalist system as a whole. To 'accuse' it of this would be as otiose as charging a nun with devotion to Christ. A more serious charge against the World Bank is that it has punitively withheld resources from left-wing governments where they have nationalized foreign enterprises, and in so doing has really acted 'bilaterally' on behalf of the member state whose assets had been appropriated. (The most notorious case concerns the Allende government of Chile in the early 1970s which nationalized – with compensation – American mining interests.) But here it was the denial of aid, not its provision which constituted 'neocolonialism' or 'imperialism'.

The charges worth making against development aid are that it is insufficient, poorly coordinated and, occasionally, harmful to the poor. (Thus, when cash crops are substituted for food crops, undernourishment sometimes becomes more frequent even though income rises – markets are too poorly organized to make good the food deficits.) The Brandt Report called, in 1980, for a doubling of aid to the poorest countries in real terms and a commitment on the part of the developed states to allocate 0.7 per cent of GNP to development assistance by 1985. By the end of the decade, the Nordic countries, the Netherlands and France (if we include her aid to overseas departments and territories) had achieved this target; the UK – in common with most other donor countries – had not.

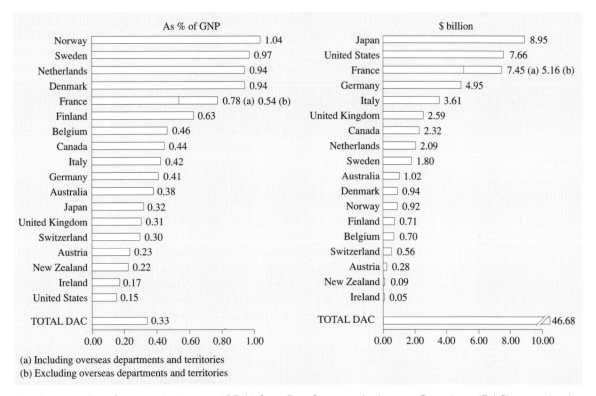

Net Overseas Development Assistance (ODA) from Development Assistance Committee (DAC) countries in 1989

Source: Organization for Economic Cooperation and Development (OECD) 1991 *Review*

Conclusions

This essay set out to trace the relationship between Europe and the Third World within the twin contexts of global economic inequality and the emergence of an international 'society' of nation-states. Several of the theses which shaped this agenda can now be seen as, at best, highly implausible. The contribution of colonial spoils to the onset of industrialization in Europe was marginal; sustained economic development in the nineteenth century did not require imperial control of the less developed regions; surplus capital did not go to colonial outlays; colonies were not important sources of raw materials for nineteenth-century industrial economies; international trade with the Third World did little to make the rich states richer. The contrary set of arguments which trace 'underdevelopment' in the Third World to the impact of Europe are more persuasive: slavery, forced labour, the compulsory growing of cash crops at fixed prices, the break-up of communal holdings – all regularly accompanied European political expansion. It is impossible to say, in a general way, whether the longer-term benefits of the imperial civil peace, administration and law 'compensated' for the frequently catastrophic impact of the initial phase of European rule. We would have to examine the issue case for case, and the moral arithmetic is dauntingly complex. Was Belgium's

65

paternalist welfare state in the Congo adequate restitution for Leopold's hell on earth? Much less persuasive is the 'strong' thesis of 'underdevelopment' and 'world-systems' theory, namely that dependent relations with the core stymied broad-based economic development in such peripheral regions as Latin America and India. One problem with this thesis is it that it exaggerates the extent to which the different regions of the globe participated in an international division of labour before the twentieth century (see the discussion of Latin America above). We could also justly argue against it that where growth has taken place it is at the points of contact with international capitalism.

Since the 1970s, the once close-knit relationships between western Europe and its former dependencies in the Third World have unravelled. This is partly because superpower rivalry reintensified during the late Brezhnev, early Reagan years, and was extended into the Middle East, the Horn of Africa and other politically-turbulent regions in the less developed world. The political influence of the old colonial powers was overshadowed, while the attempts by western European leaders untainted by the colonial past (such as Olof Palme and Willy Brandt) to promote a North–South dialogue were disrupted. The most baneful result of what has been called 'The Second Cold War' was the accelerated militarization of much of the 'Third World': during the 1980s, while US spending on developmental aid fell in nominal as well as real terms, spending on military and security aid shot up; similarly, the value of arms transfers by the Soviet Union to Africa (both north and south of the Sahara) far outweighed economic assistance. Although the superpowers have ended their confrontation, its consequences persist in, say, Somalia where rival factions deploy huge stocks of weaponry against each other, and against a brutalized and starving population.

We may finally note how this militarization has interacted with the chief global political consequence of the 'European' history of the world: the organization of humanity into sovereign states with fixed frontiers. Arms have generally flowed into regions where state borders are of questionable historical legitimacy, because imposed by colonial powers, but are at the same time essential to modern national identity. That this is an explosive conjunction is particularly evident in the Middle East, where most borders were decided by the European victors in the aftermath of the First World War; the boundaries of Kuwait, for example, were delineated by a British military officer and Iraqi claims date back to the 1920s. The unitary character of these states belies the ethnic and sectarian divisions within them, but the flow of arms has greatly increased the coercive power of the cliques who control the state over dissident minorities (such as the Kurds). So resort to 'internal' state violence mirrors 'external' aggression, which the superpowers either signally failed to resolve in the 1980s – as with the Iran–Iraq war – or, in the Gulf war, could only resolve with the massive use of force. There are analogous situations in the Horn of Africa, the Sudan and Indonesia. The political settlements imposed by Europeans in their centuries' long expansion have often been trumpeted as bringing civil order to strife-torn regions; a sceptical eye might well discern in them seeds of the present international anarchy.

References and further reading

ALBERTINI, R. VON (1971) *Decolonization: the administration and future of the colonies, 1919–1960*, New York, Holmes and Meier.

ALBERTINI, R. VON (with WIRZ, A.) (1982) *European Colonial Rule, 1880–1940*, Oxford, Clio Press.

AMIN, S. (1970) *The Maghreb in the Modern World*, Harmondsworth, Penguin.

AMIN, S. (1973) *Neocolonialism in West Africa*, Harmondsworth, Penguin.

ARNOLD, G. (1979) Aid in Africa, London, Kegan Paul.

BAIROCH, P. (1975) *The Economic Development of the Third World Since 1900*, London, Methuen.

BAIROCH, P. (1980) 'Le bilan économique du colonialisme: mythes et réalitiés', *Itinerario*, Pt.1, pp. 29–41.

BAIROCH, P. (1982) 'International industrialisation levels from 1750 to 1980', *Journal of European Economic History*, **11**, pp. 269–332.

BAIROCH, P. (1986) 'Historical roots of economic underdevelopment: myths and realities' in MOMMSEN, W. J. and OSTERHAMMEL, J. (eds) (1986).

BISSIO, R. R. (ed.) (1988) *Third World Guide 89/90. The World as seen by the Third World: facts – figures – opinions*, Montevideo, Third World Editors.

BRANDT, W. (1980) *North–South: a programme for survival*, Report of the Independent Commission on International Development Issues (the Brandt Report), London, Pan.

BROWN, J. M. (1985) *Modern India: the origins of an Asian democracy*, Oxford, Oxford University Press.

BRUNSCHWIG, H. (1966) *French Colonialism, 1871–1916: myths and realities*, London, Pall Mall Press.

BULL, H. and WATSON, A. (eds) (1984) *The Expansion of International Society*, Oxford, Clarendon Press.

CASSEN, R. *et al.* (1986) *Does Aid Work?*, Oxford, Clarendon Press.

COQUERY-VIDROVITCH, C. (1988) 'The transfer of economic power in French-speaking West Africa' in GIFFORD, P. and LOUIS, W. R. (eds) (1988).

CURTIN, P. D. (1969) *The Atlantic Slave Trade: a census*, Wisconsin, University of Wisconsin Press.

DAVIS, L. E. and HUTTENBACK, R. A. (1986) *Mammon and the Pursuit of Empire: the political economy of British Imperialism 1860–1912*, Cambridge, Cambridge University Press.

DESCHAMPS, H. (1970) 'France in Black Africa and Madagascar between 1920 and 1945' in DUIGNAN, P. and GANN, L. H. (eds) (1970).

DRÈZE, J. and SEN, A. (1989) *Hunger and Public Action*, Oxford, Clarendon Press.

DUIGNAN, P. and GANN, L. H. (eds) (1970) *Colonialism in Africa 1870–1960*, Vol. 2, Cambridge, Cambridge University Press.

ELLIOTT, J. H. (1963) *Imperial Spain. 1469–1716*, Sevenoaks, Edward Arnold.

EMSLEY, C. (ed.) (1979) *Conflict and Stability in Europe*, London, Croom Helm.

FANON, F. (1967) The Wretched of the Earth, Harmondsworth, Penguin.

FAIRBANK, J. K. (ed.) (1978) The Cambridge History of China, Vol. 10, *Late Ch'ing, 1800–1914*, Pt. 1, Cambridge, Cambridge University Press.

FERNS, H. S. (1960) *Britain and Argentina,* Oxford, Oxford University Press.

FIELDHOUSE, D. K. (1973) *Economics and Empire 1830–1914*, London, Weidenfeld and Nicolson.

FIELDHOUSE, D. K. (1981) *Colonialism 1870–1945*, London, Weidenfeld and Nicolson.

FIELDHOUSE, D. K. (1986) *Black Africa 1945–80: economic decolonization and arrested development,* London, Allen and Unwin.

FIELDHOUSE, D. K. (1988) 'Arrested development in Anglophone Black Africa?' in GIFFORD, P. and LOUIS, W. R. (eds) (1988).

FRANK, A. G. (1973) 'The development of underdevelopment', reprinted in WILBER, C. K. (ed.) (1973).

FRANK, A. G. (1978) *World Accumulation 1442–1789*, New York and London, Monthly Review Press.

FURTADO, C. (1976) *Economic Development of Latin America* (2nd edn), Cambridge, Cambridge University Press.

GALLAGHER, J. and ROBINSON, R. (1953) 'The Imperialism of free trade', *Economic History Review*, second series VI, pp. 1–15.

GALLAGHER, J. and ROBINSON, R. (1962) 'The partition of Africa', *New Cambridge Modern History*, Vol. XI, Cambridge, Cambridge University press.

GIFFORD, P. and LOUIS, W. R. (eds) (1971) *France and Britain in Africa: imperial rivalry and colonial rule*, New Haven, Yale University Press.

GIFFORD, P. and LOUIS, W. R. (eds) (1982) *The Transfer of Power in Africa: decolonization 1940–1960*, New Haven, Yale University Press.

GIFFORD, P. and LOUIS, W. R. (eds) (1988) *Decolonization and African Independence: the transfers of powers, 1960–1980*, New Haven, Yale University Press.

GLANTZ, M. H. (ed.) (1987) *Drought and Hunger in Africa*, Cambridge, Cambridge University Press.

GRAY, J. (1990) *Rebellions and Revolutions: China from the 1800s to the 1980s*, Oxford, Oxford University Press.

GRIMAL, H. (1978) *Decolonization: the British, French, Dutch and Belgian Empires, 1919–1963*, London, Routledge.

HOBSON, J. A. (1902) *Imperialism: a study*, London, Constable.

HOLLAND, R. F. and RIZVI, G. (eds) (1984) *Perspectives on Imperialism and Decolonization*, London, Frank Cass.

HOLLAND, R. F. (1985) *European Decolonization 1918–1981: an introductory survey,* London, Macmillan.

HORNE, (1977) *A Savage War of Peace: Algeria, 1954–1962*, London, Macmillan.

IRVING, R. E. M. (1975) *The First Indochina War: French and American Policy 1945–1954*, London, Croom Helm.

JONES, E. L. (1981) *The European Miracle*, Cambridge, Cambridge University Press.

KENNEDY, P. (1989) *The Rise and Fall of the Great Powers*, London, Fontana.

KUMAR, D. (ed.) (1983) *The Cambridge Economic History of India, Vol. 2: c.1757 – c.1970*, Cambridge, Cambridge University Press.

LACOSTE, Y. (1980) *Unité et Diversité du Tiers Monde*, 3 Vols, Paris, Maspero.

LENIN, V. I. (1947) *Imperialism: the highest stage of capitalism* (originally 1916), Moscow, Progress Publishers.

LOFCHIE, M. F. (1987) 'The decline of African agriculture: an internalist perspective' in GLANTZ, M. H. (ed.) (1987).

LOUIS, W. R. (1971) 'The Berlin Congo Conference' in GIFFORD, P. and LOUIS, W. R. (eds) (1971).

LOUIS, W. R. (1977) *Imperialism at Bay*, Oxford, Oxford Universtiy Press.

LOUIS, W. R. and ROBINSON, R. (1982) 'The United States and the decolonization of the British Empire' in GIFFORD, P. and LOUIS, W. R. (eds) (1982).

LYON, P. (1984) 'The emergence of the Third World' in BULL, H. and WATSON, A. (eds) *The Expansion of International Society*, Oxford, Clarendon.

MADDISON, A. (1971) *Class Structure and Economic Growth: India and Pakistan since the Moghuls,* London, Allen and Unwin.

MARX, K. (1853) 'The future results of British rule in India', *New York Daily Tribune*, 8 August 1853; republished (1959) in *Marx and Engels on Colonialism*, Moscow, Progress Publishers.

MARX, K. (1867; 1976 edn) *Capital*, Vol. 1, Harmondsworth, Penguin.

MOMMSEN, W. J. and OSTERHAMMEL, J. (eds) (1986) *Imperialism and After*, London, Allen and Unwin.

MOORE, B. (1967) *Social Origins of Dictatorship and Democracy*, Harmondsworth, Penguin.

MORRIS-JONES, W. H. and FISCHER, G. (1980) *Decolonization and After: the British and French experience*, London, Frank Cass.

MORTIMER, R. A. (1980) *The Third World Coalition in International Politics*, New York, Praeger.

MURPHEY, R. (1977) *The Outsiders: the western experience in India and China,* Ann Arbor, University of Michigan Press

O'BRIEN, P. J. (1975) 'A critique of Latin American theories of development' in OXAAL, I. *et al.* (eds) *Beyond the Sociology of Development: economy and society in Latin America and Africa,* London, Routledge and Kegan Paul.

O'BRIEN, P. K. (1982) 'European economic development: the contribution of the periphery', *The Economic History Review*, second series, **35**(1) February, pp. 1–18.

O'BRIEN, P. K. (1988) 'The costs and benefits of British Imperialism 1846–1914, *Past and Present*, 120, pp. 163–200.

OLIVER, R. and FAGE, J. D. (1975) *A Short History of Africa* (5th edn), Harmondsworth, Penguin.

PANIKKAR, K. M. (1953) *Asia and Western Dominance*, London, Allen and Unwin.

PANTER-BRICK, K. (1988) 'Independence, French style' in GIFFORD, P. and LOUIS, W. R. (eds) (1988).

PARRY, J. H. (1949) *Europe and a Wider World*, London, Hutchinson.

PERLIN, F. (1983) 'Proto-industrialisation and pre-colonial South Asia', *Past and Present*, 98, pp. 30–95.

PLATT, D. C. M. (ed.) (1977) *Business Imperialism*, Oxford, Clarendon.

PLATT, D. C. M. (1980) 'Dependency in nineteenth-century Latin America: an historian objects', *Latin American Research Review*, 15, pp. 113–28.

RAYCHAUDHURI, T. (1985) 'Historical roots of mass poverty in South Asia: a hypothesis', *Economic and Political Weekly*, **20**(18), pp. 801–6.

REYNOLDS, L. G. (1985) *Economic Growth in the Third World, 1850–1980*, New Haven, Yale University Press.

ROBINSON, R. (1980) 'Andrew Cohen and the transfer of power in tropical Africa, 1940–1951' in MORRIS-JONES, W. H. and FISCHER, G. (eds) (1980).

ROSTOW, W. W. (1956) 'The take-off into self-sustained growth', *Economic Journal*, March.

ROSTOW, W. W. (1960) *The Stages of Economic Growth*, Cambridge, Cambridge University Press.

ROTHSTEIN, R. L. (1977) *The Weak in the World of the Strong: the developing countries in the international system*, New York, Columbia University Press.

SAID, E. (1978) *Orientalism*, New York, Pantheon Books.

SCAMMELL, G. V. (1989) *The First Imperial Age: European overseas expansion c1400–1715*, London, Unwin Hyman.

SHAW, A. G. L. (ed.) (1970) *Great Britain and the Colonies 1815–1865*, London, Methuen.

SHEEHAN, J. T. (ed.) (1976) *Imperial Germany*, New York, New Viewpoints/Franklin Watts.

SKOCPOL, T. (1977) 'Wallerstein's world capitalist system: a theoretical and historical critique', *American Journal of Sociology*, **82**(5), pp. 1075–90.

SMITH, T. (1978) 'A comparative study of French and British decolonization', *Comparative Studies in Society and History*, 20, pp. 70–102.

SMITH, T. (1981) *The Pattern of Imperialism: the United States, Great Britain and the late industrialising world since 1815*, Cambridge, Cambridge University Press.

STOKES, E. (1970) 'Traditional resistance movements and Afro-Asian nationalism: the context of the 1857 mutiny rebellion in India', *Past and Present*, 48, pp. 100–118.

SURET-CANALE, J. L. (1971) *French Colonialism in Tropical Africa 1900–1945*, London, Hurst.

THORNE, C. (1978) *Allies of a Kind: the United States, Britain and the war against Japan 1941–45*, Oxford, Oxford University Press.

TOMLINSON, B. R. (1979) *The Political Economy of the Raj 1914–1947: the economics of decolonization in India*, London, Macmillan.

TOMLINSON, B. R. (1982) 'The contraction of England: national decline and the loss of Empire', *Journal of Imperial and Commonwealth History*, **11**, pp. 58–72.

VINCENT, R. J. (1984) 'Racial equality', in BULL, H. and WATSON, A. (eds) (1984).

WAKEMAN, F. (1978) 'The Canton trade and the opium war' in FAIRBANK, J. K. (ed.) (1978).

WALLERSTEIN, I. (1974) *The Modern World System: capitalist agriculture and the origins of the European world economy in the sixteenth century*, London, Academic Press.

WALLERSTEIN, I. (1979) *The Capitalist World Economy*, Cambridge, Cambridge University Press.

WEHLER, H-U. (1970a) 'Bismarck's imperialism 1862–1890', *Past and Present*; reprinted in SHEEHAN, J. T. (ed.) (1976).

WEHLER, H-U. (1970b) 'Introduction to Imperialism', in EMSLEY, C. (ed.) (1979).

WILBER, C. K. (ed.) (1973) *The Political Economy of Development and Underdevelopment,* London, Random House.

WILSON, H. S. (1977) *The Imperial Experience in Sub-Saharan Africa since 1870,* Oxford, Oxford University Press.

WORSLEY, P. (1967) *The Third World*, 2nd edn; 1st edn 1963, London, Weidenfeld and Nicolson,

YOUNG, C. (1988) 'The colonial state and post-colonial crisis' in GIFFORD, P. and LOUIS, W. R. (eds) (1988).

Essay 2
Europe and Russia

Prepared for the Course Team by Paul Lewis,
Senior Lecturer in Government, The Open University

Introduction

The very title of this essay contains an ambiguity and something of a puzzle which bring us to the heart of the subject-matter of this course. While 'Europe' can be set in the context of the 'wider world' and Europe can generally be distinguished from its global environment, it has been a matter of lengthy historical debate as to whether Russia is part of Europe or a country beyond it. That this debate continues can be seen in recent history. The persistent dictatorship and increasing inefficiencies of Soviet rule led to growing resentment and restiveness among the east European peoples in the 1980s, expressed in one form by the Czech writer Milan Kundera in terms of a reassertion of the European character of central Europe as distinct from an alien Russian culture (Kundera, 1984). Shortly after this, however, Mikhail Gorbachev claimed a place for Russia within Europe, using the idea of a 'common European house' and attempting to promote the reform of the decrepit Soviet system by tying its fate to that of the more dynamic West. That particular project has now become part of history with the demise of the Soviet Union, but the question of Russia's relationship with the West remains on the agenda as attempts are made to integrate its economy with the processes of global capitalism and steps taken to implement principles of liberal democracy.

The question of Russia's relationship with Europe is, then, one that has lost none of its relevance in the closing decade of the twentieth century – and leads on to further consideration of the fundamental question, 'What is Europe?' As on earlier occasions, Russia's relations with western Europe have undergone a sharp change of course. For much of the second half of the twentieth century, the character and behaviour of Soviet Russia tended to accentuate the contrast with the West and the central institutions of European civilization. The Soviet Union was regarded as one of the two global superpowers, a populous and strongly armed state with extensive economic resources that dominated eastern Europe and threatened the security of the West. Its 'superpower' image was formed during the course of the Second World War (it was only in 1944 that the word itself was first seen in published form: see Fox, 1944), and was reinforced by Soviet military occupation of much of eastern and central Europe and by the USSR's acquisition of nuclear weapons shortly after the United States. It was consolidated by the development of the Soviet Union's international role by Khrushchev and Brezhnev, the projection of its power throughout the Third World and the construction of a strong naval force with a global presence. The ideological claims of the Soviet leadership, already given credence by the extent of the Soviet contribution to the defeat of Nazi Germany, were also sustained by its military resources and international political role.

Towards the end of the Brezhnev leadership, however, it was becoming evident that the Soviet Union (although endowed with extensive material and economic resources), was suffering from growing technological backwardness and finding it increasingly difficult to sustain the international political and military role it had shaped for itself. As Gorbachev sharpened the focus on the complex of problems that faced the Soviet Union, the consequences of its economic, ideological and political failings became increasingly apparent. A country of obvious strength and potential, by the late 1980s it was no longer possible to regard it as a superpower in terms of anything but crude military force. The Soviet bid to play a powerful, or even dominant, global role had clearly fallen far short of its target (a similar problem of over-extension was creating major problems for the other superpower, the USA) and, within the Russian leadership, increasing attention was paid to its regional position and the establishment of new relations within a European framework. While the general thrust of the 'return to Europe' and the construction of a 'common European house' was easy to grasp, the precise nature of these initiatives and the further changes they implied were far less clear.

The idea of Europe and the extent of its community is a matter of uncertainty and it will be evident to you by now that Europe is as much a concept and cultural construct as a territorial entity. 'Europe' and its traditions have been intimately associated with particular societies which have considerable territorial continuity, but it is the values of those societies and the capacity to put them into practice that have given the idea of Europe its continuing significance. Geography and the historical development of its society have placed Russia on the margins of Europe. As a result, Russia has experienced a persistently ambiguous relationship with Europe over a number of centuries, a tradition that was continued – if in different form – with the Revolution of 1917 and the subsequent establishment of the Soviet Union.

In the ancient world, Europe was understood to be bounded by water, its frontiers in that region lying on the Sea of Azov and the River Don. It was not until the sixteenth century, as western contacts were made with Russia and cartographic accuracy was improved, that the errors in the classical view became fully apparent. Far from there being a small land bridge between Europe and Asia, it became clear that large tracts of land extended northwards from the Black Sea – and it was this expanse that came to constitute the heartland of Russia. This new awareness, however, did not have the impact on ideas of European and Asian distinctiveness that might have been expected. For it was precisely during this period that the idea of Europe was taking form as the realm of Christendom, and geographical conceptions became less significant. Muscovite Russia, meanwhile, was little concerned as it had few dealings with western Europe and what it did know it largely disliked (Bassin, 1991, p. 4). The situation changed with the accession of Peter the Great in 1694 and his recognition of the achievements of European civilization. Montesquieu's writings reflected this development and alluded to Russia as one of the nations of Europe. Post-Napoleonic Europe saw Russian participation in the Holy Alliance as a full member of the European community, although liberals now began to make the distinction between a liberal western and a conservative eastern Europe. Ideology, as much as geographical considerations, came to play an important part in Russia's relationship with Europe and has been a leading factor in the development of this relationship in modern times.

This essay will examine the relationship of Russia and the former Soviet Union with Europe, discuss its origins and development, and analyse the implications of recent changes. It will be necessary to survey, if relatively briefly, Russian traditions and the history of its relations with Europe, as the influence of that past has a particular relevance, even today. During the critical formative period of European identity during the late middle ages, for example, Russia was cut off from contact and intercourse with western Europe by the lengthy period of Mongol dominance. This had a decisive influence on its cultural outlook and subsequent social development, distancing it from the main currents of European development. Russia was only just breaking free from the Tatar yoke (as Mongol rule was also called), as western European states initiated the process which placed European civilization on a global rather than purely continental plane. The relative backwardness of Russia, its isolation on the eastern periphery of Europe, and the ambivalence it has shown towards more advanced European nations and the West – no less absent in the closing years of the twentieth century – all have deep historical roots and direct our initial attention to the origins and early growth of the Russian state, a development interrupted and crucially curtailed by the Mongol invasion.

Russia and Europe

The origins of a proto-Russian state can be linked with the dynamic impact in the ninth century of the travels of the Vikings, whose influence was also felt throughout western Europe. Warrior-traders from Scandinavia (the Varangians) penetrated along the waterways south towards Byzantium (also called Constantinople, and then Istanbul) from around AD 830 and succeeded in imposing their authority over local Slav tribes. The consolidation of their power over Kiev towards the end of the ninth century is generally recognized to mark the first founding of a Russian state. 'Rus' now came to be the term by which the mixed Scandinavian and Slavonic upper class of the Kievan territory was known, following a description (initially made by the Finns) of the Varangians who made the journey south. Svyatoslav I, who campaigned actively along the Danube in the 960s, was the first reigning prince to have a clearly Slavonic name.

The origins of the Russian state

Russia of the tenth century was obviously far removed from the modern idea of the nation-state and the first Russian princes different from later rulers. The lands they struggled to exert their authority over were vast and relatively empty. The loss of population from the Kiev area from the middle of the eleventh century was therefore of critical importance and an important element in the waning of the first Russian empire. Russia became subject to Christian influences with the conversion through Byzantium of Vladimir in AD 989. The depredations of the Polovtsy, an Asiatic tribe, gathered pace during the eleventh century and contributed to the weakening of Kievan Rus, but a more critical blow was that of the Mongol invasion. Just after 1200 the Tatars, under the leadership of Genghis Khan, challenged their existing (possibly Chinese) rulers and established their own empire in central Asia.

In 1240 they took Kiev and continued their westward march to defeat the Hungarians and Poles the following year. While Novgorod kept its independence and did not fall to the Tatars, the invasion destroyed all remaining unity and sense of integrity of the Russian people. The heartland of modern Russia to the north of Kiev was crushed and the young community, in the words of Bernard Pares, 'taken out of the orbit of Europe' (Pares, 1962, p. 85). The vulnerability of the early Russian civilization to the Asian fighters, the ferocity of the attack from the east and its effect of isolating Russians from intercourse with the west had a profound impact on Russia's historical development and continues to mark the contemporary Russian outlook. But while the Tatar yoke was in place for more than two centuries, it did not prevent other developments on the Russian lands. Although still paying formal tribute to the Tatars, Moscow's influence and territory grew and under Ivan III in 1480 it managed to throw off all vestiges of Tatar control.

It was at this stage that Ivan took the title both of Sovereign of All Russia and of Tsar (or Caesar), thus expressing the autocratic basis of his rule, primarily in terms of its independence from Tatar influence but also with reference to his own political style. Christian Constantinople had fallen to the Turks in 1453 and Ivan had married the niece, Zoe (renamed in Russian Sophia), of the last Eastern Emperor. Although this marriage had been encouraged by the Pope as a means of strengthening Christian unity, the result was quite different and Moscow was soon promoted as the third Rome, after Constantinople had fallen to the 'infidel'. Moscow had gained considerably in political strength and now developed an identity firmly rooted in the Christian tradition, which had further implications for the development of Muscovy in the light of Poland's espousal of Catholicism. Ivan declared his intention to reunite all Russian territory and had some success in imposing his authority over Lithuania, existing at this time in a loose union with Poland.

The work of unification was continued under Ivan's son, Basil III, and further progress made towards the formation of a Russian empire under his grandson, Ivan IV (the Terrible). Ivan the Terrible inherited the title of Grand Prince of Moscow in 1533 at the age of three and grew up surrounded by the intrigues and political conspiracies of relatives, major aristocratic houses and the Church. He developed, nevertheless, considerable powers of independence and in his early career as sovereign saw major successes. In 1552 he broke the power of the Tatars at Kazan, their major fortress to the west of the Urals, and opened the path of his subjects to relatively unrestricted advance to the east. Advances were also made in the Caucasus and Russian territories extended to the Caspian Sea as well as beyond the Urals. This expansion continued and by 1643 Russian colonists had reached the Pacific Ocean.

Initiatives in other areas were less successful, and Ivan failed in his attempt to gain an opening on the Baltic for Russia and thus more direct access to the centres of European civilization. Sweden, Poland and Lithuania continued to obstruct his progress in this direction. The internal government of Russia was affected as Ivan became increasingly suspicious of members of his entourage and clearly un-balanced psychologically. In 1565 he set up the *Oprichnina*, effectively a police state within the state of Muscovy, and recruited the *Oprichniki* to defend it by methods that would be recalled nearly four hundred years later with the establish-ment by Joseph Stalin of a modern police state. By this stage other features of the modern Russian state could be detected in some of the paths of development ex-plored by Moscow. The decline of Tatar power opened the way to further expan-sion eastwards and to the south-east and, by the beginning of the seventeenth

Unknown artist, Ivan the Terrible *(1530–1584), late sixteenth century, icon (photo: Nationalmuseet, Copenhagen).*

century, Russia was one of the greatest of the eastern powers and the strongest representative of Christian culture in central Asia and the Far East.

On the other hand, relations with the more developed nations and growing centres of European civilization were constrained and Russia's access contested by strong powers to the north and west. The political basis of the Russian state was also unstable. This became evident during the political and dynastic wrangles of the Time of Troubles that followed the death of Ivan the Terrible in 1584, and with the incursions of the Polish Commonwealth, which had finally been successful in incorporating Lithuania. With opponents defeated and little real competition, Russia was capable of rapid territorial expansion. But this same opportunity was also a threat when powerful enemies developed and Russia's open borders became insecure. The Russian state thus developed under conditions of frequent warfare and the necessity for perpetual military preparedness, although national finances and the level of economic development were quite inadequate to sustain on a permanent basis the forces required for this.

In keeping with these imperatives, the early Russian intercourse with the west that developed after the marriage of Ivan III to Zoe Palaeologus was directed to the requirements of the court or the military needs of the state. For example, a key contribution to Ivan the Terrible's capture of Kazan was made by a Danish engineer in his service. Although the Time of Troubles was followed by a period of greater order and the establishment of the Romanov dynasty, the experience of this period reinforced the concern with military affairs which continued throughout the seventeenth century. Russia's early relations with Europe were thus selective and determined by the particular conditions of national development – as, indeed, have been those of developing countries in more recent times. The critical role of the state and its coercive forces in the development of the Russian nation directed it to place great emphasis on issues of security and competitive relations with neighbours to the west and north; at the same time, this stance led it to set increasing store by western technology and to evolve a foreign policy which differentiated significantly between the rapidly developing European powers.

Russian ambivalence towards Europe was thus set at an early stage and rested on conceptions – political, cultural and spiritual – very different from those which developed in the west. The idea of Moscow as the 'Third Rome' contrasted with and challenged the notion of a western Christendom, founded on the Holy Roman Empire, which underlay the development of mainstream European civilization. In this sense, Russia was not so much on the edge of Europe and in intermittent contact with its development, but represented an alternative Europe founded on analogous, if ancient, Christian principles. If early modern Europe was one based on an awareness of its Christian identity, something of this development could also be seen in Russia. But it was one which lacked the dynamism and capacity for cultural and technological evolution that underlay the rise of the west and made the products of European civilization increasingly indispensable for the Russian state. It was an alternative, primitive Europe which did not experience the Renaissance and was little touched by the Enlightenment. Its spiritual authority was nevertheless rooted in a continuous line of Christian descent and reinforced by its distance from the growing materialism of western civilization.

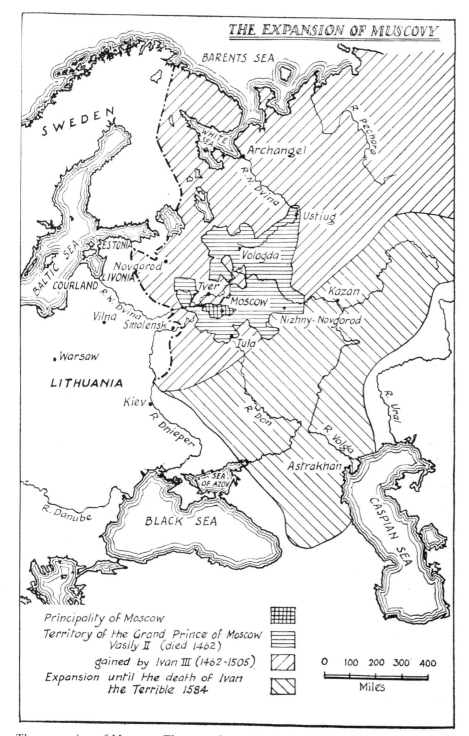

The expansion of Muscovy. The map shows that from an early period much of the development of the Russian state was to the east of the River Don and therefore on the margins of the classical conception of 'Europe' (from Grey, 1973, p. 13).

This self-conception can be traced throughout modern Russian history and was by no means absent in Soviet culture. While it is rooted in folk tradition more than in élite groups, it has also had a major impact on ruling circles and national policies. Although early Rus had indeed not differed greatly from other communities on the European continent, it had been isolated by the influence of the Tatars just as Europe had begun to consolidate its distinctive civilization and to develop a 'Western' trajectory which Russia had little opportunity either to join or to catch up with. Early on, therefore, there was a major separation from the European mainstream. At the same time, early associations and the Christian affiliation preserved a European identity in dealings with Asiatic peoples and powers and sustained feelings of 'orthodoxy' both in a general and more specific religious sense. The weakening of the Mongol empire and access to a thinly populated Siberia allowed Russia to develop this identity in the east, an extension of Russian society and its aspirations which took it way beyond any geographical conception of a European community or homeland.

Ambiguities of Russian modernization

While relations between Muscovy and the west had been strengthening since the late fifteenth century, it was between 1650 and 1700, states Sumner (1961, p. 294), that intercourse began to grow into influence. 'After 1700 influence became imitation; after 1800 came absorption.' Russian interests were at first purely those of a consumer, but they soon deepened into growing awareness of the need not just for goods but also for the techniques, skills and ideas that had produced them. In short, Europe soon became a model for Russia's modernization, although for Russia this process was rather different from the course mainstream European development had taken. The path of Muscovite development and the primacy of the state in the growth of the Russian empire meant that the impact of the west was quite differentiated in its social effects. These divisions became more clearly apparent with the accession to power of Peter the Great in 1694.

Peter actively sought the Westernization of Russia and, at the same time, the secularization of its social life. He founded the first system of secular education in Russia, which was designed for those entering the different branches of state service. He was also successful in extending the borders of Russia to the Baltic by acquiring Estonia and Livonia and gaining a predominant influence in Kurland (Lithuania). St Petersburg, named after the tsar, was founded in the early eighteenth century as Russia's window on the west. This brought Russia, and particularly its governing circles, into direct contact with the Baltic Germans of this area and opened the way for many Germans to enter the service of the Russian state. All this, however, concerned European influence primarily on the ruling class and had the effect of deepening the divisions within Russian society. Before Peter's reign, in the sixteenth and seventeenth centuries, rulers and ruled had led greatly different lives, but the difference had not been primarily a cultural one. This unity was lost as Russian society became divided into two distinct worlds.

Following Peter's turn towards the west, the eighteenth century saw the Russian upper classes increasingly involved with European culture and the accoutrements of its civilization. Increasingly distant from the 'dark people', as their own, largely

Daniel Maclise, Peter the Great at Deptford Dockyard, *1857, oil on canvas, 150 x 225 cm. In 1992 Peter the Great, regarded as the founder of the modern Russian state, was identified by 44 per cent of a sample of the population as Russia's greatest politician. Lenin and Stalin were selected by 15 and 6 per cent respectively, while Mikhail Gorbachev, Russia's last Communist ruler, was named by fewer than 3 per cent (Radio Free Europe/Radio Liberty Research Report, 12 February 1993) (photo: Mary Evans Picture Library).*

peasant masses were termed, the Russian élite became predominantly Europeanized. The ideas of the Enlightenment, too, had a ready audience amongst such groups, not least because of the enthusiasm of Catherine the Great.

The French Revolution in 1789, however, changed this situation and contributed to divisions within the educated élite between government groups and those with more critical views. While a major gulf had already developed between the rulers of Russia and those ruled, fissures now grew within the élite itself in response to the conflicting currents in western Europe which were tearing some of its established societies apart.

The more settled conditions of the eighteenth century and the continuing territorial expansion of Russia, particularly, during this period, in the Ukraine, had led to steady population growth and the growing importance of Russia as a factor in European international affairs. It was only towards the end of the eighteenth century, though, that the population of Russia (some 36 million in 1800) exceeded that of the most populous European country, France (27.5 million). With only some 13 million earlier in the eighteenth century, the subjects of the tsar had been considerably less numerous than the French. Until the late-seventeenth century the Russian population was most probably also considerably smaller than that of Poland-Lithuania. It was only in the nineteenth century that Russia became numerically preponderant in Europe; by 1871, it was more than double the size of the next largest western power, which by this date was Germany, rather than France. The growing strength of Russia, combined with increasing links with the west and gradual territorial expansion in that direction, led to fuller involvement with political developments in western Europe. In the conservative vision of Europe given practical form in the Holy Alliance, Russia was already seen as a guarantee of its Christian civilization.

The western campaigns and Russian occupation of France (1815–1818) brought large numbers of her people to the West and provided them with unprecedented direct experience of western Europe. This had a rapid effect, not least amongst some officers of the Guards, who quickly organized conspiratorial groups and mounted the Decembrist revolt in 1825. Élite dissension became a recurrent feature of nineteenth-century Russia and was tied in with the complex sequence of reformist initiatives launched by the ruling circles in response to Russia's backwardness. These in turn evoked consequences within the broader society, which were followed by further responses from the ruling group and often a turn back to reactionary policies. The reign of Alexander I (1801–1825) thus began with great liberal hopes and ended with the post-Napoleonic alliance to preserve Christian conservatism in Europe. Nicholas I's reactionary rule ended with the Crimean War (1853–1856), which provided further demonstration of Russia's backwardness and relative weakness, and was followed by Alexander II's reformist drive and the emancipation of the serfs in 1861. This opened the way to further economic growth.

Despite the vagaries of tsarist policy during the first half of the nineteenth century, the impact of European industrial development on Russia had been significant and the volume of foreign trade had more than doubled, with timber, grain and minerals as the major exports. After Russia's defeat in the Crimean War and further demonstration of Russian weakness, a concerted programme of modernization and economic westernization was adopted in which, not surprisingly under Russian conditions, the state played a major role. Foreign capital was also imported on a large scale, with France taking the lead in the process, following the worsening of Russia's relations with Germany and Austria-Hungary after 1887. By 1914, 80 per cent of Russia's external government debt was held in France. Between 1860 and 1913 the production of iron rose fifteen-fold and that of steel by several thousand times; more than one hundred times the volume of coal was mined and three hundred times the amount of oil produced. The latter part of the nineteenth century and the opening years of the twentieth thus saw the course of Russian development increasingly following the path taken by European industry and the western economies.

With the increased differentiation of Russian society that accompanied this economic development, some groups, notably the intelligentsia and parts of the middle class, became increasingly Westernized and European both in orientation and their way of life. 'Russian' society (in terms of the peoples forming the population of the Russian Empire) also became increasingly diverse as its borders extended. According to the first official Russian census, conducted in 1897, out of a total population of 129.4 million in the Russian empire, 'ethnic' Russians (i.e. those claiming Russian as their native tongue) numbered only 55 million, around 43 per cent. One of the consequences of the revolutions of 1917 and the settlement after the First World War, which detached Poland and parts of the Bielorussian and Ukrainian population from Russia, was the Russification of Soviet society. The results of the 1923 census showed that Russians then made up 72 percent of the Soviet population (Dixon, 1990, p. 21).

A consequence of Russia's Westernization at the end of the nineteenth century was its involvement in the European conflict of 1914–1918 – an involvement that was to provoke a decisive shift in Russian development. Opposition to the war mounted in the face of Russia's terrible human and material losses during the hostilities, and the increasingly evident failure of the regime to deal with the mammoth demands and costs of modern warfare. Some two-and-a-half years into the war, in early 1917, popular discontent erupted and Tsar Nicholas II was forced to abdicate in favour of a Provisional Government, initially headed as premier by Prince Lvov. There was, as George Kennan (1960, p. 24) acidly suggests, little understanding of these developments in western Europe and among the western allies – and especially on the part of US President Woodrow Wilson, whose view it was that the Romanov autocracy had been 'not in fact Russian in origin, character, or purpose'. There was, in particular, no comprehension among the western powers – although this was not the case amongst some diplomats *in situ* – that the pressures of the war, exacerbating the problems of Russian backwardness and its divided society, having brought about the collapse of the established political order, now threatened the destruction of the country's social fabric.

Seeking, at long last, to establish some elements of western democracy and European constitutionalism in the Russian context, leading figures of the interim administrations struggled to maintain good relations with the allied states and acceded to their demands for the maintenance and even intensification of the war effort. This only contributed to the further erosion of existing political authority, intensification of social turmoil and the growing incapacity of the Provisional Government. The masses who fed the military machine were increasingly inclined to rebel and desert the front, seeking what security they could find in the countryside and hoping to gain what land and resources were available as the progressive collapse of the old regime continued.

The Soviet response

Not all members of the Russian élite and the educated classes had been carried along by the tide of Europeanization during the nineteenth century, or had given their commitment to the parliamentary procedures and constitutional forms of the established western powers. There were growing currents of Russian nationalism and traditional Slavophilism in response to modernization and the establishment of western forms. Conservatives sought to re-establish links with the traditions of Russian, proto-Slavonic society and thus to avoid many of the evident evils of

European industrialism, while also, of course, losing the benefits. In reacting against the forms of modernization, those holding such views were shadowing similar developments in the west, where Rousseau and Herder had contributed to a growing emphasis on the role of collective sentiments and traditional national identity. But in promulgating traditional values the use of modern means of communication was an important factor in assimilating previously uneducated groups into the public political process.

There were others in Russia whose response was in some ways similar, but whose allegiance was directed to the growing European socialist movements and whose opposition to the bourgeois governments of the west was established on a different normative and theoretical basis. The European imprint on this line of thought was even clearer. It was a fraction of the latter group, the Bolsheviks, that seized the initiative following first the dissolution of the Romanov order and then the collapse of the unsteady parliamentary regime that attempted to take its place. The Bolsheviks, led by V. I. Lenin, were socialists and followers of the western doctrine of Marxism who sought to implement a different conception of progress from that pursued by the established European regimes. Like the Slavophils, but on a different basis, they sought to mobilize politically the Russian masses and working classes.

Their style of thought, rhetoric and action was also, of course, quite different from that of European parliamentarians and their Russian followers and it is this, in conjunction with a certain anti-western (and particularly anti-*modern* western) orientation, that leads Hough (1990, p. 9) to write of the Bolshevik revolution as the Khomeini revolution of Russian history. This involves a paradox in that socialism, not least in the form developed over several decades in Germany and England by Karl Marx, was a pre-eminently European movement whose political precepts were derived from analysis of the social and economic dynamics of modern industrial production. Lenin and other Russian socialists were, in that sense, very much in line with the direction taken by modern politics in the west and the intellectual currents prevailing in many European circles. Moreover, their seizure of power in 1917 was premised on the expectation (and hope) that the existing regimes in western Europe, themselves critically weakened by the war effort and being challenged by socialist forces, were about to experience their own revolutions and that the spark produced by the Bolsheviks would ignite a conflagration in Germany and elsewhere.

That vision was shared (and feared) by many Europeans, too, but the prospect of world revolution began to recede soon after the war and the Russian Communists (the Bolsheviks having renamed their party in 1918) were driven back on their national resources. Growing isolation and a precarious political position encouraged the party and its leaders to return to more traditional forms of political rule, a tendency already entrenched in the organization by the emphasis on internal discipline and the conspiratorial form of activity imposed on the movement by the lack of civic freedom in tsarist Russia. The Bolsheviks and their Communist successors nevertheless remained enthusiastic proponents of industrial progress and the creation of a working class along the lines of western developments. Modernization, planning and accelerated social developments were early guiding

V. I. Lenin (1870–1924), Moscow, 25 May, 1919 (photo: Mansell Collection).

principles of Communist practice. But the Communist view of western modernization was in fact a highly selective one. Modern technology and the process of industrialization were welcomed and encouraged, but the dominant values and social forms of the societies that had produced the greatest impetus for these developments were treated with suspicion and hostility.

These tensions became a major feature of Soviet Russia as elements of traditional culture – particularly in the political sphere – persisted alongside processes of economic and social modernization. The doubts and antagonism shown towards Europe became more pronounced as the Soviet system developed (the suspicions of Stalin and his entourage, moreover, appearing to be increasingly justified with the looming collapse of capitalism and the rise of fascism) and the characteristics of Soviet socialism became more clearly defined.

These features gained full clarity under Stalin during the 1930s and if, as Malcolm points out, Lenin echoed and reinforced traditional Russian apprehensiveness about Europe, while remaining hostile to the influences of Asiatic culture on Russian development and sanguine about the prospects of socialist revolution in Europe, under Stalin 'traditional nationalism, militarism and xenophobia returned with full force' (Malcolm, 1991, p. 2). The consolidation and intensification of personal dictatorship under Stalin and the increasing frequency with which reference was made to aspects of traditional Russian culture support arguments for a high degree of continuity between tsarism and the period of Soviet rule. As the Soviet project showed clear signs of falling far short of its objective of forming the basis for an alternative, superior civilization to that developed on the foundations of western capitalism, arguments for the traditionalist position appeared to strengthen (Vihavainen, 1990, p. 13).

But the Revolution also set in train processes of economic and social modernization that eliminated many of the structures of the tsarist system, swept away old élites and enshrined values that did point to the development of a new kind of social order. Even if these values were increasingly irrelevant to the course of Stalinist practice and the way in which Soviet society actually developed, they remained in place as icons of the Communist system. They were also influential outside the Soviet Union where, despite the division within the socialist movement and the split between social democracy and the world Communist movement established by the Russian leadership, Soviet ideas and even practice were admired by many on the left who were not members of a Communist party (Caute, 1977). As the context of the Soviet experiment was very different from that of western Europe, it proved to be easy for those on the left to overlook its shortcomings as historical shortcuts or necessary expedients, and to identify in Russia what the British socialist Sidney Webb called a new civilization. This perception was facilitated by the slump of the early 1930s, the widespread unemployment that followed it and the relative failure of western socialist parties when they did enter government.

Communist opposition to Hitler and the rise of fascism was another factor encouraging sympathy with Communism and the values embodied by the Soviet system. The role of the Soviet leadership in helping the reformation of German armed forces during the 1920s in breach of the Versailles treaty, and the vigour with which it had encouraged the emasculation of German socialism (thus facilitating Hitler's rise to power), were factors to which less attention was paid at the time. Plans for joint action on a European basis to forestall Nazi aggression also found little favour in either east or west and Stalin, not without reason, was highly suspicious of federative plans like that floated by Aristide Briand. Soviet policy towards Europe was exclusively concerned with national survival and Stalin was prepared to make any number of tactical proposals and agreements to that end, an approach that culminated in the Soviet–German pact of August 1939. But the differentiated strategy towards the European powers he developed during the 1930s appeared to have failed completely once Nazi Germany launched its attack on the Soviet Union in June 1941. Russia, this time under Communist leadership, seemed once more to face defeat by an advanced western power and a further instalment in its unfortunate historical experience of military involvement with more developed European states.

However, despite initial set-backs and enormous losses, Russia did emerge victorious from the Second World War, which was more than could be said of its position at the end of the First World War (when a separate peace had been signed on

German terms), or the war with Japan in 1904–1905 – or that in the Crimea (1853–1856). This could partly be attributed to factors that had saved Russia during earlier conflicts: its huge population resources and a willingness to accept heavy losses; vast territories that made retreat possible for Russian forces and advance an exhausting effort for the invading army. German errors and miscalculations also played their part. Participation in a powerful alliance that could draw on the resources of the American economy was a major benefit. But victory was also due to the planned (if selective and limited) modernization of critical portions of the Russian economy and a conscious attempt to achieve levels of production characteristic of the developed European economies. The emphasis placed on heavy industrial development in the thirties seemed to have paid off in this context.

Despite early losses, war-time confusion and the enormous demands made on it. Soviet industry proved capable of producing the weapons and turning out the necessary supplies. Soon after the battle of Stalingrad in 1943, a balance was reached whereby in the early summer of that year the Russians could not now lose the war and the Germans could not count on winning it. Although Hitler's allusion to a 'crisis for Europe' at this point of the war reflected a very partial vision which saw Europe fused with German domination, Stalingrad certainly was a watershed in the conflict and pointed to the establishment of a post-war Europe very different from that of 1939. This would be a Europe in which Soviet Russia had a considerably more prominent presence and played a larger direct role there than it had since the Revolution.

Russia in Europe

Russia had emerged as a major European power at the time of Peter the Great and had played a significant role in European relations for most of the time since then, having presented itself as a leading member of the conservative Holy Alliance after the defeat of Napoleon. Even after the Revolution, although isolated in some ways from European affairs, it was nevertheless active in power politics and diplomacy. Furthermore, in exercising Communist influence within left-wing political life, it was effectively a major presence in the domestic counter-establishment of most European countries. Following the shock of the German invasion, Stalin's devotion to the security concerns of the Soviet Union retained its primacy and this factor was to be critical in the development of Soviet policy towards Europe after the War. As the German forces began to be turned back, his commitment to the enhancement of Soviet security seemed to be barely separable from the traditional thrust westwards which had given Peter the Great control of the Baltic coast and, later, delivered most of Poland into Russian hands. As had been the case in the war with Napoleonic France, war with the major continental power brought Russian forces far to the west. This time, however, they were far slower to withdraw.

The origins of post-war eastern Europe

Immediately after the German attack on the Soviet Union on 22 June 1941 there was a widespread belief that the German forces would prevail within the Soviet territory as completely as they had in the west of the European continent. The advance had been halted outside Moscow before the end of the year, although German troops were in the very suburbs of the capital. The following year the German front line failed to advance in the north, although progress was made in the south along the eastern shores of the Black Sea and towards the Caucasus, reaching as far as Stalingrad in the east. It was here, on the Volga, that the German army suffered what turned out to be a critical reverse and, by the time the Battle of Stalingrad ended in February 1943, the victory of Stalin's forces had 'set the Soviet Union on the road to being a world power' (Erickson, 1985, p. 57). Russian success had a major impact on relations within the wartime alliance and thus on prospects for the future European order.

When the Western allies – primarily, at that stage, the UK – had been joined by the Soviet Union in the conflict with the Nazi dictatorship, their initial priority had been to keep the Soviet ally in the war by preventing its defeat (Lend-Lease was particularly significant in helping to remedy the chronic Soviet deficit of motor vehicles) and by discouraging any thoughts of a separate peace. Pre-eminent among Stalin's objectives were the preservation of the frontier of the Soviet Union operative at the beginning of June 1941 (thus including the territorial gains made in agreement with Nazi Germany) and the alleviation of the military burden placed on the Soviet Union, principally by pressing for the opening of a second front in western Europe. The first of Stalin's objectives presented Britain and the United States with a major problem, particularly over the question of Poland.

It was Poland over which Britain had gone to war in 1939 and it remained, of course, a military and political ally. No action had been taken by Britain, on the other hand, when the Soviet Union invaded Poland from the east two weeks after this. The Soviet Union only joined the war nearly two years later when German forces crossed its western frontier – then set well into what had been Polish territory in 1939. It was understandable that the Soviet Union intended to regain the frontiers it possessed at the outset of its involvement in the hostilities. However, the fact was not only that Britain (generally in this matter in accord with the United States) had different objectives from the Soviet Union, but that their wars had actually started at different times and, while sharing the same enemy, they were in a sense engaged in a different conflict. These differences would turn out to be of paramount importance for the future contours and character of central Europe. The Soviet victory at Stalingrad, momentous as it was in military terms alone, had considerable significance also in structuring the form and process of negotiation between the allied powers, and thus in shaping the post-war future of central Europe.

Significant developments in relations between the allies took place around this time. At Teheran in November 1943 Stalin was essentially granted what he wanted over the border with Poland and gained a firm commitment on the opening of the second front. Two months after the meeting at Teheran, Soviet forces crossed the former Polish border and began the liberation of central Europe, although it was some time before any significant centres were taken. Toward the end of July 1944 military detachments neared the suburbs of the Polish capital on the east bank of the Vistula, across the river from the centre of Warsaw. Dismayed by the outcome of western treatment of the Polish issue, and apparently faced by the imminent Soviet liberation of the capital, the Polish underground (with some encouragement from Soviet broadcasts) rose against the Germans and launched their own liberation. Initially relatively successful, they were soon faced with unexpectedly fierce German retaliation, while assistance from the Soviet side was significantly unforthcoming.

There were certainly some practical reasons for Soviet passivity, though it was difficult to understand why aircraft from western bases were not even allowed to drop supplies and land behind Soviet lines. Having set up the nucleus of a pro-Soviet government on Polish territory in Lublin during July, Stalin was clearly unlikely to extend much sympathy to the Warsaw insurgents or to recognize the validity of their political objectives, which were identified with those of the emigré government.

The Soviet army remained inactive across the river as the German army methodically put down the insurrection (at the cost of some 200,000 Polish lives) and then razed the city. The necessity for the western powers to maintain the military alliance with the Soviet Union had eventually come to have dire consequences for less powerful allies. Soviet behaviour in Poland, and the full-blooded pursuit of Russian interests in the Balkans, was giving rise to the conviction in the West that a 'fundamental change of policy had taken place in Moscow' and that the underlying principles of the military alliance had virtually disappeared (Mastny, 1979, p. 212).

The course of events in Czechoslovakia was little more promising. In contrast with the conditions of German occupation in Poland, the invasion of Czechoslovakia had been followed by the establishment of a puppet state in Slovakia. In April 1944 Soviet advance forces had reached the borders of pre-war Czechoslovakia. Both the Soviets and the Czechoslovakian emigré government in London began making preparations for armed struggle, but the critical plans were those made in the Slovak Ministry of Defence by resistance leaders who concealed them from pro-fascist forces. Communist guerrillas, however, acted prematurely in late August 1944 and the situation got out of hand, attracting an effective German counter-attack. Disagreements between the emigré government and Soviet representatives prevented the swift coordination of a military relief effort. By the end of October the bloody suppression of the uprising was almost complete. In two countries of central Europe, then, the critical consequences of military vulnerability and political disagreement had been made clear to the indigenous population before the end of 1944. Such experiences gave an indication of the future pattern of development in central Europe.

The second of the 'Big Three' meetings (involving the UK, the USA and the USSR, represented by Churchill, Roosevelt and Stalin) was held in the Crimean resort of Yalta in February 1945. Although 'Yalta', particularly in relation to central Europe, has become a symbol and shorthand for an arbitrary process of decision-making by distant power-holders unconcerned for the nations and people, whose fate they were determining, it is now clear that many of the decisions of Yalta had effectively been taken earlier. The Soviet refusal to allow virtually any support for the Warsaw uprising could be deplored by the western powers but hardly countered. In other areas, for example, the occupation of Romania, Stalin had been given a free hand in return for leaving Britain free to act in Greece, where there was a strong Communist resistance movement.

What was made clear at Yalta was that Stalin regarded the 'Big Three'– the principal powers in the struggle against fascism – as having superior rights to smaller countries. He articulated further his refusal to compromise any major Soviet interests in relation to Poland, and it was clear that assuring the future security of Soviet borders was one of Stalin's major objectives, and this went a long way to explaining his emphasis on the Soviet interest in securing what he regarded as an appropriate frontier with Poland. Ensuring the protection of the Soviet Union, and particularly the Russian heartland, against the kind of attacks from the west

Stalin and Roosevelt at the Livadia Palace, Yalta, 7 February 1945 (photo: Imperial War Museum).

mounted in both 1914 and 1941 was an understandable objective. It helps to explain why Stalin was eager to see also a Poland that was 'friendly' to the Soviet Union – effectively, one that was not likely to enter into an alliance with Germany or permit the easy transit of its forces towards the east.

The Soviet vision of a future central Europe was, on the other hand, also significantly determined by the threat of ethnic division *within* the Soviet Union. The desire to incorporate Bielorussians and Ukrainians within the Soviet border and then to seal Soviet nationalities from potential external contamination was a further major security concern. A final summit meeting, which opened in the Berlin suburb of Potsdam in mid-July 1945, developed little in the way of practical solutions to these problems. The Potsdam talks ended very much in stalemate. The failure to reach agreement was to allow developments in central Europe their own momentum, which itself confirmed Stalin's famous statement made in April 1945 that whoever occupies a territory now 'also imposes on it his own social system (Djilas, 1963, p. 90).

Europe's shifting frontier

For many, the extension of Russian control over its western and southern neighbours meant a diminution of Europe. Russia's relationship with Europe had been, as we have seen, an ambiguous one and its role in European development was contested. For Count Richard Coudenhove-Kalergi, Russia marked the eastern border of Paneuropa, while in the view of Max Scheler, it represented an independent and separate 'cultural sphere'; according to Christopher Dawson, Russia was a collectivist entity which lay outside the bounds of an authentically Catholic Europe. The extension of Soviet power after the Second World War into the heart of Germany could, therefore, be interpreted as a significant limitation of the role of Europe and a reduction of its influence. Some of these territories had fallen under Russian control during earlier times. Large areas of modern Poland (including Warsaw, its capital) had formed part of the tsar's empire. But while Paris had been occupied by the Russians for a short period after the Napoleonic wars, Russian power had never been established so far west for such a lengthy period. Even for those who denied its European character, Russia was now very much 'in Europe'.

The countries over which Russia now consolidated its control certainly displayed important historical and cultural differences from Russia. Unlike Russia, for example, they had escaped domination by the Mongols and remained more European, or western, in orientation by maintaining links with Rome and embracing Catholicism. Their roots were closely linked with the major currents of European history. Czechs could look back to the Kingdom of Bohemia-Moravia whose capital of Prague in the fourteenth century was one of the leading cultural and scientific centres in Europe. Poland, too had fostered major cultural and scientific developments and had been the home, for example, of Nicholas Copernicus. The countries of post-war central Europe thus had deep historical roots, and the resurgence of some of their traditions and values within the Soviet empire confronted Russian leaders again with the challenge of specifically European conceptions and aspirations.

But, while it seems clear that central Europe did not experience the same problems of isolation and backwardness that have so conditioned relations between Russia and Europe, some have questioned the degree to which central Europe pursued the values more obviously characteristic of western Europe and have queried the existence of any general European model of development. Taking an equally broad historical perspective, they have directed attention to the divisions that run through the centre of Europe itself and suggest the ambiguous character of central Europe and its peoples. Berend (1986) noted the division marked by the western border of the Soviet zone of occupation in Germany in 1945 and observed that it was the Roman Catholic/feudal society to the west of that line that began in the tenth century to develop and monopolize the idea of Europe itself. Between the eleventh to thirteenth centuries, the frontier of this 'Europe' had shifted to the east to take in nations more recently converted to Christianity, including the inhabitants of the lower Danube, the eastern Carpathians and the forest area separating Poles from Russians. It is the cultural frontier of this period that modern central Europeans have often been prone to emphasize.

But in socio-economic terms, another, more recent but still ancient, division can be detected: this shifts the major fracture to the line running from the Elbe down to the Mediterranean at Trieste. It is described by Polonsky (1975, p. 3) as 'perhaps the most fundamental frontier in European history' and divides the areas where serfdom disappeared in the fifteenth and sixteenth centuries from those in which it survived until the nineteenth. Szücs (1988) distinguishes three historical regions of Europe. The basis of these ancient cultural and socio-economic distinctions retains considerable validity in the twentieth century and even the oldest, referring to the eastern border of Christendom, remained of considerable significance to a central Europe bordering the Soviet Union which proclaimed atheistic adherence to Marxism-Leninism.

Later conceptions of central Europe overlaid this with the subsequent concerns and realities of European history. The political challenge of a unified German state was of more recent provenance than the long-established Russian regional presence, and it was in distinction to the German conception of *Mitteleuropa* that conceptions like that of T. G. Masaryk's central Europe was developed. Its origins lay with the establishment of the new national states after the First World War, and the central Europeans in question were the subjects of the independent states sandwiched between the major regional powers of Germany and the Soviet Union. The borders between western and eastern Europe thus changed over the centuries, like the location of 'Europe' itself and the idea of its 'centre', and the meaning and most appropriate political form to be taken by a modern central European identity was not easy to pin down.

Considerations of ethnicity and national identity emerged with renewed force following the collapse of the multi-ethnic empires at the end of the First World War. While national identity was the dominant principle underlying the formation of new political units in the region following the First World War – and, most significantly, was enthusiastically accepted as such by US President Woodrow Wilson – the application of the principle proved to be enormously difficult. Nationalism had certainly been a major factor producing the conditions that led to the outbreak of the First World War and was recognized as such with great clarity by many of the relevant policy-makers at the time. The post-war attempt to create political structures that would satisfy nationalist sentiments and aspirations nevertheless provided conditions that were hardly less destabilizing than those that had characterized the pre-1914 period. One problem was the sheer diversity of nationalities and ethnic groupings in central and eastern Europe. While eastern Europe, in the sense of the lands lying to the east of the German – and Italian – speaking areas, had roughly the same area as the western portion, it contained three times as many different nationalities.

A second problem was the dispersal of national groups throughout large areas and the rich ethnic mixtures that were found in many parts. Some rulers had made specific invitations of settlement to non-indigenous nationalities. This had been the case of the Russian ruler Catherine the Great with German settlers and the Polish monarchy with the Jews. Numerous Jewish refugees had arrived in Poland from Germany under Casimir the Great (1333–1370) and further immigration was encouraged by Sigismund I (1506–1548). Spontaneous migration, and the effects of successive waves of immigration from the east (compounded by a long-established German tendency to settle attractive or sparsely populated areas in the east), was also a major factor and produced multiple layers of settlement and many small ethnic enclaves within broader national areas. It was reflected in the different view taken of the same area by different nations and governments – none of which could necessarily be described as wrong (although territorial claims were often highly exaggerated). The problems of drawing ethnic frontiers were demonstrated as much by the post-Munich solution applied by Germany in Czechoslovakia as by the problems of the 1918–1939 period itself (Rothschild, 1974, p. 134). A third problem was the dissatisfaction engendered by the treaties signed at Versailles in 1919 and elsewhere and the desire of many groups to secure revision of the post-First World War settlement.

This was felt most strongly by nations which been directly defeated during the First World War. East Prussia, for example, was separated from the bulk of the German state by the Polish Corridor which gave the new Polish state access to the Baltic sea at the Free City of Danzig. Areas of Silesia, valuable for their deposits of coal, were disputed by Poland and Germany, the matter eventually being decided by a plebiscite conducted by the League of Nations, whose outcome the Poles nevertheless refused to recognize and which led to the partition of the region. Hungary, as part of the Austro-Hungarian empire defeated with Germany, emerged from the post-war settlement stripped of much of its territory. Two-thirds of its former lands and 60 per cent of its former population were taken from it, most awarded to Czechoslovakia, Romania and Yugoslavia. In 1920 around 30 per cent of ethnic Hungarians (Magyars) lived outside the post-war state. But ethnic tensions during the inter-war period were not restricted to international relations and conflicts between states.

The territorial provisions made for the new Czechoslovak state meant that it included nearly three million Germans, a factor that caused considerable domestic problems and made it particularly vulnerable to German expansionism as it developed under Hitler and became transformed in 1938 into direct aggression against the Czechoslovak state. Whilst, too, it was only Czechoslovakia among the central European states during the inter-war period that had any claim to have maintained and put into practice the democratic principles that prevailed in the immediate post-war period, it was the dynamic of internal ethnic relations that placed this claim in the greatest doubt and the demographic composition of Czechoslovakia that 'compounded all the other weaknesses of the state' (Pearson, 1983, p. 151). Polish experiences with its large Ruthene minority (14 per cent of the population) and with its Bielorussians also played an important part in the country's move towards increasingly dictatorial methods of rule. Such problems made a significant contribution to the instability of the countries of 'middle Europe' between the wars and subsequently set limits on the capacity of Soviet Russia to impose its form of social and political order on these more European parts of its new empire.

The establishment of Soviet Europe

The establishment of Communist power throughout central Europe was a complex and gradual process, with Soviet and domestic Communist influence being exercised in a variety of ways and through diverse institutions. The direction of change, located in a hardening international context that was rapidly turning into the Cold War, was nevertheless quite clear and the immediate post-war years saw the steady strengthening of Russian control over the region. Communist forces had been active in the wartime resistance in a country like Poland, which had lengthy experience of German occupation, but they were relatively small and far outnumbered by non- or anti-Communist resistants. The Communist base in the region on which Soviet-style rule could be established was quite small. The scene was set for a period of wide-ranging political conflict and a more complex pattern of Communist advance. It corresponded to the first of the three stages of Sovietization outlined by Seton-Watson (1950, p. 169) which involved the formation of genuine political coalitions and competition between political contenders under conditions not yet fully controlled by Soviet agents.

The first stage was followed by the establishment of bogus coalitions composed mostly of Communist front representatives and then the final imposition of a monolithic Communist regime. Political developments in the immediate post-war years also took place in a context characterized by diverse forms of economic change which involved different forms and levels of production from those which had prevailed before the war. Developments in the countryside, which saw the enactment of long-awaited land reform, contributed in particular to a reduction in the level of opposition to the Communist takeover, while the rapid pace of post-war reconstruction and accompanying social mobility tended to reduce stability and attachment to existing forms of organization in urban and industrial areas. The process of immediate post-war recovery broadly coincided with the period during which genuine government coalitions were in existence – although in countries like Poland and Hungary conditions for the survival and articulation of independent political forces rapidly became less favourable.

The coalitions that were formed as a result of the elections held in Poland in January 1947 and later the same year, during August, in Hungary were of a far less genuine character and considerably more subject to Communist manipulation. The Czechoslovak coalition held until February 1948 and then collapsed with the resignation of most of its non-Communist ministers and the staging of a Communist coup, after which the pattern of increasingly monolithic Communist rule was followed there too. The coalition element in the provincial councils in the Soviet zone in Germany was also qualified following the elections of October 1946. The developments that took place in the Soviet zone of occupation in Germany were initially hesitant, following developments elsewhere rather than initiating them in terms of political development and state formation. Soviet authorities were, however, aggressive and ambitious in trying to define policy for the whole of Germany and seeking to maximize Communist influence. This mixture reflected the ambiguity and duality in developments within central Europe during the immediate post-war period. Relations with the western forces of occupation rapidly worsened and the Americans ceased reparations deliveries to the Soviet Union from their zone in May 1946. By the time a People's Council was elected in the Soviet zone prior to the establishment of the German Democratic Republic in 1949, the political situation was under rigorous Communist control.

The rapid transition from what appeared to be relatively moderate Soviet policies in central Europe, involving the acceptance of genuine political coalitions and the holding of free elections (Hungary and Czechoslovakia in 1945 and 1946, as well as voting in the Soviet zone of Austria), to outright Communist aggression and manipulation, seemed to reflect a marked duality of outlook on the part of the Soviet Union – if not sheer duplicity in terms of political manoeuvring. The Soviet authorities and local Communist leaders expended considerable effort on constructing the appropriate Marxist theoretical view to be taken of regimes in the newly liberated areas. Such regimes were clearly not (despite some later, cruder formulations) the revolutionary consequences of a domestic upheaval, and the standard Marxist-Leninist conception of the dictatorship of the proletariat did not fit the new state forms. It was accepted that Russian experience of social developments was not directly applicable to post-war central Europe, if only because the role and presence of the Red Army had been itself a major factor in the establishment of what came to be termed the 'People's Democracies'.

But signs soon began to emerge from the Kremlin that the Soviet leadership was not fully satisfied with the performance of national Communist leaders in central Europe. Once installed, the leaders, not surprisingly, became increasingly conscious of local conditions and more preoccupied with domestic issues. Tendencies towards 'domesticism' began to trouble the Soviet leadership. Problems encountered in building socialism in central Europe, not always the ideal location for such an enterprise, naturally turned the attention of local Communists to reconsider the importance of national conditions and review policy errors of the past. The question of nationalism was thus one that emerged during 1947 in Poland, while similar echoes were also detectable amongst Czechs, East Germans, Hungarians and Romanians (Brzezinski, 1967, pp. 53–54). Poles and Czechs also looked further afield and responded positively in July 1947 to American proposals concerning participation in the Marshall Plan.

The task of striking the right balance was clearly a difficult one for the new Communist rulers and, as Stalin told Tito in straightforward terms, the basic problem was not one of whether mistakes were being made: 'the issue is conceptions different from our own'. The foundation of the Cominform (Communist Information Agency) in September 1947 was the major Soviet response to this set of problems. Most European Communist leaders, with the notable exception of Władysław Gomułka in Poland, did not just accept the Soviet initiative but received it with some relief, as the accelerating pace of change and growing political conflict in central Europe was in any case leading to greater dependence on the Soviet Union. The foundation of the Cominform helped dissipate the illusions of some 'fellow-travellers' and enhanced the strength of the Soviet model that underlay the process of building socialism in central Europe. The foundation of the Cominform also meant the end of the phase of relative diversity and the beginnings of full Stalinism, the period of near-total uniformity in relations between the countries of Communist central Europe and the Soviet Union (a development which was a source of great disappointment to Communist forces in France and Italy).

The Communist takeover in central Europe was not a smooth or uncontentious process. The international context had initially served to restrain Communist domination but then, ironically enough, as the Western powers expressed more firmly their resistance to the Communist advance, to accelerate it. The consolidation of Soviet power in central Europe was nevertheless clearly signalled by the establishment of the Cominform in 1947; the Communist takeover of the social democratic parties, mostly in the following year, firmly established the Communist monopoly of the left, while the organization of non-competitive elections provided these phoney parties with a spurious political legitimacy. Communist uniformity in central Europe made a further advance with the establishment of the German Democratic Republic in 1949. The effective imposition of the Stalinist model on neighbouring European countries in the late 1940s made the incorporation of the People's Republics with the USSR a feasible option and it was presented at one juncture as a real possibility. The degree of Soviet influence already achieved, however, was soon recognized to be fully adequate to ensure the imposition of the Stalinist pattern.

Soviet–European relations after 1945

The latter half of the twentieth century was marked by the unambiguous existence of an area of 'Soviet Europe' (Carrère d'Encausse, 1987) more obviously 'European' than Russia itself though also, in the views of some, historically distinct from western Europe and not having always been harnessed to the main thrust of European developments. As the reach of Soviet power extended westward, though, the focus of Soviet attention in terms of the identification of an alternative model of social organization and development (both as a threat to the USSR and as an example to emulate) moved from western Europe to the United States. The idea of the superpower emerged towards the end of the Second World War and, although Britain was originally regarded as a member of the exclusive group of superpowers, it rapidly became clear that only two major powers had the resources, commitment and military capacity to take on the global role that the status implied. The Soviet Union though, unlike the United States, had suffered a high level of economic and material losses during the war and was far from having reached the same level of socio-economic development.

Europe in the age of superpower rivalry

The Soviet Union's awesome military record during the war (with some 80 per cent of German casualties having been inflicted on the Eastern Front), its continuing post-war presence in the heart of Europe, and growing international support in the form of new Communist states and evident political influence, lent it a superpower status fully equal to that of the United States. From a later perspective, with a greater understanding of the strength of the United States and its economy in the immediate post-war period and of the intrinsic weakness of the centrally directed Soviet command economy, with its poor growth prospects, the power, potential global role and much-publicized threat of the Soviet Union in the immediate post-war may seem to have been grossly exaggerated. That, however, was not the view at the time. In his book conceived during that period, George Kennan could refer to the developments which had carried the Western community in the space of forty years (ie. immediately after the Russian Revolution) from a 'seemingly secure place at the centre of world happenings to the precarious and isolated position it occupies today, facing a world environment so largely beyond its moral and political influence' (Kennan, 1960, p. 36).

This, it should be noted, was written by a well-informed American during the period after the Second World War when the United States enjoyed unprecedented global economic dominance (it produced around 50 percent of global GNP by the end of the war) and wide-ranging political power (even if the US felt isolated and somewhat marginalized by the strength of the Soviet presence in Europe). US sentiments of vulnerability further increased with the surprisingly rapid Soviet development of atomic weapons. However, despite Soviet military advances and subsequent shocks to the West like the launching of Sputnik in 1957 (which seemed to imply that the Soviet Union had developed the capability to deliver nuclear missiles to American territory), America retained a clear technological lead and military superiority over the eastern superpower. It was only towards the end of the 1960s that the Soviet Union gained nuclear parity in the sense of having the capability to launch a significant arsenal of inter-continental ballistic missiles against the United States.

American forces did remain in Europe at the end of the War and took the lead in maintaining an integrated military structure which, though smaller than the Soviet military presence and subject to potential problems of supply and reinforcement from across the Atlantic, acted as a significant balance to Soviet forces and, according to one's point of view, either as a major deterrent to aggression or as a significant threat to Soviet security. But the Soviet perception of the post-war situation in Europe was by no means negative. West European military forces were fairly small and the American presence distant from its home base. The US preponderance in terms of nuclear weapons was a significant factor, but its arsenal was hardly likely to be used aggressively in view of even the limited Soviet ability to respond in like fashion and the proximity of the conventional forces of the Soviet Union and its allies in the restricted European theatre. More important, the American presence in Europe justified the maintenance of significant numbers of Soviet forces in advance positions (up to 400,000 in the case of those stationed in East Germany) and legitimated Moscow's tight military and political control over its European allies.

The Kremlin had acquired a valuable defensive shield of obedient satellites and Sovietized allies, whose relations were reflected first in a range of bilateral military agreements and then, from 1955, in the regional security arrangements of the Warsaw Pact. Germany remained divided and while Stalin lost the opportunity to influence developments in the whole of the defeated country, the Soviet position in the Eastern sector was consolidated and any fear of the unconstrained resurgence of German military power as seen during the Hitler years effectively eliminated. At the same time, Soviet acquiesence in the continuing American presence in Europe did not prevent the Kremlin making considerable political use, particularly during the immediate post-war period, of its numerous supporters in western Europe and especially of the sizeable Communist parties of France and Italy. There was also the heritage of war-time military cooperation with those previously seen by Lenin and Stalin as major enemies of the Soviet state.

This particularly concerned Britain and France, the established European capitalist powers, who had been perceived in this respect as somewhat more dangerous than the upstart German state. Collaboration and military alliance with the West, however, had clearly been of advantage to the Soviet Union during the war and been instrumental in securing its post-1945 territorial and political gains. Stalin had also had some success in building differentiated relations with the allies, exploiting the not inconsiderable differences between them and playing one off against the other. The capitalist nations had certainly not proved to be an indivisible bloc. There had also been signs of a western willingness to continue cooperation and offer some assistance to the Soviet Union even after the growing differences between the allies that had become apparent towards the end of the war. Stalin's conviction of the hostility of western imperialism towards the Soviets had, despite the worsening of East-West relations and the onset of the Cold War, by no means been fully vindicated.

Neither were Soviet forecasts of western capitalism's growing weakness and incipient collapse substantiated. The American economy emerged from the war strong and considerably expanded, conditions which enabled it to transfer resources to western Europe and facilitate its post-war recovery and steady development. The condition of post-war Europe stabilized. Berlin, an enclave within Soviet-controlled East Germany, survived (by means of a year-long airlift) the attempt to subject it to Soviet authority and cut it off from western supplies. But, despite extensive rhetoric, the West did little in practice to lift the Iron Curtain or to remove the Soviet Union from its forward position in central Europe. Increasingly, the paranoia of Stalin's last years and his fears of capitalist infiltration and subversion seemed misplaced and out of step with the course of development in the developed world.

In fact, the signs were of internal weakness rather than external threat. As the capitalist economies benefited from the conditions of post-war recovery and continued with a steady rate of growth (in some cases, like that of West Germany, with increasingly spectacular signs of success), the Soviet Union was showing serious signs of economic stagnation. Disappointing results followed the early quantitative successes of the accelerated growth strategy of the 1930s and the process of post-war recovery, supported as it was by significant levels of German reparations and the assistance of grossly unequal trade relations with its satellites in eastern Europe (it was estimated that the Soviet Union extracted from the region resources roughly equal to those poured into western Europe under the Marshall Plan). Following the considerable gains it had achieved during the war, primarily in terms of military power and territorial expansion, the limits of Stalinist power were becoming increasingly apparent to its political heirs.

Developments after Stalin

Stalin died in March 1953 and already in 1954 complaints were being voiced in the Council of Ministers (or government) about the slowing rate of growth and worsening prospects for economic development. The Iron Curtain had economic as well as military implications, and it was clear that the Stalinist emphasis on autarky did not provide favourable conditions for the maintenance of patterns of steady economic growth. By 1958 Anastas Mikoyan, the Soviet Minister for Foreign Trade, asserted that while separate capitalist and socialist markets continued to exist they were both reflections of a deeper unity, a single world economy; the attitude of the Soviet Union to this global economy was at best ambiguous. Similar changes in view were occurring in the area of security and politics. It took some years for the conflicts of the post-Stalinist succession to work themselves out, but by 1956 Nikita Khrushchev had emerged politically dominant and launched a major criticism of Stalinism in his 'secret speech' during March of that year.

Political conditions were relaxed both within the Soviet Union and in dealings with foreign countries: capitalist, socialist and non-aligned. A period of 'peaceful coexistence' with capitalism was announced; this meant that systemic conflict was to be conducted in political and ideological terms rather than in an atmosphere which anticipated the imminent outbreak of armed engagement. International relations on this basis proved to be somewhat tempestuous and unpredictable because of the novelty and insecurity of the international structure that developed and because of the continuing conflict between the interests of the major powers involved. The unpredictability was at least partly due also to the personality and shifting views of Khrushchev himself and the insecurity of his position in the post-Stalin leadership. But the greatest instability was seen in eastern Europe, where the economic privations of the Stalin period and the impositions of political dictatorship were keenly felt, creating greater tensions within the countries with a stronger national identity like Poland and Hungary than they had in the Soviet Union or in the less developed Balkan states.

Nikita Khrushchev at his desk in the Kremlin (photo: Camera Press, London).

The first signs of disturbance came in Germany and Czechoslovakia as popular opposition to Communist rule, the economic policies pursued and their grave implications for living standards became apparent in 1953 with demonstrations in Pilsen (Czechoslovakia) and East Berlin, where workers' opposition to wage reductions soon developed into a national movement against Soviet domination and Communist rule. With firm attachment to the dictatorial methods of Stalinist rule still holding and, in East Germany, the substantial presence of Soviet troops, control of the demonstrations posed few problems and opposition was soon contained. In Hungary and Poland, countries with stronger traditions of anti-Communism and opposition to Soviet influence, conflict was slower to develop but more difficult to control. The greater problems involved in maintaining Communist rule in those countries were evident both to the post-Stalin Soviet leadership and, naturally enough, to the domestic Communist élite. The gravity of the problems involved was responsible for the development of serious differences of opinion between Moscow and the local regimes on how to cope with them.

Such differences were most apparent in Hungary. Stalinist repression, party purges and religious repression had been considerably more intense there than in Poland, and the death of Stalin, rapidly followed by realignment of the leadership in the Soviet Union and significant shifts in policy, prompted similarly swift leadership changes in Hungary. There ensued a pattern of political instability between 1953 and 1956. When Imre Nagy became prime minister for the second time in 1956, with the acquiescence of Soviet representatives, he was unable to control the situation or satisfy Hungarian demands in ways which could also be accommodated to Soviet requirements. He finally moved to re-establish multi-party government and proclaimed Hungarian neutrality, withdrawing the country from the Warsaw Pact. Existing Soviet military units were now reinforced and others invaded to engage in the armed repression of the thousands of Hungarians who had now become anti-Communist revolutionaries.

In the first two weeks of November 1956 some 3000 were officially recorded as having died in hostilities, with 13,000 wounded. Nagy was seized by Soviet troops and executed in 1958. Even after the hostilities many remained on strike and János Kádár, the new Communist party leader, was compelled to deal diplomatically with the Central Workers' Council of Greater Budapest, which coordinated popular opposition. In January 1957 the pattern of Communist repression was restored and special courts established to accelerate the proceedings. By the time the structures of Communist power had been fully restored some 2,000 Hungarians had been executed. Hungary therefore suffered the full rigours of totalitarian dictatorship and a period of post-Stalinist instability before encountering the limits of Soviet tolerance and experiencing a further spell of Communist repression.

Poland, a similarly unlikely prospect for Communist rule in view of its lengthy period of conflict with Russia, nationalist traditions and strong attachment to Catholicism, was dealt with more cautiously during the Stalinist period and avoided abrupt changes in personnel and policy after the death of Stalin. The impetus of the dynamic of Communist change slackened after Stalin's death, as it did in other countries of Soviet Europe, and restrictions on political life in Poland began to be slowly relaxed from the beginning of 1954. The picture changed again with Khrushchev's speech of 1956 – definitively so for Polish Communist leader Bierut, who died in Moscow of a heart attack on 11 March – although this did not interrupt the course of relatively controlled change in Poland. However, this did come to a turning-point in June with workers' demonstrations and their violent repression in Poznań. Like the upheavals in Pilsen and Berlin, these events originated in economic disputes which affected workers' living standards and grew out of a long-standing dispute over wages and tax allowances. The changing political situation nevertheless gave them particular significance and, amidst the uncertainties about the parameters of change in central Europe at this stage, evoked an armed response which left 53 dead and some 300 wounded, according to the official record.

It was at this stage that disagreements over the response to these developments in Poland began to show amongst the Communist authorities – initially primarily between the Soviet élite and the Polish leadership as a whole, but then increasingly within the Polish ruling group. The return to prominence of Władysław Gomułka, the Polish Communist leader removed from his post with the onset in eastern Europe of full Stalinism in 1948, appeared increasingly unavoidable. In October he was restored to the leadership in time to lead the Polish side to a show-down with Soviet leaders. The major part of his argument concerned the need to endow the Polish party with a greater level of national autonomy and to permit it to evolve its own solution to the increasingly tense situation within the country (developments in Hungary had still to reach their denouement and bloody resolution). While not tainted with the Stalinist excesses that had marked the record of Rákosi, Gomułka was by no means a liberal or unorthodox Communist either, and Khrushchev acquiesced in his return to the leadership and his desire to devise a national, though in no way liberal solution to growing social unrest.

The developments in Poland and Hungary marked the end of the first phase of the post-Stalinist period and contributed to a clarification of the principles of Communist rule that were emerging in eastern Europe. The attitude of the Soviet leadership had also evolved with respect to the areas of central Europe over which it now exercised a quasi-legitimate authority (the West's response to Soviet actions in Hungary, for example, having been relatively muted and clearly not signalling any possibility of positive action by NATO or any other western organization). The Soviet leadership certainly showed greater flexibility than under Stalin and was willing to tolerate a measure of domestic autonomy and some degree of policy variation (as shown in the tolerance of the Catholic Church and a private farming sector in Poland). But no retreat from Soviet rule over the extensive areas of central Europe that came under its authority in 1945 was envisaged, a point on which Gomułka soon showed himself to be in full agreement with his Soviet comrades, and the continuing military integration of the Communist bloc also emerged as a major priority.

The sequence of events in Hungary seemed to suggest that it was Nagy's attempt to abandon overall Communist leadership and control and to return to the immediate post-1945 form of coalition that triggered the return of the Soviet military in force to Hungary on 1 November 1956. Both Gomułka and Kádár, although they had fallen into disfavour under Stalin, understood this and took care to apply the lesson. The apparently mutual comprehension and acceptance of these rules of the game, whose significance and urgency had been reinforced by the tragic Hungarian experience, was reflected in a period of relative stability in central Europe during the late 1950s and early 1960s. The immediate post-Stalin years had also seen a revision of economic policy and priorities which contributed to a rise in living standards, further assisting in a process of relative stabilization. The changes that had taken place in 1956 had an important political influence on subsequent political developments and contributed, in different ways, to the consolidation of a new course in Soviet-controlled central Europe.

Détente and the resurgence of Europe

In conjunction with the relatively stable constellation of forces and conditions for growth in western Europe, Soviet–European relations as a whole in the post-Stalin period, and particularly after 1956, were subject to little major change – especially as under Khrushchev Soviet policy was more concerned with international détente, the shifting character of relations with the United States and the changing conditions under which global competition was pursued. During Khrushchev's tenure as Soviet leader, the tenor of relations with Europe was not fundamentally changed. The conditions of Soviet domination of central Europe were relaxed but not transformed – the limits were shown not only by the events in Hungary, but also in the renewed crisis over Berlin from 1958 to 1961. The post-war allied occupation of Austria ended and Soviet forces withdrew in 1955, but security concerns remained paramount in Soviet–European relations, and the military focus was central on both sides. There were changing emphases in policy and temperamental shifts in approach under Khrushchev – but they were more critical for the conditions of global rivalry and for Soviet–US relations than for those with Europe.

Partly because of his unpredictability, Krushchev was removed from power in 1964 and replaced by what turned out to be a more authentic collective leadership under the looser guidance of Leonid Brezhnev. Now greater emphasis was laid on consistency and continuity, but the consequence of this was to make clearer some of the inherent contradictions within Soviet policy as a whole. Brezhnev aimed to combine military détente and greater economic cooperation with the West with firmer domestic control. Ideological competition and political rivalry persisted on the international plane – the latter theme receiving stronger emphasis and greater substance with the Soviet achievement of broad nuclear parity towards the end of the sixties and a more prominent Third World presence in the 1970s. This policy did not, however, spell any relaxation of Soviet control over central Europe, and the Brezhnev leadership was significantly more conservative in this respect than Khrushchev had been. The course taken by the Dubček leadership in Czechoslovakia during 1968 to maintain Party supremacy while pursuing a course of political and economic reform did not prevent Soviet forces invading in August of that year.

However, Europe also became more important to the Soviet Union under Khrushchev's successors. The growing economic strength of western Europe and the revival of its political fortunes in terms of growing confidence and autonomy (both elements reflected in the increasing importance of the European Economic Community) were one cause of this. Political developments also played a part. France's departure from the integrated NATO command alerted Moscow to the possibilities of developing a more differentiated approach to western Europe, a line of development that gained further impetus with Willy Brandt's elaboration of an *Ostpolitik* (closer relations with countries to the east) during his tenure as leader of the Federal Republic of (West) Germany. Initiatives in this area, too, tended to compensate for the relative inaction in relations with the United States and for continuing difficulties with the Chinese. As Khrushchev's Third World initiatives had brought few successes, future relations with Europe and its leading western powers came to look increasingly promising. West German signature in 1969 of the non-proliferation treaty concerning the acquisition and use of nuclear weapons, and, the following year, further German treaties with Poland and the Soviet Union concerning the permanence of the post-war European frontiers removed major problems to the improvement of Soviet–German economic relations, an increasingly attractive option in the light of Germany's growing economic strength and the USSR's persistent weakness.

Growing Soviet interest in strengthening links across Europe and advances in détente with the Americans, reflected in the conclusion of an Anti-Ballistic Missile Treaty and the SALT (Strategic Arms Limitation Talks) agreements, led to the participation of the Soviet Union and all other European states, together with the United States and Canada, in the Conference on Security and Cooperation in Europe, whose final act was signed in 1975 in Helsinki. It was in many ways a loose and abstract agreement which was entered into by the different states with different expectations and different intentions in mind. Its utility, though limited, nevertheless was proved in subsequent years as conditions within the Soviet Union and eastern Europe went through various phases and periods of rapid change. The state of superpower détente and Soviet relations with west European states began to change soon after the signature of the agreement as the stock of Soviet intermediate-range missiles was built up and NATO announced the 'double-zero' option, leading to the installation of Cruise and other limited range missiles.

Political relations within Soviet Europe also worsened as the domestic Communist élites came under pressure as a result of growing economic problems and, in some cases, political opposition. The existence of a general crisis of the Communist system became evident during 1980 in Poland, and its protracted nature reflected both the severity of the problems it posed and the poverty of Soviet strategy in this area. Both East Germany and Hungary registered years of zero, or minimal, economic growth in the early 1980s, and, in general, the Communist economies of eastern Europe showed their fundamental failure to develop. No longer could rising living standards be offered in compensation for the persistence of authoritarian government and the unpopularity of Soviet influence. The build-up of nuclear weapons and new missile systems in Europe, part of the onset of a new Cold War, combined with overall lack of success in Soviet policy in the Third World, reinforced the tendency of Soviet leaders to pay more attention to European countries and their problems. Domestic problems and the increasingly apparent obstacles to securing the economic development of the Soviet Union pointed in the same direction and meant that attitudes to Europe were as ripe for reappraisal as other areas of Soviet policy when a new leader, Mikhail Gorbachev, acceded to the leadership in 1985.

Russia in the 'common European house'

After years of stagnation and a succession of ageing leaders at the head of the Soviet Union, Gorbachev arrived at a time when most areas of Soviet policy (including those concerning Europe), were due for overhaul. The relative neglect of the European dimension of Soviet policy had proved to be costly. The return of Cold War elements in superpower relations following the Soviet invasion of Afghanistan and the hardening of US policy under President Reagan, had led to the closer military integration of Europe with the United States and a stronger NATO. Trade and technology transfer remained relatively underdeveloped and subject to western political restrictions. Meanwhile, the slow-down of the domestic economies reached critical proportions in the Soviet Union and the countries allied with it. Having opted to play for high stakes in the superpower contest it was becoming clear that the Soviet Union had lost. The process itself had already shown the negative consequences it carried for relations with Europe: given the primacy of the superpower framework, relations with Europe were subordinate to those forged with the United States.

Attempts to run the alternative track and conduct a form of public diplomacy (in support of national peace movements for example) with west European publics were also counter-productive in that the governments were irritated and, while little effective advantage was gained, progress in terms of mainstream diplomacy was probably held back. As long as there was no sign of Soviet military decommitment from central Europe – a measure also forestalled by the looming collapse of parts of its allies' economic and political systems (as had become evident in Poland during 1980 and the subsequent period of martial law) – there were likely to be few improvements on either side. The European aspect of Soviet external relations was, therefore, more than ready for review. The position of Europe itself had also changed dramatically by the 1980s.

The Cold War framework within which superpower relations continued to be set became the object of increasing criticism in Moscow and the prospects for Europe perceived more favourably, making Russia's west European neighbours increasingly attractive partners. The consequence of the 'new thinking' in the Kremlin, which became evident with Gorbachev's accession to power, was a significant switch of attention to Europe, with diplomatic relations finally being established between the Soviet Union and the European Community in 1989. Economic factors played an important part. The success of EEC developments was one major element and provided an attractive example for the growing proponents of domestic reform, who detected both the growing problems of US economic development and its close association with military expenditure and technological development, which tended to mirror the existing Soviet pattern and thus reinforce existing structures in both camps.

Gorbachev and the 'new thinking'

The reduction of the security emphasis in Soviet thinking and the apparent exhaustion of the possibilities in established superpower relations meant that

Europe now provided Soviet Russia with a more attractive model and opened the way for the exploration of an alternative path. Gorbachev's rise to supreme power did not bring about an immediate change in Soviet foreign policy and the priorities that could be detected within it, but it certainly facilitated the emergence of the 'new political thinking' that many saw as necessary in the context of Russia's increasingly problematic domestic and international position. Specialist advisers and their political allies who had argued for the revision of Soviet foreign policy and proposed greater East–West rapprochement had not been absent, but they had remained at some distance from the decision-making centres of the Soviet political system. With the leadership change that followed the death of Chernenko in 1985, those supporting the adoption of such new thinking now gained prominence in the Soviet Foreign Ministry, the Party's International Department and leading positions in the various institutions engaged in foreign affairs research. Some even joined the Presidential Council or became members of the Politburo.

There were several components to the new political thinking. The emphasis on military strength and the role of power in international relations was deplored. Talk of the 'anti-imperialist struggle' and the pursuit of class war was increasingly replaced by references to compromise, interdependence and common human interests. In this context, for many in the more influential sectors of the intelligentsia, 'Europe' took on particular significance as a symbol of modernity, as it had in earlier times (Malcolm, 1991, p. 12). This orientation was supported by more specific shifts in perceptions of the international situation. While international relations were perceived in terms of a zero-sum conflict, in which advantage for one party could only be secured at the cost of the other, the superpower conflict that had been dominant since the end of the Second World War had directed attention overwhelmingly towards the United States and left little room for a significant role to be played by European actors. The situation changed with the advent of the new political thinking.

A second change in perception concerned relations within the capitalist camp and the implications they carried for the Soviet position. While developments in superpower relations pointed by the mid-1980s to a more decisive US dominance in global terms, America's role within the constellation of western powers was far less assured in view of the rise of Japan and Germany as major economic forces. It was not clear what this was likely to mean for the Soviet Union and its future, but it certainly suggested the likelihood of some decline in America's relative position and an enhanced political role for Europe as the emphasis on the military dimension of international relations was reduced. The importance of Europe was still less than that of the United States for Soviet foreign policy, but it was greater than it had been – and was considerably greater than that of Asia in terms of Soviet perceptions (Iivonen, 1991, p. 34). The overall course of developments thus encouraged the direction of Soviet attention towards Europe.

The 'common European house (or home)' was one expression of this orientation and one made considerable use of by Gorbachev in developing his new policy. (The Russian term is open to either translation – although their implications are rather different. 'House' has architectual implications and directs attention to structure; 'home' implies the existence of relations and suggests a family network.

Mikhail Gorbachev being sworn in as Soviet President at the Third Extra-ordinary Congress of the USSR People's Deputies in the Kremlin, 15 March 1990 (photo: Camera Press, London).

The difference, however, is in other respects primarily one of emphasis, as any satisfactory pursuit and realization of the principle would involve aspects of both meanings (Brzezinski, 1989, p. 2)). The term itself was not particularly original, as it had already been used in the Soviet political context by Brezhnev in 1981 in a more traditional sense, to suggest the exclusion of the United States from any European role (and had even, at an earlier date, been associated with Hitler). Gorbachev put his version of the origin and nature of the idea in the following terms:

> Having conditioned myself for a new political outlook, I could no longer accept in the old way the multi-colored, patchwork-quilt-like political map of Europe ... I felt with growing acuteness the artificiality and temporariness of the bloc-to-bloc confrontation and the archaic nature of the 'iron curtain'. That was probably how the idea of a common European home came to my mind and at the right moment this expression sprang from my tongue by itself ... developing the metaphor, one may say: the home is common, that is true, but each family has its own apartment, and there are different entrances, too. But it is only together, collectively, and by following the sensible norms of coexistence that the Europeans can save their home, protect it against a conflagration and other calamities, make it better and safer, and maintain it in proper order. The concept of a 'common European home' suggests above all a degree of integrity, even if its states belong to different social systems and opposing military–political alliances. It combines *necessity with opportunity*.
>
> *(Gorbachev, 1988, pp. 194–95)*

As Gorbachev also pointed out (1988, p. 191), his conception was a response to those who sought to exclude the Soviet Union from Europe and to equate 'Europe' with 'western Europe', a tendency that had gained strength in eastern Europe as the stagnation and reactionary character of the Brezhnev years prompted fears that Soviet Russia would never regain the dynamic shown by European civilization. As Czechs and Hungarians in particular reclaimed an identity as central Europeans, so they also tended often to stress a divide between 'Europe' and 'Russia' and their separation in cultural and social terms over the centuries. Gorbachev's idea represented, therefore, a response to the changing position of both western and eastern Europe as well as to shifts in the superpower relationship. In addition to underpinning Gorbachev's efforts to tie the fate of Soviet Russia more closely with that of Europe – particularly, of course, the leading western forces within it – his view also incorporated a particular vision of Europe which, placing greater emphasis on cultural and historical factors, distanced it even more from established Communist analysis.

Once the new principles were established, the pace of change quickened throughout 1987 and, particularly, 1988. Soviet changes met with a sympathetic German response which provided an international basis for more substantial developments. These soon emerged in the form of progress in discussions on conventional disarmament and significant improvement in economic relations with the European Community. In the rapidly changing context of the late 1980s, the 'common European house' idea thus underwent several major changes. During the first phase, the approach taken towards western Europe since 1945 – in which it had principally been treated as a subordinate member of the US-dominated alliance – was broken with and a view of Europe as an autonomous power-centre developed.

In 1989 and 1990 Russia's relationship with Europe underwent further reappraisal as it became clear that the idea of two systems within a single Europe was no longer to be imposed by the application of external pressure. The gravitation of former Soviet allies towards the western power-centres was accepted as the inevitable tendency that it had surely become. To the extent that this conception involved the abandonment of the 'Brezhnev doctrine', which sanctioned Soviet involvement in the internal affairs of Communist allies, its formulation is difficult to date. Although the Brezhnev doctrine had clearly become inoperative by 1989 (and had been replaced, in government spokesman Gerasimov's happy formulation, by the 'Sinatra' doctrine – in which those concerned do it 'their way') the date of its abandonment as an operative principle is a matter of some uncertainty. A further phase of the 'common house' view finally directed attention to the position of the Soviet Union itself, and its own relationship with Europe (Malcolm, 1991, pp. 50–1). Gorbachev's initiative, indeed, had implications for central Europeans, Warsaw Pact allies and – ultimately – Russia itself that were considerably more momentous than for western Europe.

The return to Europe

As far as central Europe was concerned, it soon became clear that the 'common European house' had little credibility if a large part of the family was held in the basement under armed guard. In parts of 'Soviet Europe' the economic situation was just as serious as in the Soviet Union, if not more so (while living standards might be higher, their material basis was more precarious, and popular expectations were certainly greater than in the Soviet Union). Central Europe was, therefore, from an early stage a prime candidate for greater openness to economic links with the West, a process which promised important and much needed political advantages, too. Rather than a barrier to western influence, the central European area could play a more positive role as a bridge and path for innovation. This idea, however, was also not a new one and Gorbachev soon discovered, like other Soviet leaders, that measures of economic liberalization and greater openness to the West had little positive effect unless major steps towards political reform were also taken.

The Poles launched a new programme of economic reform in 1987 (which was, formally, the second stage of a programme supposedly in operation since the early 1980s – including the period of martial law). This soon turned out, however, to be just one more in a long line of economic initiatives dating back to the 1950s. Poland had already shown signs of economic liberalism in areas like agriculture, where private farming had been widely retained, and had been quite open to dealings with the West, particularly during the leadership of Edward Gierek (1970–1980) when extensive credit agreements were made with foreign institutions. The succession of reform programmes, the relatively small part played by the state in agricultural production and a willingness to establish relations with foreign markets had done little to help the Polish economy, however, and often seemed to worsen the situation. The more consistent reform programme implemented in Hungary since 1968, with the adoption of the New Economic Mechanism, was also showing considerable weakness by the mid-1980s and had few prospects of further development. A major consequence was that these two countries had the highest levels of absolute and per capita foreign indebtedness in eastern Europe, high levels of popular frustration and wide-spread élite disillusion with the prospects of further reform.

The two countries thus offered fertile ground for the surfacing of currents favouring more radical change and contained influential groups within the leadership disposed to take advantage of the more relaxed view of developments within the region evident in the Soviet élite. Significant movement in this respect could be seen in 1988. Dissatisfaction grew in Hungary with the continued leadership of János Kádár, installed as party leader during the Soviet invasion of 1956 but who had, nevertheless, overseen the implementation since 1968 of an economic and political programme which had been quite radical within the contemporary east European context. The recognition that Gorbachev's approach contained prospects of more radical change coincided with evident signs that Kádár had ruled the country long enough and had lost much of his former political touch. He was removed from office in May 1988, opening the way for the advancement of younger politicians more sympathetic to current specialist economic opinion and prepared to contemplate more radical forms of political change.

In Poland change occurred under the pressure of two waves of strikes, one in the spring and a second during August 1988. Although significant, they were hardly as cataclysmic as the events of 1980 which had brought Solidarity into being. Nevertheless, they showed the possibilities for industrial unrest that continued even with the neutralization of Solidarity and persistence of the problems that further economic reform would encounter in the ramshackle Polish economy. More significantly, they directed leadership attention to the new context of national political activity in central Europe and encouraged the pursuit of more radical solutions. This involved the opening of negotiations with Solidarity representatives and an attempt to reach agreement with opposition forces on a new plan of action which foresaw the establishment of structures to stabilize the political situation and open the way to a path of more coherent and effective reform.

The opposition movements that contributed to these events, limited in their membership in some countries but by no means without influence, were also developing new perspectives and putting forward different ideas. The European dimension in the activities of the oppositions became prominent and developed in various directions (Sabata, 1988). It built on a number of elements. Relations between the different opposition groups in central Europe, particularly those of Czechoslovakia, Hungary and Poland, were becoming stronger, and a common vision was being formed (Lewis, 1992). Links with western peace groups, particularly those within the European Nuclear Disarmament movement (which had taken care to accommodate central European perspectives and distinguish itself from Communist-inspired peace fronts), were important. The emergence of human rights movements with a common interest in the nature and implications of the

Helsinki Final Act was a further factor. A final and – in the context of the later 1980s – decisive element was a growing awareness of the implications of the changes under way in Soviet Russia and the developing vision of the 'common European house'. This was increasingly understood to be the prime means for overcoming the post-war division of Europe and removing the obstacles to change on both sides of the divide. It was, however, particularly significant in this respect to independent movements in central Europe and it was for them especially that the changes suggested possibilities of a 'return to Europe'.

Yet it is by no means clear how far Gorbachev meant this opening to the West to go or whether central Europe was really intended to return to Europe – or the West. Opinions on this matter differ – and Gorbachev has, at the time of writing, not pronounced on it either (although close colleagues have expressed their views on the issue). Henry Trofimenko, chief analyst at the Institute of the United States and Canada attached to the USSR Academy of Sciences, wrote that to 'answer this question truthfully, one must admit that neither Gorbachev nor anyone else in the Soviet leadership really anticipated the extent of the radical change' that was taking place in central Europe (Trofimenko, 1991, pp. 12–13). An American observer like Jerry Hough, however, seemed to read the situation quite differently: 'Most persons in the West were shocked by the events in Eastern Europe, and they assumed that Gorbachev too must be surprised. Many thought that he was acting in panic. It was a fundamental misreading of the situation' (Hough, 1990, p. 233).

The questions of the direction of change and the speed at which it occurred are, however, different ones and it is perhaps here that the real distinction should be drawn. While the construction of a 'common European house' without major internal divisions was the accepted goal, the rate at which this should take place was initially understood to be a fairly gradual one – sufficient, for example, to secure equivalent military disengagement on the western side, the creation of pan-European security structures and with significant steps being taken to integrate the Soviet Union within a broader European system of political and economic collaboration (Malcom, 1991, p. 30). While the general trend of development might have been that foreseen by Gorbachev (although certainly not at the very outset of his leadership), the pace of change was almost certainly not. His understanding of the direction that changes were taking, however, meant that he had a profound comprehension of the transformation that was under way and of the factors that spoke against any attempt to slow down the rate at which change, once underway, took place.

Forces within central Europe, predominantly those identified with movements of opposition and dissidence and organized as independent groups outside the Communist establishment, thus took the lead, with Gorbachev and proponents within Soviet Russia of the new thinking, to identify and develop the prospects of a return to Europe of the countries and peoples that had been largely divorced from it since 1945 – or, in the case of Russia, considerably earlier. The sequence of events that led to the return to Europe contained many surprises – the carefully arranged Polish elections of June 1989 with a built-in establishment majority that the Communist authorities nevertheless lost, the determined attempts throughout the summer and autumn of East German citizens to flee to the West and the assistance they received from foreign governments. However, the process of post-Communist development and integration with Europe also turned out to be more problematic and ambiguous than many had anticipated.

Russia and the new Europe

The prospects for Russia's 'return to Europe', or (more in keeping with Gorbachev's terminology) reinforcement of the structure of the 'common European house', were influenced by the conditions under which several critical junctures of overall European development were occurring. Following the withdrawal in 1989 of the countries of central Europe and the Balkans from the Communist camp, the turning-point for Soviet Russia came in 1991. The short-lived putsch of August 1991 spelt the end of the Soviet Union in practical terms, although the formal demise of the union only came at the end of the year with the formation of a Commonwealth of Independent States. With these actions the 74-year period of Communist rule within Russia and its possessions came to an end, as did Russian rule over the former Soviet republics, most of which had formed part of the tsarist empire – Ukraine since the seventeenth century; Bielorussia, Georgia since the eighteenth; Moldavia, Armenia, Azerbaijan, etc. since the nineteenth – with, in some cases, only a brief period of independence after the Revolution of 1917. Some of the former Soviet republics (like Bielorussia, Kazakhstan, Kirghizia) had no experience of independent statehood at all.

The critical implications of the events of 1989–1991 for the countries of central and eastern Europe could, therefore, hardly be overlooked. Yet, if somewhat less dramatic than the weakening and final collapse of Communist power, developments in western Europe also showed features of a process of fundamental transition. Something of a 'new Europe' was emerging in the west and raised further questions about the direction and character of common developments within Europe as a whole. The 1980s had seen the strengthening of tendencies toward greater integration within the European Community, movements in the direction of monetary union and acceptance of a commitment to the creation of a fully integrated internal market by the end of 1992. The development of closer co-operation within western Europe and the strengthening of EC structures was undeniable. But friction and conflicts had not been absent – over levels of funding and the distribution of the common financial burden, the relative competence of national decision-making bodies and EC institutions, as well as more general questions of sovereignty and the exercise of power.

The 'deepening' of the European Community, the strengthening of existing structures and the extension of joint processes, now also coincided with demands for its 'widening', the embrace at least of the countries of central Europe and the development of closer relations with (and the provision of material support for) others emerging from Communist rule. The Community thus faced a multiplicity of problems whose concurrence was a serious matter and could be judged to be rather unfortunate, bearing both on its own development and on relations with the other half of Europe (Calvocoressi, 1991, p. 255). Fundamental questions of con-

tent and structure were involved. The economic disparity between the two halves of Europe and the requests (on occasion escalating into virtual demands) from the former Communist states for material support were one major aspect. The effects of continuing economic crisis and the costs of the beginnings of transition to a market economy were already marked in central Europe in 1990 and 1991 (particularly so in Poland, which took the lead in the latter process). The economic results of the final phase of Communist rule in Soviet Russia were hardly more encouraging. In 1991 the gross national product of the eleven republics that subsequently formed the Commonwealth of Independent States was officially reported to have fallen by 17 per cent, just one of a range of dire statistics pointing also to rising inflation, unemployment and declining health standards (*Radio Free Europe/Radio Liberty Research Report*, 1992, pp. 39–41).

This took place as even the most dynamic western European economies were suffering from the effects of global recession as well as significant domestic problems (deriving, in the case of Germany, from the costs of unification and the controversial form that the assimilation of the East German currency had taken). The demands of the eastern economies posed, therefore, considerable problems for the EC and members of bodies like the G7 (the group of the seven richest world economies). The EC was not unresponsive in economic terms. 700 million ecu[1] were allocated in 1990 under the PHARE programme to support the process of post-Communist reform in central Europe and the Balkans. Commitments of ecu

Boris Yeltsin addressing a victory rally to celebrate the failure of the coup, 22 August 1991. The first popularly elected leader of a Russian state, Yeltsin received further endorsement of his position and his policies in the referendum of April 1993 (photo: Camera Press, London).

[1]   An ecu was equivalent to US $1.2 in April 1991.

850 million and 1 billion were made for 1991 and 1992. Further to such grants, Community institutions had by January 1991 provided ecu 2 billion in the form of loans, while member governments had allocated a further ecu 1.6 billion of grants and 4.9 billion of loans – in addition to contributions made through the IMF, World Bank and European Bank for Reconstruction and Development.

Estimates of the cost of economic reform produced figures that rose far above these levels, however. According to one estimate, the provision of the physical structure for the construction of competitive economies in Bulgaria, Czechoslovakia, Hungary, Poland and Romania together might range from $103 to $226 billion per year. Such requirements were considerably higher even than the relatively generous provisions of Marshall Aid made to western Europe between 1948 and 1952 by a globally dominant United States whose economy had emerged from World War II in a strong and productive state. If the 1.3 percent of US GDP devoted to Marshall Aid during this period were translated into equivalent figures for the contemporary EC, it would have been providing at an annual rate of over ecu 50 billion (Pinder, 1991, pp. 31, 47, 98–9). Such figures were way above the level of provision proposed by the EC. Even the one-third of 1 per cent of GDP regarded as realistic by EC President Delors was considered excessive and to be treated as an opening bid rather than a serious proposal when originally made.

Pizza Hut in Moscow, December 1991. A symbol of fast-food modernity – but the express route to European integration may be less certain (photo: Derek Branford).

The economic demands of Russia and post-Communist Europe were only one aspect of the problems surrounding the broader process of European integration and the pattern of future European relations. Another aspect concerned the nature of the structures within which the course of future social development was conceived and the contrasting trajectories of political change that were evident in the two halves of Europe. The trend since 1989 within the former Soviet camp was one of enhanced national autonomy and the assertion of sovereignty in central Europe, the Balkans (where the forms of state sovereignty had been maintained throughout the Communist period in the absence of any great exercise of national independence), and in the republics of the former Soviet Union (where the complex structures of formal union had been accompanied by the continuing practice of imperial rule). The weakening of central Russian authority was, not surprisingly, seized on as a rare opportunity for the expression of national and regional identity and escape from alien rule, seen as either Russian or Communist – or as both.

In western Europe, on the other hand, the tendency had been towards the pooling of sovereignty and a slowly growing recognition of the limited powers of individual European states under the political and economic conditions that had come to prevail in the second half of the twentieth century. Although this trend gained some momentum during the 1960s, it still met with considerable national resistance, particularly in Britain but also – over particular issues – in France and Germany. Nevertheless, the movement towards greater integration within the European Community was a steady one which was endorsed, with varying degrees of enthusiasm, by all leading political forces. It had, quite simply, been increasingly recognized by the great majority of European decision-makers that there was little choice for the nations of western Europe (with the possible exception of Germany) but to join forces and maximize their regional capacity. In distinction to the countries of eastern Europe, the members of the European Community based this perception on extensive experience of state sovereignty and knowledge both of the opportunities it provided and on its limitations under the conditions that prevailed in modern Europe.

Indeed, Calvocoressi begins his study of modern Europe with the observation that 'for Europeans the state is almost a fact of nature, although this has not been entirely true of any particular state at any particular moment' (Calvocoressi, 1991, p. 3). The rise of diverse nationalisms in western Europe and the establishment of a variety of states to express and contain them gave rise to numerous conflicts – but also to the development of a system for restraining their effects and regulating relations between the states (which was by no means uniformly successful). Western Europe thus saw the development of statesmanship (first explored as a specific skill and praised by Niccolo Machiavelli in sixteenth-century Florence) as an alternative to, and improvement on, military might as a form of political management. This tradition did not take firm root in Russia and many of the countries of eastern Europe. Claims to post-Communist sovereignty in these regions and the inevitable conflicts over territory and resources in some cases provided conditions for the early resort to military might.

This could most obviously be seen in the former Yugoslav federation as well as in the more peripheral areas of the disintegrating Soviet Union (Armenia and

Azerbaijan, the Baltic states, and disputes between Russia and the Ukraine over rights to the military resources themselves). Analogous tendencies could be seen in central Europe in the conflicts between Romania and Hungary, and disputes between Czechs and Slovaks within their own republic – but in the latter cases statecraft was more sophisticated and the threat of military conflict or civil violence correspondingly less. Such events have been far from absent in west European history – and it was the devastation experienced during the Second World War that provided the impetus for the contemporary European movement towards integration. But the development of statecraft and the gradual evolution of constitutional order have also been an important thread in European history and a leading principle in the civilization it has fostered.

In this sense, it is western Europe that has been the core of Europe as a whole (Wallace, 1990, p. 4). While much attention is, rightly, paid to the economic dimensions of Russia's relations with the European Community and to issues of democratic development, general questions of state development and political management are also of prime importance. Whilst they have been of critical significance to the historical character of western Europe, their influence on the emergence of the European Community and the continuing evolution of political structures and processes within that framework seem to mark a further stage in the development of that aspect of European society. Whether the countries of eastern Europe and, particularly, Russia itself will succeed in these dimensions of their further social development is likely to be decisive both for the evolution of their relations with western Europe and their place within Europe as a whole.

References

BASSIN, M. (1991) 'Russia between Europe and Asia: the ideological construction of geographical space', *Slavic Review*, **50**(1), pp. 1–17.

BEREND, I. T. (1986) 'The historical evolution of Eastern Europe as a region', *International Organization*, **40**(2), pp. 329–46.

BRZEZINSKI, Z. K. (1967) *The Soviet Bloc*, Cambridge, Mass., Harvard University Press.

BRZEZINSKI, Z. K. (1989) 'Toward a common European home', *Problems of Communism*, **38**(6), pp. 1–10.

CALVOCORESSI, P. (1991) *Resilient Europe: a study of the years 1870–2000*, London, Longman.

CARRÈRE D'ENCAUSSE, H. (1987) *Big Brother: the Soviet Union and Soviet Europe*, New York, Holmes and Meier.

CAUTE, D. (1977) *The Fellow Travellers*, London, Quartet.

DIXON, S. (1990) 'The Russians: the dominant nationality', in SMITH, G. (ed.), *The Nationalities Question in the Soviet Union*, London, Longman, pp. 21–37.

DJILAS, M. (1963) *Conversations with Stalin*, Harmondsworth, Penguin Books.

ERICKSON, J. (1985) *The Road to Berlin: Stalin's War with Germany*, vol. 2, London, Grafton Books.

FOX, W. (1944) *The Super-Powers*, New York, Harcourt Brace.

GORBACHEV, M. (1988) *Perestroika*, London, Fontana.

GREY, I. (1973) *Ivan III and the Unification of Russia*, Harmondsworth, Penguin (first published 1964).

HOUGH, J. (1990) *Russia and the West: Gorbachev and the politics of reform*, New York, Simon and Schuster.

IIVONEN, J. (1991) 'New thinking in practice: general changes in Soviet policy towards Europe', in IIVONEN (ed.), *The Changing Soviet Union in the New Europe*, Aldershot, Edward Elgar, pp. 28–44.

KENNAN, G. F. (1960) *Russia and the West under Lenin and Stalin*, New York, New American Library.

KUNDERA, M. (1984) 'The tragedy of central Europe', *New York Review of Books*, 31 (7), pp. 33–8; translated from the French by Edmund White.

LEWIS, P. G. (ed.) (1992) *Democracy and Civil Society in Eastern Europe*, London, Macmillan.

MALCOLM, N. (1991) 'The Soviet concept of a common European house', in IIVONEN, J. (ed.), *The Changing Soviet Union in the New Europe*, Aldershot, Edward Edgar, pp. 45–82.

MALCOLM, N. (1993) 'The Soviet Union and Europe', in J. STORY (ed.), *The New Europe*, Oxford, Blackwell, pp. 91–114.

MASTNY, V. (1979) *Russia's Road to the Cold War*, New York, Columbia University Press.

PARES, B. (1962) *A History of Russia*, London, Methuen.

PEARSON, R. (1983) *National Minorities in Eastern Europe*, London, Macmillan.

PINDER, J. (1991) *The European Community and Eastern Europe*, London, Pinter/Royal Institute for International Affairs.

POLONSKY, A. (1975) *The Little Dictators,* London, Routledge and Kegan Paul.

Radio Free Europe/Radio Liberty Research Report (1992) Munich, **1**(12).

ROTHSCHILD, J. (1974) *East Central Europe between the Two World Wars*, Seattle, University of Washington Press.

SABATA, J. (1988) 'Gorbachev's reforms and the future of Europe', *East European Reporter*, **3**(2), pp. 7–8.

SETON-WATSON, H. (1950) *The East European Revolution*, London, Methuen.

SUMNER, B. H. (1961) *Survey of Russian History,* London, Methuen.

SZÜCS, J. (1988) 'Three historical regions of Europe', in J. KEANE (ed.), *Civil Society and the State*, London, Verso, pp. 291–332.

TROFIMENKO, H. A. (1991) 'Soviet policy *vis-à-vis* Europe, a Soviet view', in J.IIVONEN (ed.), *The Changing Soviet Union in the New Europe,* Aldershot, Edward Elgar, pp. 3–27.

VIHAVAINEN, T. (1990) 'Russia and Europe, the historiographic aspect', in V. HARLE and J. IIVONEN (eds.), *Gorbachev and Europe*, London, Pinter, pp. 1–21.

WALLACE, W. (1990) 'Introduction: the dynamics of European integration', in W. WALLACE (ed.), *The Dynamics of European Integration*, London, Pinter/Royal Institute for International Affairs, pp. 1–24.

WEBB, S. and B. (1935) *Soviet Communism: a new civilisation?*, London, Longman, Green.

Essay 3
The United States and Europe, 1945 to 1991

Prepared for the Course Team by Alan Sharp and Ken Ward, University of Ulster at Coleraine

Introduction

In 1945 Europe was at its lowest ebb, much of its industry, its housing stock and its transport systems were in ruins, many of its people were homeless, starving, refugees, or all three. The fate of the continent seemed to lie in the hands of the two extra-European superpowers, the Soviet Union and the United States, whose victorious troops had met on the River Elbe on 25 April. In defeated Germany, soon to be divided between the competing Soviets and Americans, 1945 was *die Stunde Null* (Zero Hour), a political, cultural and physical vacuum. But the sensation of an obliteration of previous identities spread far beyond the borders of the crushed Third Reich. The experiences of the war had, apparently, exposed the frailties of the national state as an adequate safeguard of security, undermined the faith of many in nationalism itself and had negated many of the basic tenets of liberalism leaving the entire continent, winners and losers alike, unsure of where the future lay. It seemed as if the old certainties had been destroyed and it was not clear what would replace them.

In 1919, in a bitter critique of the performance of the American leader, Woodrow Wilson, at the Paris Peace Conference, the British economist J. M. Keynes argued that:

> When President Wilson left Washington he enjoyed a prestige and a moral influence throughout the world unequalled in history ... Never had a philosopher held such weapons wherewith to bind the princes of the world ... [but] ... He had no plan, no scheme, no constructive ideas whatever for clothing with the flesh of life the commandments which he had thundered from the White House.
>
> *(Keynes, 1919, pp. 38 and 43)*

In 1945 the advantages enjoyed by Wilson in 1919 had been multiplied many times over. America's enormous economic and industrial strength (it was responsible for nearly 50 per cent of world production) was accentuated by its massive and well-equipped armed forces, whilst, for the second time in a generation, the Europeans had plunged the world into war. Would it now prove possible for the United States to stamp its values and political and economic philosophies on the physically exhausted and morally bankrupt Old World? Was Europe about to be 'Americanized'?

In the immediate post-war period there was no doubt about the dominant military and economic influence that America could exercise if it chose in a world where its own strength was exaggerated by the weakness of all around it. But would the reconstruction of west European society entail an Americanization of European cultures? It was not a new fear, since from the beginning of the century there had been a continuing critical debate about the effect of the expansion of American industrial and marketing methods and outlooks upon fundamental cultural values in European societies. Georges Duhamel's *America the Menace* was a French bestseller in the 1930s, whilst Robert Aron and Armand Dandier enjoyed acclaim for their 1931 book, *The American Cancer*. The new methods of industrial organization entailed large-scale production of a standardized product for the mass market, which was backed up by advertising campaigns using the new forms of mass communication. This was often given the epithet 'Fordism', after the automobile manufacturer who not only pioneered industrial mass production, but also the encouragement of a docile workforce through the 'doctrine of high wages'. It was pointed out in the inter-war period that such a development might be suited to the United States with large amounts of capital available for mechanization, an extensive domestic market making standardization possible and a relatively scarce workforce (de Grazia, 1991, pp. 64–5). These conditions hardly applied to Europe before 1939, but in the post-1945 period the reconstruction and development of industry could and would call on the American experience.

It is within the context of the 'modernization' of European countries that one needs to place the argument about the extent of the Americanization of culture. There is no doubt that the dominant position of the United States encouraged the acceptance of ideals which were seen as essentially American, not least the belief in individualism and capitalism as the underpinning of the moral and material superiority of that country. The cultural industries through which these ideas were disseminated, the cinema, publishing and advertising, were part of the modernizing process and, many people felt, the means by which American cultural influence was developed.

After 1945 the United States had a clear interest in utilizing all the means possible to influence the reconstruction of western Europe, but it would be simplistic to equate the reconstruction process with Americanization. The fact was that the United States was the most advanced industrial society and if other countries wished to emulate it or compete they had to find either a new form of industrial organization or work from the American model. The reason that in western Europe they chose the latter was in part the result of the American presence. But the construction of a modern industrial society was bound to raise questions of how far the indigenous cultural experience of European societies might be lost. Part of the narrative of the period from 1945 to the 1990s is how European states attempted to cope with this dilemma.

The answers suggested by this essay are not simple. Whilst there are obvious examples of American domination in the post-war world in commercial, industrial and communication and, above all, military and defence contexts, this essay will argue that the process is much more complex than that of American attempts to seek a permanent dominance on the European continent. American perceptions of the role and purpose of the United States did not remain constant or unanimous and equally the reactions and alternative visions of the future advanced by Europeans revealed a wide variety of aims and methods. Ambiguity and ambivalence will be key ideas in the discussion of the interactions which took place between the two continents. This may seem to make more complicated and difficult an already massive topic but it would be impossible to do justice to the paradoxes and contradictions encompassed by the developments over the half-century that this essay spans without some reference to the uncertainties experienced by contemporaries and later commentators.

It was not always clear to the participants what various terms meant. Sometimes the confusion of definitions was deliberate, sometimes unintended. What indeed was Europe? Alternative definitions were advanced by political and cultural opinion-makers at different times, sometimes using a continental land mass as the central identifier, sometimes meaning only part of that land mass, sometimes appealing rather to a spiritual and intellectual community of ideas that bridged oceans. Some American decision-makers had a strong commitment to European unity (an ideal with a variety of possible meanings) but when the European Community came to challenge the trading and economic interests of the United States the reality became less attractive. In entertainment and communications the American domination of the 1950s (always limited outside the United Kingdom by problems of language) was replaced in the later period by a much more complex situation, with European ideas, programmes and personnel and the involvement of finance and influences from other continents creating a different pattern that was multinational rather than American or European in character. The position of Great Britain was pivotal but never satisfactorily resolved in any of the areas of concern and the question of its own identity – European, Atlantic or imperial power – was defined only in the negative sense that, by the 1960s, a European role was all that remained available; a solution even then only partially accepted by some British decision-makers. The whole phenomenon of the Cold War was an enormously complicating factor, dividing Europe into east and west, though it might be argued that this development was the solidification of earlier separate identities rather than something entirely new. In one sense their fear of the Soviet Union drove the west Europeans to seek American protection, recognizing that this entailed American control – the idea of 'empire by invitation' – yet there was also resentment of that control that helped to encourage alternative strategies (Lundestad, 1984, pp. 1–21). The juxtaposition of resentment and admiration is also obvious in the envy of American troops during the war ('Oversexed, overpaid and over here') and the appearance of graffiti demanding 'Yanks Go Home!', yet at the same time in a willingness to accept American largesse ('Any gum, chum?').

It is the purpose of this essay to investigate how Europe (mainly western Europe) and the United States have created or suggested new or changed perceptions of their own and each other's identity in the post-1945 world and how their reactions

Understandable in any language (credit: Hulton Deutsch Picture Collection).

have reshaped and redesigned those relationships into patterns that are sometimes discernible but never static. We seek, as far as possible, to combine the major international, military, economic and cultural developments, into a series of inter-connecting arguments and definitions.

The inter-war background

It has been argued that both the United States and the European states adopted a fundamentally different approach to their relationships after the Second, as opposed to the First, World War. This is a defensible proposition but one that requires careful consideration and modification. Recent American research has indicated the influence in the 1920s of Jean Monnet in the shaping of French policies towards Germany that would re-emerge in a more developed form in the 1940s. Thus western European integration was not an entirely novel concept after 1945. The American rejection of the Treaty of Versailles and the defeat of Woodrow Wilson's ideas in the 1920 presidential election meant that the United

States withdrew from its military role in Europe and took no part in the political enforcement of a treaty that it had a vital role in shaping. It would, however, be unwise to neglect the continuing and expanding economic and cultural role played by the United States in Europe, even during the apparent period of 'isolation'. The mid-western perception of Europeans as cunning tricksters and welchers might continue to dominate American domestic and international politics but American funds flowed into Europe. Large American loans to Germany under the Dawes and Young plans, designed to ease the payment of reparations after the First World War, and heavy investment by the United States, particularly in Germany, even during and after the Wall Street Crash of 1929, profoundly altered the economic balance and relationship between the two continents. Coca-Cola – 'the essence of American capitalism' according to company president Robert Woodruff – was established in Essen in 1929, it flourished through the thirties, despite Nazi disapproval, with sales of four-and-a-half million cases in 1939. One of the earliest communications between Germany and the United States after the Allied victory in 1945 read 'Coca-Cola GmbH survives. Please send the auditors' (Willett, 1989, p. 103).

American cultural influences were also recognized in European countries well before the Second World War. Features of the mass circulation press were borrowed from the United States, broadcasting organizations were developed in the light of the American experience of unrestricted commercial activity, and the Hollywood cinema, jazz and American danceband music became the models of successful popular entertainment. The responses were ambiguous, since many intellectuals and politicians equated commercial success with an undermining of national cultural values, while recognizing the necessity to find forms of press, film and broadcasting material that could popularly express a national culture. In the case of authoritarian and fascist states, embargoes were placed upon American films and a well-funded production facility developed. In democratic societies there was no less concern and there was legislative intervention in film production and distribution.

Thus there were stronger links between the two continents than the political relationships suggested and the Second World War made a profound difference. Some three million American troops brought their mores, political and cultural outlooks and forms to European populations. Victory brought the seductive opportunity to reshape Germany into a democratic society on an American model, at first in the zone occupied by the United States in the south, but rapidly throughout the whole of what would become the Federal Republic. The political, economic and cultural advantages of the Americanization of West Germany and, later, western Europe were both severally and jointly obvious, particularly as the Cold War developed. But, just as it would be unwise to discount American interest in European affairs in the inter-war period, so it would be foolish to neglect the survival of a desire to disentangle the United States from European involvement and commitment. In other words there was no simple pattern that emerged at the end of the fighting in May 1945.

The Cold War declared: 1945–1953

The early stages

At the Yalta Conference on 5 February 1945 President Roosevelt told the Soviet leader, Joseph Stalin, that:

> ... he did not believe that American troops would stay in Europe much more than two years ... he felt that he could obtain support in Congress and throughout the country for any reasonable measures designed to safeguard the future peace, but he did not believe that this would extend to the maintenance of an appreciable American force in Europe.
>
> *(Feis, 1957, pp. 531–2)*

Whilst it is true that Roosevelt later qualified this statement by accepting that the United States might play a more major role under the auspices of an international organization like the United Nations, the continued unbroken presence of American (and Canadian) forces in Europe forty-six years later requires some explanation. Indeed the months following the Allied victory in Europe saw a rapid fall in the number of United States service personnel from a high point of 3 million in May 1945 to 391,000 by 1946 and twelve poorly trained and ill-equipped divisions by 1948. The demand to 'Bring the Boys Back Home' remained a powerful factor in American politics. By 1950, on the eve of the Korean War, American forces in Europe reached their lowest point in the post-war era, 116,000 (US General Accounting Office, 1989, p. 13). Thus the pattern established by the First World War – decisive American intervention in both the waging of war and the making of peace followed by a withdrawal from military and political responsibility afterwards – seemed to be reasserting itself after the Second World War. Yet this did not happen, and since this must be the fundamental factor in any assessment of the relationships between the United States and Europe in the post-1945 era, the crucial question must be why?

There was a change of president; Roosevelt died on 12 April 1945, and Harry S. Truman brought an abrasive and astringent style to his dealings with the Soviet leadership. At his second meeting as president with the Soviet foreign minister Molotov, Truman declared in robust tones that cooperation between the United States and the Soviet Union must cease being a 'one-way street'. Molotov claimed he had never before been addressed in such a manner; 'Carry out your agreements and you won't get talked to like that' was Truman's reaction (Ambrose, 1971, p. 114). This was not decisive. Of greater significance was a general change in the mutual perceptions of the relationship between the Soviet Union and the United States that occurred in the period between 1945 and 1947 and an accompanying revision of the relationship between the United States and, in particular, western Europe.

Roosevelt's vision of the post-war world assumed continuing Soviet–American cooperation. He believed that the Soviet Union had limited external ambitions based upon its security needs rather than any ideological crusade, that its post-war resources would preclude adventures in foreign policy and that he could control the world after the defeat of Germany and Japan in a cooperation with Stalin that would also include Great Britain and China – the 'Four Policemen' (Loth, 1988, p. 29). He estimated that he had two major advantages – the Soviet need for American credits and an American monopoly in nuclear weapons – and he thought that he had Stalin's assurance that the new governments of eastern Europe would allow democratic structures a fair chance to operate. He was also suspicious of British attempts to present Soviet policy in a less favourable manner, fearing that Churchill and his advisers anticipated a post-war Anglo-Soviet confrontation and were seeking to align the United States with Britain (Loth, 1988, pp. 30 and 63–6; Watt, 1984, pp. 103–4). His close adviser Harry Hopkins commented:

> The Russians had proved that they could be reasonable and far-seeing,
> and there wasn't any doubt in the minds of the president or any of us
> that we could live with them and get along with them peacefully for as
> far into the future as any of us could imagine.
>
> *(Spanier, 1971, p. 25)*

Roosevelt's hopes for a cooperative rather than a confrontational post-war world were not realized, instead a Cold War of opposing Soviet and American camps emerged. There were serious difficulties and problems facing the United States and the Soviet Union but these were exacerbated by a series of misconceptions, misapprehensions and a growing mistrust that frequently verged upon paranoia. This created a vicious circle of mutually exaggerated misperceptions which confirmed existing suspicions. Even during the war tensions began to appear; Stalin perceived the Anglo-American reluctance to open a 'Second Front' in western Europe as part of a long-term plan to let the Nazis and Soviets exhaust each other; America seemed to him to require too high a price for its projected economic aid; he suspected German collusion in the rapid Anglo-American advance in the spring of 1945, fearing a new anti-Soviet alignment might be about to emerge (Zametica, 1990, p. 46); he believed that he had Roosevelt's acceptance of the need for a Soviet domination of eastern Europe, whereas Roosevelt's domestic political situation and his ideological stance could not permit such an outcome in the brutal form that seemed to be emerging as the Red Army 'liberated' the area. For its part American policy was based upon the delusion expressed by the Secretary of State, James Byrne, that it was possible to achieve: '... a government [in Poland] both friendly to the Soviet Union and representative of all the democratic elements of the country' (Ambrose, 1971, p. 104). There was a discrepancy between the idealistic policy that Roosevelt espoused for internal consumption in the United States and the more realistic stance that he adopted when dealing with his external partners. This discrepancy, suggests Wilfried Loth, created an impossible situation for Roosevelt, but more especially for his successor, which encouraged a harder line towards the Soviet Union (Loth, 1988, pp. 21–2).

Poland was indeed the key to the growing rift between the two main victors in the Second World War, though the country that was most affected in the short term was Germany. The Yalta agreements had spoken of a 'reorganization' of the arrangements for governing liberated Poland, where the Soviets had installed the Lublin government formed under Soviet auspices and sympathetic to their cause. The Anglo-Americans expected that this administration would be reformed with important posts for the London-based Polish government-in-exile, eventually leading to democratic elections in Poland, but the Yalta wording was open to differing interpretations. The Soviets thought the Anglo-Americans had accepted their need to install friendly governments in eastern Europe whilst, perhaps naïvely, there were many members of the United States Congress who believed that western values and democratic practices could and would be established in the areas liberated by the Red Army. Stalin's plans to push the whole Polish state one hundred miles west to the Oder-Neisse line, deporting between six and nine million Germans in the process, with the Soviet Union moving its own boundary with Poland correspondingly west to the Curzon line, also alarmed the Anglo-Americans, though they accepted that they had little option but to acquiesce.

The resulting confusion and growing suspicion between the Anglo-Americans and the Soviets was fuelled and spread by the difficult task of administering defeated Germany. Although the original intention of the Yalta agreements had been to divide Germany into regions of military occupation but to govern the country as a single unit under Four Power control (with the French as junior partners), what emerged from an increasingly hostile relationship between the erstwhile allies was a political, economic and social division of Germany into Soviet and Anglo-American-French spheres. The military zones, which had not been intended to have political significance, thus came to represent the lines upon which Germany was divided, leaving the former capital, Berlin, an island of Four Power control deep in the Soviet area. During the war the United States had supplied her European allies with much wartime equipment, effectively for no payment, under the lend-lease scheme, originally a device whereby Britain, lacking the dollars to buy armaments, received American destroyers in return for granting the United States leases on bases in the West Indies. The abrupt termination of American lend-lease aid to Russia after 8 May 1945, VE Day (a decision rapidly disowned by Truman as a mistake), the 'loss' by the United States of a Soviet request for a loan and the confirmation of American nuclear capability with the explosion over Hiroshima on 6 August 1945, all did little to heal the growing rifts in Germany over Soviet demands for reparations from the Anglo-American zones and their own reluctance to allow food deliveries to flow westwards from their zone. Roosevelt's relatively benign assessment of Soviet intentions was gradually replaced by the suspicion that Stalin intended to utilize eastern Europe and his occupation zone in Germany to launch an ideological crusade against western Europe, deemed vulnerable by the United States because of the economic and political disruption left in the wake of the war.

The end of the war did indeed find Europe in a sorry state:

> … This wasteland of rubble, rags and hunger was a prison without
> privacy or dignity; and like all prisons it smelled. It smelled of dust, oil,
> gunpowder and greasy metal; of drains and vermin; of sweat and vomit;
> dirty socks and excrement; of decay and burning and the unburied dead.
> *(Mayne, 1970, p. 30)*

Over 16 million Europeans (not counting Russian dead) had died in the war, many more were refugees; one fifth of the houses in France were destroyed or badly damaged; in the Soviet Union twenty five million people were homeless. Coal was scarce; the Ruhr produced only 25,000 tons daily instead of 400,000 tons; industrial production across Europe was rarely more than a fifth of the pre-war levels and in southern Germany it was one-twentieth. Communication by sea, road, rail and river was severely disrupted; food production was down; everything from pit-props to bailer twine was in short supply. Even after the war had ended over 140 million Europeans were living on less than 2,000 calories a day and 100 million on less than 1,500 calories a day; the normal requirement of an active worker is between 3,200 and 5,500 calories a day (Mayne, 1970, pp. 30–5). The danger that this economic and social distress would find a political expression unfavourable to the needs and aspirations of the United States was reinforced by the prominence of the communist parties of western Europe, their popularity boosted by their involvement in resistance against the Nazis and by a negative reaction to the parties that had enjoyed power before the Second World War. In the October 1945 elections to a Constituent Assembly the French communists and their associates with 160 seats represented the largest party, whilst in the corresponding elections in Italy in June 1946 the communists took 19 per cent of the votes and 104 seats. In France and Belgium the communist party was part of an uneasy tripartite coalition government with Socialists and Christian Democrats, whilst in Italy it was part of a wider coalition (Morgan, 1972, pp. 23–5, 67–8 and 73).

The United States, increasingly nervous about Soviet intentions and believing that a strong European market was necessary if it was not to suffer a crisis of over-production, began to realign its policies but this was never a simple or a one-dimensional process. Anglo-American relations were rarely as warm as Churchill hoped they might be and there was a strong body of official opinion in Washington that believed that the financial and trading arrangements of the British Empire and sterling area represented a further grave threat to American prosperity and that the United States should use its present superiority to enforce its will upon the British. Lend-lease was cancelled, collaboration on atomic research was interrupted and the reconstruction funds that Keynes hoped to negotiate from the American government in late-1945 emerged as a loan, not a grant, the terms of which were castigated by Robert Boothby, a Conservative MP, as '... our economic Munich ... selling the British Empire for a packet of cigarettes' (Watt, 1984, pp. 106–7; Loth, 1988, p. 25). Aware of its own international weakness and vulnerability the British Labour government, and in particular the Foreign Secretary, Ernest Bevin, worked hard to maintain an American involvement in Europe yet could not escape entirely from resentment at becoming a junior partner in the relationship. The British perception of their three areas of influence – Europe, the Atlantic partnership and the Empire – did not accord easily with the mainly European role envisaged for them by the Americans, nor was Bevin committed to an anti-Soviet stance from the outset, preferring a settlement agreed between the three major allies (Bullock, 1983, pp. 117–18 and 413–17). For the Americans the empires to which their British, French, Dutch and Belgian friends sought to cling were a complicating factor. Ideologically opposed to the concept, but increasingly a recruit to the ranks of the reluctant imperialists, the United States found itself torn between its principles and its pragmatic need for partners in distant parts.

1946 saw a significant shift in attitudes. The hostile reaction to a speech (5 March) in Fulton, Missouri by former Prime Minister Winston Churchill in which he referred to an 'Iron Curtain' descending across Europe and appealed for an Anglo-American alliance against the Soviets, forced Truman to deny he had prior knowledge of what Churchill intended to say. American perceptions of the Soviet Union as a trusted ally and partner began to fade. For its part the USSR began to direct its attacks increasingly upon the United States rather than Britain. The famous 'long telegram' from George Kennan in Moscow (22 February) in which he advocated the 'containment' of Soviet ambitions world-wide was followed by confrontation in Iran, the unilateral ending of reparations deliveries from the Anglo-American zones in May and a growing competition for the hearts and minds of the German people arising from Molotov's speech in July and Secretary of State Byrne's Stuttgart speech (6 September). This committed the United States to maintain troops in Germany for as long as anyone else did and signalled the end of any lingering vestiges of 'Morgenthauism' (the policy of destroying or limiting German industrial capacity advocated by the American Treasury Secretary, Henry Morgenthau, during the war) in American policy towards Germany.

The Truman Doctrine, the Marshall Plan and NATO

The crucial developments came in 1947. On 21 February Britain, faced with crippling demands upon its resources at home and in India and the Middle East, informed the United States that it could no longer afford to sustain its efforts in the protection of Greece and Turkey against an implied Soviet internal and external threat. This placed Truman in an awkward position, since Greece, where a civil war had broken out in 1944, was not the most promising example of democracy and a Soviet threat to either power was less obvious than it might have been. His answer was the 'Truman Doctrine' of 12 March that declared 'it must be the policy of the United States to support free peoples who are resisting attempted subjugation by armed minorities or by outside pressures'. This used the fears of the American public and Congress about Soviet expansion to achieve the necessary funds and to disguise American support for the Greeks and Turks as a universal principle. In the short term it was a triumph for the president but observers like George Kennan feared the longer-term and wider consequences of a policy that deliberately encouraged American apprehensions about the Soviet Union and presented the issues in an over-simplified and stark manner. McCarthyism was part of the long-term price of Truman's initial success (Mayne, 1970, pp. 93–4; Loth, 1988, p. 142). The Moscow Four Power meeting of foreign ministers in March to discuss a German peace treaty failed to reach agreement and relations between the Soviet Union and the United States continued to deteriorate though they had not yet reached the point of outright confrontation.

Even the weather took a hand. The winter of 1946–47 was exceptionally severe whilst the summers of 1946 and 1947 saw drought. Harvest, production and transport were all disrupted once more. Western Europe was already living on American credit worth $9,500 million; now more and more imports were needed of American grain, coal and manufactured goods but there was no money to pay for them. Europe's industry entered a vicious circle of decline; without the funds to buy raw materials and food it saw output and productivity fall thus cutting its capacity to earn foreign currency for essential purchases or the repayment of earlier debts. Europe's dollar deficit on its current account with the United States was nearly $5,000 million. The financial problems that had forced Britain to turn to the United States in the Near East also caused Bevin to demand an increase in German production so that less of the burden of feeding and supplying the occupied power fell upon Britain. Former President Herbert Hoover had reached a similar conclusion following a tour of Germany, arguing that:

> There is only one path to recovery in Europe. That is production ... The productivity of Europe cannot be restored without the restoration of Germany as a contributor to that productivity.
>
> *(quoted in Mayne, 1970, p. 98)*

These difficulties were mirrored in France which found itself forced to pay $200 million instead of the expected $30 million for American wheat. In August it stopped all inessential imports (Mayne, 1970, pp. 94–5; Monnet, 1978, p. 264). It became obvious that the funds that the United States had lent to the western European nations in 1945 and 1946 would not be sufficient to restore the prosperity and stability for which both the lender and borrowers had hoped. A crisis loomed.

The implications for the United States were immense. The collapse of the European market for American goods would bring recession and unemployment at home whilst decision-makers in Washington perceived that the temptation for Stalin to threaten the internal stability and external security of western Europe might prove irresistible. What, asked James Forrestal, about to be appointed Secretary of Defense in June 1947, should the United States do if faced 'during this summer with a Russian *démarche* accompanied by simultaneous coups in France and Italy' (Edwards, 1990, p. 28)? The Truman doctrine required the United States to take action. Secretary of State George Marshall, returning disillusioned from the Moscow Conference, broadcast on 28 April that Europeans were crying out 'for help, for coal, for food, for most of the necessities of life ... The patient is sinking while the doctors deliberate' (Mayne, 1970, p. 99). He began planning for aid to Europe and, in a speech to the Harvard alumni on 5 June, he declared:

> The truth of the matter is that Europe's requirements for the next three or four years of foreign food and other essential products – principally from America – are so much greater than her present ability to pay that she must have substantial additional help or face economic, social, and political deterioration of a very grave character ... It is logical that the United States should do whatever it is able to do to assist in the return of normal economic health in the world, without which there can be no political stability and no assured peace.

Marshall was more subtle than Truman in his approach, claiming that:

> Our policy is directed not against any country or doctrine but against
> hunger, poverty, desperation and chaos … Any government that is
> willing to assist in the task of recovery will find full cooperation, I am
> sure, on the part of the United States Government.

There was, however, little doubt that his initiative dovetailed with that of the
president – 'two halves of the same walnut' was Truman's description – and
Marshall was adamant that:

> Any government which maneuvers to block the recovery of other
> countries cannot expect help from us. Furthermore, governments,
> political parties, or groups which seek to perpetuate human misery in
> order to profit therefrom politically or otherwise will encounter the
> opposition of the United States.

In offering this assistance, however, Marshall insisted that 'The initiative … must
come from Europe … The program should be a joint one, agreed to by a number,
if not all, European nations' (Mayne, 1970, pp. 103–4).

The Truman Doctrine and the Marshall Plan (or European Recovery Programme)
represent the foundations upon which the United States and Europe built their relationships for over forty years and it would be difficult to exaggerate their importance. There can be no doubt that American policy was shaped mainly by the

President Harry S. Truman and Secretary of State George C. Marshall 'Two halves of the same walnut'
(credit: Camera Press, London).

perception of what constituted America's interests but there was also a significant element of both governmental and private altruism and generosity involved. The reaction to this American initiative would create and shape many of the crucial developments in Europe and the world until, at the very least, the late 1980s and arguably beyond. The first, perhaps unintended, consequence of the Marshall Plan was the intensification of the division of Europe between East and West. Although Bevin and the French foreign minister, Georges Bidault, seized avidly upon Marshall's offer and invited their Soviet counterpart, Molotov, to discuss proposals to implement it, the meetings in Paris from 27 June resulted in a Soviet withdrawal on 2 July. The Soviets feared that Marshall's offer would mean American intervention in the economic affairs of the participants and a diminution of sovereignty. Thus it was the British and French alone who invited all European states (with the exception of Spain and the Soviet Union) to a conference in Paris on 12 July. The states in the Soviet sphere showed initial interest but came under heavy (and successful) Soviet pressure not to participate; Czechoslovakia accepted the invitation – and then, overnight, changed its mind. Bidault's definition of Europe on 27 June was 'all countries of Europe, allies, ex-enemies, or neutrals, with the provisional exception of Spain' but the Committee of European Economic Cooperation established in Paris on 16 July was an organization of sixteen western European states (Austria, Belgium, Denmark, France, Greece, Iceland, Ireland, Luxembourg, the Netherlands, Norway, Portugal, Sweden, Switzerland, Turkey and the United Kingdom; with Germany represented by the military governments of the British, French and American zones) without any eastern European representative. Whether the United States was relieved or disappointed is a matter of historical debate. There is some evidence that the Americans had already written off eastern Europe; Will Clayton, one of the American governors of the World Bank and International Monetary Fund, had declared in November 1946 that 'no, repeat no, loans or credits from the Import bank or other official US sources were contemplated by the United States for Poland, Czechoslovakia, Romania, Bulgaria or Albania' (quoted by Edwardes, 1990, p. 22). Wilfried Loth argues persuasively, however, that there were several strands intertwined in American policy and that the establishment of either Europe-wide or western European economic cooperation could be judged to have been in American interests, either opening a wider market to the penetration of American production or consolidating a political and security bloc in the west (Loth, 1988, pp. 147–50). The latter proved to be the outcome and the Soviet response was to establish (in September) the Communist Information Bureau (Cominform), consolidating relations between the states in their sphere. This brought Soviet–American confrontation closer, whilst at the same time making any resumption of pre-war trade between eastern and western Europe much less likely.

The second consequence was that the relationships between the United States and western Europe existed within a framework of prosperity. Although it has been argued (notably by Milward, 1989, pp. 231–53) that European recovery would have occurred without Marshall aid this was not a common perception at the time. American government grants and credits to western Europe between 1948 and 1952 totalled $13,150 million supplemented by a further $500 million of private generosity. After a shaky start the plan was a spectacular success in economic and industrial terms. American machinery and expertise boosted productivity, American food and raw materials ensured that this could be sustained. Trade between the United States and western Europe more than doubled between 1947 and 1950, recovering to its pre-war levels in 1949. Western Europe's industrial production was 43 per cent above pre-war levels by 1951 and its farm production was 10 per cent better (Mee, 1984, pp. 246–52; Mayne, 1970, p. 117). This rapid and sustained recovery was a key factor in future developments, particularly in restoring the rather battered self-confidence of the west Europeans, but it also undermined the position of the communist parties in western Europe and boosted that of liberal and conservative groups. There was however, a price to be paid in terms of the American domination of the west European markets, defence and, potentially, in cultural and entertainment terms as well.

The third consequence related to the future political and international organization of western Europe. The Soviet concern for national sovereignty was not unfounded. There were a number of ideas, not necessarily articulated in the original offer but which were, for some, its unspoken assumptions. Of these the most persistent was an American desire to play the role of Founding Father to a European version of the United States – a federal Europe (Watt, 1984, p. 121). This was not the policy of the administration in the early stages when the main priority was intergovernmental cooperation and recovery. In a speech in Cleveland, Mississippi on 8 May 1947, declared later by Truman to be a trailer for the Marshall programme, Under Secretary of State Dean Acheson declared:

> European recovery cannot be complete until the various parts of
> Europe's economy are working together in a harmonious whole. And
> the achievement of a coordinated European economy remains a
> fundamental objective of our foreign policy.
>
> *(Beloff, 1963, p. 19)*

Nonetheless, Senator William Fulbright's attempt to amend the Marshall aid bill to call for the encouragement 'of the political unification of Europe' was judged inexpedient rather than undesirable by an American government which did not wish to be seen to be dictating to its friends (Beloff, 1963, pp. 27–8). Although the State Department believed in June 1947 that 'There is a possibility of developing tremendous emotional drive in western Europe behind the supranational idea of European unity', it recognized that 'sensitive feelings of nationalism' required any such policy to be expressed in terms of the economic benefits of 'the "functional" unification of Europe' (report by Kindelberger, van Buren Cleveland and Moore, 12 June 1947, quoted in Mayne, 1970, p. 123). Thus a longer-term consequence of Marshall aid was a growing and persistent American pressure upon western Europe, especially after 1949, to move from cooperation towards integration, though as Richard Mayne commented there was to be a 'struggle between this American vision and the stubborn, untidy realities of western Europe' (Mayne, 1970, p. 124).

Developments in Europe and beyond continued to encourage the consolidation of the two blocs that were to confront each other in the Cold War. The Soviet establishment of the Cominform and the marked tightening of their grip upon the governments of eastern Europe in 1947 and 1948 culminated in the dramatic events in Czechoslovakia in February and March 1948 when a communist coup overthrew the existing coalition. In China the Americans anticipated that the communists led by Mao Tse Tung would win the civil war against Chang Kai Shek and his Kuomintang forces. In Germany the Anglo-American efforts to reform and revitalize their zones of occupation alarmed the Soviets who reacted to the establishment of a new currency confined to the western occupation zones with an attempt to isolate the western zones in Berlin, announcing that all rail, road and canal links from western Germany towards Berlin were closed for repair. By 6 August 1948 West Berlin was cut off. The western response was firm – 'We are going to stay period' declared Truman – but designed to avoid a direct confrontation with the Soviets (Ambrose, 1971, p. 173). A massive airlift, inadequate and disorganized at first but later amazingly successful, kept West Berlin supplied with nearly double the necessary 4,500 tons of freight daily until, in May 1949, Stalin decided the repairs were complete and called off the blockade. Most significant of all, was the signing, on 4 April 1949, of the North Atlantic Treaty by the United States, Canada and ten European states (Belgium, Denmark, France, Iceland, Italy, Luxembourg, the Netherlands, Norway, Portugal and the United Kingdom), designed, according to its first Secretary-General, Lord Ismay, 'to keep the Americans in, the Germans down and the Russians out' (quoted in Rummel and Schmidt, 1990, p. 263). NATO (North Atlantic Treaty Organisation) framed the security of western Europe firmly in an Atlantic context. The presence of American troops, even in numbers that were always inadequate to deal with a serious conventional Soviet threat, gave Europe the belief that these American 'hostages' would ensure that the United States could never abandon them with honour. Whilst this was the logical consequence of the Truman and Marshall policies, NATO was a further fundamental American commitment to Europe, a guarantee that the isolationism of the inter-war period would not reappear.

European responses

This was something for which Europeans were grateful and indeed were anxious to maintain, but there were those who were, nonetheless, anxious about the future. Writing to Robert Schuman from the United States in April 1948 Jean Monnet declared:

> I cannot but be struck by the relationship that threatens to develop between this great and dynamic nation and the countries of Europe, if they remain as they are, and in their present state of mind. In my opinion, Europe cannot long afford to remain almost exclusively dependent on American credit for her production and American strength for her security, without harmful results both here and in Europe.

Monnet's conclusion was that 'the countries of western Europe must turn their national efforts into a truly European effort. This will be possible only through a federation of the West' (Monnet, 1978, pp. 272–3). The need to establish a 'partnership of equals' was a constant theme in Monnet's thought as was the idea that 'The contribution that an organized and living Europe can make to civilization is indispensable to the maintenance of peace' (Monnet, 1978, p. 295). In one sense

Marshall aid destroyed the hopes of those like Leon Blum in France, Paul-Henri Spaak in Belgium and Alcide de Gasperi in Italy, who hoped that east–west cooperation in Europe would enable an independent Europe to emerge as a 'third force' in addition to the two superpowers. In another, however, it encouraged a variation of the idea, that of the integration of western Europe for which some were more enthusiastic than others. The British, conscious of a role in a world larger than Europe, were not among the enthusiasts. French plans for a customs union received a mixed reaction from Britain, where Bevin was persuaded that such a venture, under British leadership, might be helpful to its wider interests, but the Treasury overruled the Foreign Office and thus the plans collapsed.

Bevin had a vision of western European cooperation which he saw as being much wider than the military obligations of the Brussels Treaty (17 March 1948) but although he hoped that 'the Commonwealth and western Europe might grow together … [and] make a really great Third Power in the world', he was anxious to preserve British governmental control over its own destiny and to keep Britain separate from Europe in the minds of the Americans. He was suspicious of European integration, declaring of the Council of Europe, 'If you open that Pandora's Box, you never know what Jack-in-the-Box will jump out' (Warner, 1984, p. 69; Roberts, 1984, p. 35). Britain was thus a limiting factor in the early attempts to develop European institutions and, when the Organisation of European Economic Cooperation (OEEC) was formed on 6 April 1948, it was an intergovernmental agency without supranational powers. There was little progress towards European integration under its aegis but it did help to coordinate the reconstruction needs and plans of its members, though its form forced the United States to take greater initiatives than it had envisaged (Loth, 1988, pp. 179–84).

The problem of Germany's place in these developments was also of enormous importance. As, in 1948 and 1949, the western zones of Germany began to evolve new political institutions taking them nearer to the re-establishment of political sovereignty and independence there was also a growing need for the great dynamo of the German economy to be restarted. This was partly because of the requirements of the United States, particularly in the military and defence fields after outbreak of the Korean War in June 1950, but also because western Europe too needed German production to be increased, though this need was, understandably, tempered by fear of what might ensue if effective safeguards were not established to an unbridled restoration of German power. Jean Monnet's notebooks in 1950 reveal both the complexity of the problem and his determination that 'We must not try to solve the German problem in its present context. We must change the context by transforming the basic facts' (Monnet, 1978, p. 291). This transformation did not, however, include German reunification; the division of Germany into East and West was now assumed to be a long-term reality. His thoughts in May 1950 reveal a traditional fear of German economic dominance and an awareness of the consequences – French protectionism, an attempt to thwart increases in German production that the United States would insist upon, French eclipse. He concluded that France must act, if not:

> A group will form around the United States, but in order to wage the
> Cold War with even greater zeal. The obvious reason is that the

countries of Europe are afraid and are seeking help. Britain will draw
ever closer to the United States; Germany will develop rapidly, and we
shall not be able to prevent her being armed. France will be trapped
once more in her old Malthusianism, and this will inevitably lead to her
eclipse.

(Monnet, 1978, p. 294)

His answer to this dilemma was the integration of the French and West German
coal and steel industries, as he told the French foreign minister Robert Schuman:

This proposal has an essential political objective: to make a breach in
the ramparts of national sovereignty which will be narrow enough to
secure consent, but deep enough to open the way towards the unity that
is essential to peace.

(Monnet, 1978, p. 296)

On 9 May 1950 Schuman proposed Monnet's idea which attracted support from
West Germany, the Benelux countries and Italy but not the United Kingdom. The
Americans were initially suspicious but later enthusiastic, revealing one further
ambiguity in their relationship with Europe – a doubt as to the extent to which
independent European initiatives were welcome.

Bevin's reaction to this and the Pleven plan for a European army, (the European
Defence Community, EDC) proposed by the French premier on 24 October 1950,
was that it represented an attempt by France to establish a continental bloc under
its leadership 'which, while linked with the Atlantic Community, would constitute
in world politics a force with some measure of independence'. What had been appropriate under British leadership in 1948 was now condemned as 'a sort of
cancer in the Atlantic body. We must nip it in the bud' (Ovendale, 1984, p. 75).
Monnet's notes at the time record his opinion:

Britain has no confidence that France and the other countries of Europe
have the ability or even the will effectively to resist a possible Russian
invasion ... Britain believes that in this conflict continental Europe will
be occupied but that she herself, with America, will be able to resist and
finally conquer. She therefore does not wish to let her domestic life or
the development of her resources be influenced by any views other than
her own, and certainly not by continental views.

(Monnet, 1978, pp. 316–7)

However, whilst Britain remained the strongest of the European powers in 1950
and could congratulate itself on the establishment of an Atlantic community, the
new Franco-German relationship, fragile as it was, represented the beginnings of
an interesting alternative strategy for western Europe.

Cultural and economic developments

Thus the jealousies and national *amour propre* of the erstwhile European world
powers remained a complicating factor in the jigsaw puzzle of relationships. The
underlying reality of their decline was sharply emphasized by the domination of
the European markets established by the United States in the wake of the Marshall

plan. Jean-Jacques Servan-Schreiber lamented that Europe had become 'a new Far West for American businessmen. Their investments do not so much involve a transfer of capital, as an actual *seizure of power* within the European economy' (Servan-Schreiber, 1969, p. 22). Whatever the immediate success or failure of the European Recovery Programme in the long term it provided a model of a modern society which emphasized the links between economic power and cultural hegemony. 'It was American goods which were to be the revolutionary mission-aries for the American way of life' (Willett, 1989, p. 27). The physical rehabilitation of Europe made possible by the United States' economic domination provided a canvas upon which to promote the ideological superiority of a capitalist society. Americanization is a concept with a long history, referring to a range of manifestations from the profit motive, efficiency and standardization to equality of opportunity, boundless energy and enthusiasm. Attitudes towards the phenomenon have been dictated by the political, economic and cultural stance of the observer, and from the late nineteenth century many European intellectuals considered the growth of the United States as a world power to be inimical to cul-tural standards. Their pessimism was based on the emergence of an industrialized culture that was pre-eminently concerned with commercialism, consumerism and entertainment and the fear that this would affect the cultural standards of the Old World.

The necessary economic subvention by the United States was accompanied by an ideological belief in a free market, not only in a range of tangible industrial goods, but the products of a range of 'cultural industries' whose influence was difficult to measure but represent an important aspect of European–American relationships. A study of the marketing of Coca-Cola in Europe in the immediate post-war period offers one of the best examples of the link between economic and cultural pressure of the United States in European countries. In order to provide the beverage for servicemen in Europe during the war the Coca-Cola company established sixty-four bottling stations abroad, which acted as the springboard for an attempt to capitalize on the European market. By 1949 bottling operations had begun in France, the Benelux countries, and the newly-established German Federal Republic. The *Time* magazine cover of 15 May 1950 presented a picture of a globe drinking Coke with the caption; 'World and Friend: love that piaster, that lira, that tickey and that American way of life' (Kuisel, 1991, p. 99). It was as much a statement of belief as fact, since the marketing operations of Coca-Cola in Europe had provoked opposition in many countries on economic and cultural grounds; an opposition led, in the main, by local communist parties.

In France the perceived threat of Coca-Cola united communists, wine-makers and Christian Democrats, worried about the damage to French culture, and the Finance Ministry, alarmed at its effect on the balance of payments. It was not the product, suggested *Le Mond*e, but the consumerism and marketing devices:

> We have accepted chewing gum and Cecil B. de Mille, *Reader's Digest*, and bebop. It's over soft drinks that the conflict has erupted. Coca-Cola seems to be the Danzig of European culture. After Coca-Cola, *Hola*.

Not until 1953 did the opposition to Coke collapse. It had been a symbolic contro-versy but, as with all cultural symbols, represented economic and political issues

(credit: Copyright 1950 Time Warner Inc. Reprinted by permission.)

of some substance. To many in France, of all political persuasions, it was symbolic of an attempt by one European country to find a 'middle way' in the course
of the developing Cold War. To the chief executives of the Coca-Cola company,
Robert Woodruff and James Farley, there was no middle way – to reject
Coca-Cola was equivalent to siding with the Russians. There were fewer inhi-
bitions in the western sector of Germany. Coca-Cola was relaunched in 1949, a
month after the establishment of the Federal Republic, and by 1950 six factories
were in operation, with an aggressive marketing policy that was modelled on

American style and content. The development of the West German economy not only followed the American model but, as Ralph Willett suggests, 'It was appropriate that the underlying message of some advertising should appear to declare that social redemption now lay not only in work but also in leisure and consumption' (Willet, 1989, pp. 105–6).

Coca-Cola raised the fundamental question of the relationship between the state and private industry, not only in the United States but in other countries that could be influenced by it. It was the task of the United States' government to construct an international environment in which there would be no restraint of trade and which would allow the maximum penetration of American private companies. As with trade so with freedom of information, which in effect would allow the free flow of information from the United States through the expansion of private media organizations. This policy had been accepted by UNESCO (United Nations Educational, Scientific and Cultural Organization) which, as a result of successful French lobbying, had been established in Paris and was administered by Europeans. Because of its control of resources the United States role in UNESCO was crucial, and effectively developed in 1945–46 by US Senator William Benton, an advertising executive and Assistant Secretary in the State Department. He had been involved in the Office of War Information and was concerned with continuing the funding of what was to become the 'Voice of America' in the post-war period, but he knew that the key to American influence lay with private firms and an international framework that would allow them to operate effectively. As he commented in 1950, three years after leaving the State Department:

> If we work through UNESCO, we cannot be charged with cultural imperialism. Indeed, there are many areas where UNESCO can be far more effective than the United States alone. Germany may be such a one, where UNESCO can work across zonal boundaries.
>
> *(Guback, 1986, p. 249)*

The idea of 'free-flow' of information was an ideological and propaganda weapon in the Cold War where the influence of commercial mass communication media was restricted.

In Europe, in the aftermath of the war, this influence of the United States was greatest in Germany where 'generals did quite literally set up newspapers, license radio stations, select senior personnel, and veto everyone else' (Tunstall, 1977, p. 137) but 'generals can scarcely command a society to be more democratic' (Edward Petersen quoted in Willett, 1989, p. 27). After 1945 the American aim was to impose a 'free' mass media structure in their occupied zone, which would encourage the development of democracy based upon a decentralized, regional, but financially viable press and broadcasting structure. Such a system lacked the basic component of competition, which underlay the concept of a 'free-flow' of information in a capitalist democracy. The media structures imposed by the occupying powers as part of the 're-education' process were not dismantled after 1949 and their decentralized character was written into the basic law of the Federal Republic so posing problems for a government and politicians who desired a more 'national' framework for political debate and information. Germany offers the only European example of direct intervention by the United States in press and broadcasting after 1945. There was some control of news agency material in Italy, but since the Rome government regained jurisdiction over the bulk of its territory after December 1945 there was no attempt to 're-educate' on the German model, partly because of the belief that Fascism had only ephemeral influence upon the Italian population. However, the fear of an internal communist takeover after 1947 did activate an American campaign to publicize the European Recovery Programme, arguing that 'Prosperity makes you free'.

The most popular medium in European countries was the cinema, which was the epitome of Americanization in its production methods, commercialism, and ephemeral character. While it was impossible to measure the effect of the films upon the manners and morals of the populations that went to the cinema each week, there was a general assumption in most European countries that social behaviour and political outlooks could be affected, very possibly for the worst. In the two decades before 1939 many European governments produced measures that sought to control the import of American films. While concerned apparently with economic aspects of the film industry, there was an underlying cultural and political motive that was to encourage the production of films that represented specific national values. A protected cinema, it was argued, would be a source of protection against the undermining cultural values of the American cinema.

The Second World War obviously disrupted the European market for Hollywood films, not only through the occupation of the mainland by National Socialist Germany, but also the unwillingness of the United Kingdom to spend scarce currency on the product. With a backlog of undistributed films and half a continent as a potential market, heads of studios were not slow to emphasize to the US government the importance of their films to the 're-education' of European populations in the 'American way of life'. As the Cold War developed it was a message that was asserted even more strongly. In the early 1950s the Motion Picture Export Association Inc (MPEA) claimed that 'each film … carries important social and ideological by-products that have a tremendous impact on film-goers around the world' and 'they serve as global show-cases for American techniques, products and merchandise' (Guback, 1986, p. 267). The MPEA had been set up by the major Hollywood studios in 1945 under US legislation, which allowed the construction of cartels engaged in foreign trade; its aim was to keep international markets open to American films. This was done either through influencing US economic policy or dealing directly with individual European governments where appropriate. In London they called themselves the 'little State Department' (Sorlin, 1991, p. 93). In 1948 the US government instituted the Information Media Guaranty Programme (IMG) by which producers would receive payment in dollars when exporting to countries without currency conversion. This was of particular importance in occupied Germany, and affected not only film companies but authors and publishers who wanted a return in hard currency for their cooperation in a 're-education' policy.

Hollywood films as the standard-bearers of freedom may have made economic sense to the producers, and influenced some admirers in Washington, but the underlying antagonism towards America among élite groups in Europe had been exacerbated by the outcome of the war. The United States was the most powerful force in international society, but the question of how far American values should be the basis of a new international order was still under discussion. Economic and military power were almost impossible to challenge, but in the late-1940s there were some challenges to aspects of 'cultural imperialism' in western Europe. Films were an important arena for this debate, as broadcasting would become in the 1960s and 1970s, and invariably the challenge succumbed to the powerful economic interests backing up the American intrusion into areas of culture.

In the late-1940s the Labour government in Britain, which had embarked on a substantial programme of national reconstruction with a bankrupt economy, sought to control the import of American films to help the balance of payments problem and to encourage the development of a film industry seeking a reciprocal market in the US. The response of the MPEA was to place an embargo on all US films to the United Kingdom, and within a year cinema exhibitors, faced with a catas-trophic decline in attendances, forced the government to negotiate a compromise, which was essentially a victory for the MPEA. In Italy the film-makers who responded to the fall of fascism with a form of indigenous production that became known as 'neo-realist' found that they could not compete in popular appeal with Hollywood films and found little support for their socially conscious productions from the Roman Catholic Church and the powerful Christian Democrat party. By 1948 only 11 per cent of films exhibited in Italy were domestic productions while 73 per cent were American in origin (Tunstall, 1977, p. 154). Yet this was not to suggest that conservative forces in Italy subscribed to all the values inherent in Hollywood films, particularly when the moral probity of those involved in their production was brought into question. The cultural response to Hollywood films in France was also ambivalent. While many critics continued to represent them as forms of debased art, emphasizing the ways in which European directors had been sucked into the commercial maw, others, led by Andre Bazin, emphasized the nar-rative realism of the popular genres developed by Hollywood and their cultural value in exploring the nature of the individual's role in society. Anti-establishment critics praised the iconoclasm of thrillers and 'low-brow' comedies. Intellectuals opposed to the conservatism of the government after 1947 emphasized the vitality and 'existential alienation' of the American popular cinema and novels. It was, as Elsasser suggests, a 'state of the imagination, a frame of mind' (Elsasser, 1975, p. 208) and one that dissolved in the 1950s under the contradictions of the Cold War. The interest in Hollywood productions led many of the film critics (who had sup-ported aspects of the Bazin position, like Truffaut and Chabrol) to make films that actively explored the possibilities of popular genre cinema and that developed into the 'new-wave' cinema of the 1960s. By the same decade young West German film directors, critical of an indigenous film industry that presented a cosy picture of society through its *Heimat* productions, felt it possible to launch the New German Cinema, which demonstrated the influence of fifteen years of exposure to Hollywood movies upon their ideas of representation of 'real' life. As Wim Wenders suggested, 'The Americans had colonized our unconscious' (Guback, 1986, p. 246).

Whatever the economic, cultural and political aims of the American producers in exporting films to Europe, the ideological response has been shown to be ambivalent and impossible to quantify. As with many forms of popular culture, films were enjoyed and negotiated with by different audiences. As the Hollywood cinema itself began to disintegrate economically in the 1950s there was less emphasis on film export and more on the support of film production in other countries. Indigenous European film industries would survive and develop, but under the aegis of American money and servicing an increasingly consumer-oriented world, a world based on the belief that social and political stability could be achieved by raising living standards everywhere, presenting the simple American message, 'You can be like us' (Ellwood, 1985, p. 227).

Summary

The period between the end of the war and Stalin's death in March 1953 established the framework for much of the future in the relationships between the United States and Europe and hence deserves detailed analysis. The early American impulse to withdraw once more across the Atlantic was gradually transformed into a realization that responsibilities went with world power and, perhaps with characteristic national exaggeration, became instead a world-wide crusade against the communists with whom Roosevelt had hoped to cooperate. The Truman Doctrine was translated by the military plans and expenditure envisaged by National Security Council paper 68 (NSC 68) into an overwhelming American military superiority in everything except conventional ground forces in Europe. (In September 1950 14 NATO divisions faced 175 Soviet divisions (Ball, 1968, p. 50).) In the wider world the United States had stepped into Britain's shoes in the Near East and was taking tentative steps to replace France in Indo-China. The United Nations forces in Korea were dominated by the American contingent, but American troop numbers in Europe were also expanded to deter a perceived Soviet threat on two fronts. Roosevelt's four policeman of the world were reduced, at least in American perceptions, to one.

This role was one with which the majority of Americans agreed, a remarkable construction of a consensus that overcame earlier isolationism with surprising ease. According to Gallup Polls, a substantial majority of Americans believed that they had a unique mission to create a just and moral international order on a global scale; that the Soviets constituted the primary threat to world peace; that containment was the right policy to adopt; that nuclear weapons were necessary to deterrence; and that America should lead the world economy and play a dominant role in the United Nations (Melanson, 1991, pp. 4–8). At the same time, however, the very success of the administration in promoting the image of a Soviet threat returned to haunt it with Senator Joseph R. McCarthy's claim on 9 February 1950 that there were 57 (though the figure soon climbed to 205) card-carrying communists or communist sympathisers in the State Department. The resulting witch-hunt for hidden Reds hit particularly hard at the entertainment industries and at left-wing intellectuals, especially those of recent European origin and left Truman's administration heavily on the defensive, with important advisers fighting to clear their names of treason. Yet McCarthyism had the support of newly-arrived east Europeans and the Catholic Church and seemed to offer an explanation for the successes of the Soviets in eastern Europe, China and in atomic research –

'Joe One', the first Soviet atomic bomb, was exploded in 1949 (Ambrose, 1971, pp. 184–7).

In the political, military, economic and cultural spheres western Europe, encouraged by, and grateful to, the United States, nonetheless sought to discover, with varying degrees of success, its own alternative solutions to its problems, including the first attempt at European supranationality in the ECSC. Predictably the United Kingdom was not a founder member of the ECSC and continued to see a role for itself beyond Europe. West Germany, to the obvious displeasure of France and the United Kingdom, was rearmed at the behest of the United States. None of these developments was, however, simple or single-facetted and there were ambiguities and unexpected complexities in the relationships that resulted.

America dominant: 1953–1973

This period saw American influence and prestige at their height, at the point at which their aims and capability of achieving them were best matched – B52s, Coca-Cola and 'B' movies circled the globe. Americans were at their most expansive in foreign policy terms in the late-1950s and early-1960s. Congress was particularly supportive of presidential initiatives.

> United States membership in the United Nations, NATO, the
> Organization of American States (OAS), and the South East Asian
> Treaty Organization (SEATO); aid to Greece and Turkey; the Marshall
> Plan; ratification of the Japan Peace Treaty, the Korea Defense Pact, the
> Formosa Security Pact and the Nuclear Test Ban Treaty; and regional
> resolutions covering Formosa, the Middle East, Berlin, Cuba, and
> Indo-China all received at least 70 per cent of the vote with several
> claiming virtual unanimous support.
>
> *(Melanson, 1991, p. 10)*

One of the more interesting developments was the attempt by the French President Charles de Gaulle to challenge the Atlantic framework of west European defence and the political conception of a divided Europe inherited from the 1940s. His success was limited, not least because his alternative vision of a 'European Europe' was only a possibility because of an American nuclear and conventional forces umbrella that devalued the whole concept. Certainly, despite France's withdrawal of its forces from the NATO command between 1958 and 1966 (though it remained a signatory of the alliance), the existence of an independent, if scarcely credible, French nuclear deterrent (the *force de frappe*), and the attempt to create a closer Franco-German axis, de Gaulle was forced, not least by West German pressure, to recognize that the United States was a necessary element in the present European security equation. Furthermore, his ideas on the military, political and economic future of Europe were challenged as out-dated, inadequate and unrealistic. As in his attempts to restore the purity of the French language so in his international policies, de Gaulle's stance was often ambiguous and based on wishful thinking tinged with the cynicism of a follower of *realpolitik*. Nonetheless, the American position faced increasing challenges from within western Europe,

B-52s around the Earth, Alexander Kortner (US Air Force Art Collection)

though these were restrained by the sporadic reminders of the Soviet presence. Yet, if America was an imperial power in Europe (even if by invitation) and was seeking hegemony, then its policy of encouraging European economic and political integration was indeed 'a policy of decline by design' (Rummel and Schmidt, 1990, pp. 264–6; Lundestad, 1992, p. 254).

International developments

The death of Stalin in 1953 brought an improved international atmosphere and a Soviet withdrawal from Austria in 1955 but this was balanced by a vigorous Soviet repression of a brief workers' revolt in East Berlin in 1953 whilst the apparently more liberal views of Khrushchev, encouraging some independence amongst the Soviet satellites, were unmasked by the brutal Soviet invasion of Hungary in October 1956. Twelve years later the illusion of another apparent loosening of the shackles of the Soviet empire ended dramatically in the invasion of Czechoslovakia in August 1968. These events, reinforced the perceptions of a Soviet threat, even though they were confined to the Soviet sphere, and, for many, put the argument for a continued American presence in Europe much more effectively than any propagandist. In the west the ill-fated Anglo-French attack on Egypt in the 1956 Suez expedition strained their relationship with the United States and, in Britain's case in particular, encouraged its attempts to shed its remaining imperial responsibilities. President Eisenhower's commitment to the defence of western Europe was rarely doubted but his attempt to reduce and contain armaments expenditure increased the reliance of the west on nuclear weapons that were relatively cheap but dangerously inflexible. The fear of nuclear war brought attempts by pressure groups like the Campaign for Nuclear Disarmament to remove the threat, or at least the weapons, from European soil. CND argued that it had no quarrel with the United States, only with its bombs and missiles but, inevitably, given the heavy dependence of NATO strategy on the Americans and their weapons, the movement became associated with anti-American feeling. It was also closely associated, at least in the public's perception, with left-wing politics and, in common with the later and broader 'Peace Movement', was sometimes portrayed as the naïve (more rarely as the deliberate) agent of Moscow (Barnett, 1984, pp. 416–23).

Meanwhile the attempts by Jean Monnet and his associates to restart the movement towards west European integration that had stalled after the failure of EDC bore fruit in the Messina conference (June 1955) which established two new European agencies, the European Atomic Energy Committee (Euratom) and the European Economic Community (EEC) both of which came into being on 1 January 1958. Once again the British stood aside but attempts by various British prime ministers to boost their prestige by acting as 'honest brokers' in the superpower relationships of the USA and USSR met with little success, whilst the problem of Germany, and particularly of Berlin, over which crises arose in 1958 and 1961, continued to cause alarm. Eisenhower's hopes of an improved Russo-American relationship foundered when the Soviets shot down an American spy plane (May 1960), and it was left to the new president, the youngest ever in the history of the United States, John F. Kennedy, to try to create a new framework for dialogue, especially in the context of a more satisfactory arrangement of European affairs. The early signs were not encouraging, though in retrospect the building of the Berlin Wall in August 1961 allowed the Soviets to find a solution to a problem that they had threatened to escalate into continuous crisis. The tense moments of the Cuban missile crisis in October 1962 were frightening reminders of the dangers of the Cold War. Its successful resolution did lead to more hopeful developments, in particular the signature of the Nuclear Test Ban Treaty in August 1963, but Kennedy's assassination and the growing American involvement in Vietnam with its accompanying escalation of the military budget created a new phase of the relationship with Europe.

Alternative visions: Kennedy, de Gaulle and Monnet

This was a phase in which America's moral advantage was rapidly eroded by Kennedy's Bay of Pigs fiasco in 1961 and the growing opposition to the Vietnam war, its economic superiority dented by budgetary and trade difficulties and its domination of the entertainment industries challenged by European intellectuals and British pop groups. The focus of American attention moved from Europe to South-East Asia and American troop numbers in Europe declined from a post-1945 high of 400,000 in 1961 to less than 300,000 by 1970, whilst American forces reached their peak in Vietnam in April 1969 at 543,000. Even so, the essential framework of west European defence remained Atlantic with the United States paramount in this field. Elsewhere, however, the west Europeans were working more closely together and their very success could be seen as a challenge to the structures in place since 1945.

Here was another aspect in which American aims and aspirations were often confused. The American commitment to encouraging west European integration remained strong; George Ball, Under Secretary of State to Presidents Kennedy and Johnson, and a close associate of Jean Monnet, commented:

> … we all arrived at the conclusion that the logic of European unity was inescapable … Only within the framework of a united Europe could there be a settlement of the major unfinished business left over from the Second World War – the division of the German people – on terms that Europeans would be prepared to accept
>
> *(Ball, 1968, pp. 44–5)*

However, when American interests were involved European sensibilities might be overridden, as they were during the Suez crisis or when the United States insisted upon West German rearmament during the Korean War despite both Soviet objections and Anglo-French reservations. As Ball admitted:

> Saved from the searing scars of invasion and occupation, we Americans found it easy to take a more flexible line. We foresaw the first glimmerings of a workable German democracy. Moreover, we had special responsibilities as Europe's banker and policeman. Our occupation costs were immense, our Marshall aid substantial, and our world responsibilities were large and growing larger. If Germans were capable of making a financial and military contribution to lighten the burden, why not? Why should they enjoy the privilege of security without contributing to it?
>
> *(Ball, 1968, p. 50)*

After difficult negotiations West Germany was permitted to re-arm and join NATO in October 1954, but only after President Eisenhower's Secretary of State, John Foster Dulles, had hinted at an American withdrawal from Europe if its wishes were not met.

The alliance was saved but it was episodes of this nature that encouraged the ideas of de Gaulle, recalled as French president in 1959. His concept of Europe, and especially the place of France within that context, was formed partly by his wartime experiences as the embarrassed and embarrassing third wheel in the Anglo-American relationship and partly by his perception of the unreliability of the United States as a partner, a view encouraged by the Suez affair. He believed that Europe/France needed to develop its own defence and political initiatives independent of the United States, whose willingness to risk nuclear destruction in the interests of its European allies he doubted, particularly after the Soviet launch of *Sputnik* in 1957 implied an early inter-continental ballistic missile capability, rendering the American homeland vulnerable for the first time. Yet de Gaulle's ideas were not simple, neither were they universally accepted. If the alternative to the United States was Europe it would not be, in the General's mind, a United States of Europe. Thus he was suspicious of the early moves towards European integration, fearing American domination. Monnet records him as saying:

> We're offered a mishmash of coal and steel, without knowing where we're heading, under some sort of cabal … Here is a crafty scheme for

a so-called 'European' Army which threatens to put a legal end to
France's sovereignty. It would make our Army disappear in a hybrid
creation under the deliberately misleading label of 'Europe'. But since
Europe does not exist as a responsible sovereign entity – because no
one has done what is needed to create it – this force will be entrusted to
the American 'chief'.

(Monnet, 1978, p. 366)

De Gaulle's vision of Europe was a collection of sovereign states based on a continental definition or, according to George Ball, two definitions:

General de Gaulle, who regards the word 'Europe' as synonymous with
'France', employs the expression 'European unity' in two quite different
ways. When he uses it with approbation he refers to a kind of
Latin–Teutonic confederation of 'the Rhine, the Alps and the Pyrenees',
presumably run from Paris, or 'a Europe from the Atlantic to the Urals',
presumably run by a Franco-Soviet directorate.

(Ball, 1968, p. 57)

Monnet was dismissive:

General de Gaulle's proposals are based on notions that are out of date,
they forget the lessons of our most recent history. They completely
ignore what a series of failures has taught us: that it is impossible to
solve Europe's problems among States which retain full national
sovereignty.

(Monnet, 1978, pp. 433–4)

Despite Monnet's condemnation, however, these ideas did not disappear and, to a
large extent, remain at the heart of contemporary debates over the future shape of
the European Community.

De Gaulle's definition of a Europe that stretched from the Atlantic to the Urals
conflicted with the vision of John F. Kennedy, who hoped to create a community
of interests in an area from Vancouver to the Elbe. For the one the Atlantic was
the boundary, for the other the vital communication link, a pond in the garden, not
the sea at the edge of the property. De Gaulles's aspiration was:

… to persuade the states along the Rhine, the Alps, and the Pyrenees to
form a political, economic, and strategic bloc; to establish this
organization as one of the three world powers and, should it become
necessary, as the arbiter between the Soviet and Anglo-American camps.

(quoted in Ball, 1968, p. 125)

In early-1961 Monnet visited Washington and discovered a quite different conception of Europe that stressed spiritual values rather than a continental land mass. As
he enthused to Adenauer:

The men around [Kennedy] have been well chosen … In the work they
have been given … they have all come to the same conclusion: that it is
urgently necessary to organize the West – that is, the free world, which
essentially comprises continental Europe, Britain, the United States and
Canada.

(Monnet, 1978, p. 454)

President John F. Kennedy – expecting more from Europe (credit: Camera Press, London).

Kennedy himself, speaking in Philadelphia on 4 July 1962, developed the idea of partnership so vital to Monnet's vision:

> We believe that a united Europe will be capable of playing a greater role in the common defense, of responding more generously to the needs of poor nations … We see in such a Europe a partner with whom we can deal on a basis of full equality in all the great and burdensome tasks of building a community of free nations.
>
> *(Ball, 1968, p. 60)*

Kennedy's vision partly shared Monnet's philosophy but was also a response to a growing feeling in the United States that Europe was 'not pulling its weight', leav-

147

Harold Macmillan: imperial sunset, European dawn? (credit: Camera Press, London)

ing the Americans to carry too much of the burden of defending and maintaining the free world.

All saw Britain as an important player. Monnet believed that Prime Minister Harold Macmillan's 1961 application for Britain to join the European Economic

Community had been prompted by Kennedy who saw Britain as the vital bridge between the United States and Europe. 'Washington believes that Britain ought to be part of the Common Market and of Europe on the same footing as France or Germany, as a full member and not as an associate' (Monnet, 1978, p. 455). This view was, in a rather strange way, endorsed by de Gaulle's unilateral rejection of the British application in January 1963 because he believed it was an offshore imperial power seeking to act as an American Trojan Horse, although ironically, the United States was encouraging Great Britain to become a European rather than an imperial power. As George Ball argued:

> ... I think it is a mistake for us to press the British government to maintain a significant presence east of Suez; that is, under any circumstances, a wasting asset, since the realities of Britain's limited power and declining interests will sooner or later force her withdrawal ... I think we should recognize that we are doing harm to both Britain and ourselves by insisting that she should perpetuate the pattern of an imperial past.
>
> *(Ball, 1968, pp. 94–5)*

It has also been argued that the 'special relationship' between Britain and America ended with the retirement of Macmillan and the death of Kennedy (Watt, 1984, p. 144). Yet Britain's entry, according to the General, would lead to a 'colossal Atlantic Community under American dependence and leadership which would soon swallow up the European Community' (quoted in Urwin, 1989, p. 214). Whilst de Gaulle remained in power British entry into the Community was blocked but his retirement in 1969 saw a rapid re–opening of negotiations and British entry (along with Denmark and Ireland) in 1973. This was a welcome development for the United States and, apparently, resolved the British debate about its own identity, but it had important implications for the relationship between Washington and the enlarged Community.

Economic and cultural developments

In cultural and entertainment terms the debate between the concepts of Americanization and modernization was also at its height. Europe became more prosperous and efficient, but was this Americanization or modernization, and how did this relate to the domination of cultural industries and markets by organizations controlled from the United States? In the decade after 1945 there was a clear correlation between the two, but the high point was reached in the middle of the 1950s. While there would be continuing modernization in western Europe that was associated with the growth of a consumer goods market, advertising, and the achievement of a standard of living impossible in the communist dominated states, the influence of the United States communication industries became less direct, although substantial investment crossed the Atlantic, particularly for the production of films. The most obvious reasons for this were the decline of the cinema as a major entertainment medium in the late-1950s and 1960s with the growth of television (except in Italy), the simultaneous break-up of the old Hollywood studio structure and the subsequent undermining of confidence in a key area of cultural influence. As costs rose and the market declined American producers found it cheaper to use facilities in Europe, recognizing at the same time the explosion of creative activity among film makers in Britain, France and West Germany.

In the late-1950s and 1960s the American film industry appeared moribund in sharp contrast to the products of European directors who sought to reflect and comment on the changes occurring in their own countries, often in forms that challenged and subverted film conventions. The success of directors like Truffaut and Godard in France, Richardson and Schlesinger in Britain, Bertolucci and the Taviani brothers in Italy and Kluge and Straub in West Germany in finding finance and distribution for their films was impressive and American companies became interested in capitalizing on European productions. The result was an increasing dependence on American finance, co-productions, with the added incentive of guaranteed distribution, not only in the United States but in European countries as well. In the pre-war period European talent had gone to Hollywood, but in the 1960s the film industries in western Europe were given a short lease of life, only to find at the turn of the decade that, as the audiences continued to decline and a stockpile of unexhibited films began to accumulate, American producers withdrew their investment. For the next two decades the international film industry would be dominated by large-scale, multinational productions, reflecting the character of an industry dominated by multinational companies, not exclusively, nor primarily American. National film industries would continue to exist satisfying a smaller, more intellectual market, mainly subsidized by government and television companies.

The emergence of television as a major source of public entertainment and of cultural identification was not equally developed in all west European countries. The reasons were mainly financial. There were not only the costs of providing an efficient transmission service and a reasonable standard of programmes, but also the disposable income available for the purchase of a television set. By the 1960s, however, a substantial part of western Europe was able to satisfy the demands of the developing 'consumer society' and television became a crucial element in the cultural and political development of individual societies and Europe as a whole. Television, like radio broadcasting, was regulated within individual states, normally by the government, although sometimes, as in Britain, this was accomplished through an 'independent' institution. The political power of the medium was quickly appreciated by politicians, although sometimes it was overestimated, not least in their assessment of it as a factor in the success of John F. Kennedy in 1960. There was also the cultural dimension, since television programming could be controlled and an emphasis placed upon the indigenous culture if there was adequate finance. Technical cooperation throughout Europe, established and developed in the 1950s, opened the possibility of a 'European dimension' to television but the fact that sport, *Jeux sans Frontières* and the Eurovision Song Contest have been the main reasons for cooperation over thirty years may open up some debate about the nature of a European culture.

This may be considered an élitist comment, but it raises a fundamental issue about the content of 'popular television' and its effect upon audiences in societies with differing cultural and social outlooks. For many Europeans the experience of American radio and television broadcasting had reinforced the view that a service based upon advertising was another aspect of the construction of an Americanized 'mass culture'. The question for governments was how best to regulate and finance the new medium. The answer tended to be forms of 'mixed economy'. In 1955 the United Kingdom started a commercial channel with a 'public service' bias to compete with, and complement the output of the BBC. On the mainland of Europe governments set up television channels that were wholly or predominantly funded by licence fees. The restriction of advertising was not for cultural reasons alone, but reflected the opposition of newspaper interests to a potential loss of revenue. Advertisers would have hardly been attracted to the initial audiences, particularly in France, where by 1960 only one million sets had been sold. The fact that these were on a totally different transmission system to the rest of the world emphasized the independence of the French, a feeling reinforced by the cultural output of the medium (Smith, 1973, pp. 160–1).

Numbers of sets sold or licences bought can be misleading. In Italy, although only a million licences were issued in 1958 the evening television audience was estimated at 10.5 million since much of the viewing took place in bars and other public venues. By 1964 over 5 million licences had been issued, and over 20 million people watched television each week. One of the most popular programmes was a game show. The fact that the Christian Democrat government of Italy controlled the broadcasting organization RAI, and thus had extensive influence over programming, raised the question as to how far they were actively encouraging a form of Americanized culture in order to legitimize the character of their conservative rule. As David Forgacs suggests, it is not clear that the development of new cultural forms encouraged a Catholic political hegemony and, as one part of the 'consumerism' of the 1960s, created a 'revolution of rising expectations' and a youth culture that led to the political challenges of the late 1960s (Forgacs, 1990, pp. 125–6).

The cultural relationship between America and Europe in the 1950s and 1960s might be best seen in the development of a youth culture related to the expansion of a new consumer market influenced by the development of popular music, which in the main originated in the United States. The American Forces Network in Germany was a formative influence on tastes in popular music among servicemen and civilians alike, (Willett, 1989, pp. 92–3) and commercial radio stations in Europe in the 1950s not only provided a range of popular music unavailable on other channels, but stimulated the growth of a young record-buying public, which found new heroes among the practitioners of commercialized, modernized blues: rock 'n' roll. The constructed sexuality of Elvis Presley challenged old conventions, and found a host of imitators in Europe, from Cliff Richard in Britain to Johnny Halliday in France. Once more, critics, influenced by the manifestations of social disruption that accompanied rock 'n' roll bemoaned the continuing moral depravity of American culture. However, the challenge of this new music was soon diluted as performers sought a wider audience and film producers offered them vehicles whereby their popularity might help to save an ailing industry. Elvis Presley in *GI Blues* singing *Wooden Heart* perfectly represents the relationship of American popular music to Europe in 1961.

Within two years the challenge to American leadership in popular music came from Britain, offered by a group from Liverpool, influenced by rhythm and blues music from the United States but experienced in the culture of Hamburg night life. Irrespective of the subsequent eulogizing of the group and its individual members, it is important to see the Beatles as a crucial influence on the development of popular music in Europe and the United States. They developed their own material, made use of technological innovations in sound recording and voiced the immediate concerns of the audience who bought their records. They were crucial in revitalizing American popular music, not only in encouraging interest in the black exponents of rhythm and blues, but encouraging folk singers like Bob Dylan to enter the field of popular music. In turn, American folk artists articulated a critical political outlook that eventually focused on the American presence in Vietnam and, in conjunction with drugs-oriented music centred on San Francisco, offered a model for popular music challenging 'old fashioned' American and European values.

The European mainland had only a secondary role in this cultural interchange, since the United Kingdom acted as an *entre-pôt* for English-language products, but the influence of this new youth-oriented culture was clearest in France where the purity of the language appeared increasingly threatened by English loan words. The social and cultural changes in France were not reflected in a political establishment that sought to isolate France and Europe from American influence, though the attempt by de Gaulle to construct a Europe around the predominant position of France was symbolically undermined by references to *le weekend*. The rejection of Britain's application to the EEC and the political axis with Adenauer emphasized the unwillingness, or maybe, inability, of de Gaulle to accept the necessity of change. The restructuring of the French broadcasting service in 1964 did not include the weakening of government control since the president had recognized the political importance of television, particularly with the increase in the audience in the 1960s. The 'modernization' of France was taking place, irrespective of the attempts by de Gaulle to halt or at least channel its progress.

This was recognized by Jean-Jacques Servan-Schreiber in 1967 with the publication of his book, *Le Défi americain*, which sold over 400,000 copies in the first three months, the greatest number for any book, fiction or non-fiction to be sold in France in that space of time. United States investment in Europe during this period increased both in amount and as a proportion of its overseas investments. Whilst Britain remained its largest single area of investment there was a steady movement of American capital towards the Community and by 1972 the book value (in millions of dollars) of American investment in West Germany (6,262) and France (3,432) totalled more than that in Britain. In 1950 American investments in the ECSC (637) and Britain (847) represented 14.8 per cent of its total foreign capital outflow (11,788). By 1972 the EC (15,745) and Britain (9,509) accounted for 26.8 per cent of the 94,031 million dollars the Americans invested abroad. In 1950 there were 1,000 subsidiaries of American firms in the ECSC and 700 in Britain; by 1966 the respective figures were more than 4,000 and 2,300 (Grosser, 1980, pp. 221–2). According to Servan-Schreiber:

> Fifteen years from now it is quite possible that the world's third greatest industrial power, after the United States and Russia, will not be Europe, but *American industry in Europe*.

He accepted the predominant economic position of the United States in Europe, and the concomitant political and cultural effects. However, rather than present a totally negative outlook, he argued that Europe as a whole, including Britain, should take up the 'American Challenge' by creating a federal structure, pooling resources, and utilizing the best American methods. Since Servan-Schreiber was the owner of *L'Express*, a news magazine modelled on *Time* and *Newsweek*, it is clear that he was sympathetic to forms of American culture. The key aspect was that Europe should manage its resources more dynamically; as Arthur Schlesinger noted in the Foreword to *The American Challenge*, from this perspective the European problem 'was not so much economic or scientific' as it was 'cultural and political'. The book was essentially anti-Gaullist, arguing for a vision of the future which adapted American experience to European traditions (Servan-Schreiber, 1969, pp. 17, 11).

Within a year of the publication of *Le Défi americain* de Gaulle faced the crisis of the May Revolution when the elements of resistance in French political and social life erupted. Adenauer had died in 1967, and West German politicians began to reassess their relationship towards East Germany and the USSR, not least in the wake of the challenge from their own student body. A culture of student revolt seemed to stretch from the campus of Columbia University to that of the Free University of Berlin. Students challenged the assumptions about American ideological and cultural superiority in the light of the Vietnam experience and the willingness of western governments to offer tacit support. It was a crisis for the American domination of politics developed through cultural means since the Second World War. The economic and military position of the United States in western Europe could not be challenged, but the moral reasoning behind it seemed less assured. Yet, paradoxically:

> The Americanization of the anti-American protest in Europe was carried out through the language of student action (sit-in, teach-in), through clothes, through music. In a certain sense, anti-Americanism became a kind of fashion which derived its mode of appearance, its forms of conduct, and even its intellectual base, from America.
> *(Grosser, 1980, p. 247).*

A changing balance: 1973–1989

This period began with the United States embroiled in a war in South East Asia that it was not winning and which was causing deep dissension at home and undermining its prestige abroad, a process in which television pictures of the conflict had a major part to play. Anti-war demonstrators utilized the medium, as civil rights campaigners had done earlier, to influence the political agenda. The Cold War consensus on foreign policy issues was shattered (Melanson, 1991, p. iii). Europe was thus not the focus of American attention but this was partly because the patterns were already well-established in that theatre. America remained committed to west European defence, with over 300,000 military personnel (or 723,000 Americans, including civilian employees and dependents) stationed in NATO Europe (US General Accounting Office, 1989, pp. 3, 19) but it concentrated its main attention upon Vietnam and the Middle East, where increased tension and the Arab attempt to use oil as a weapon threatened both peace in the region and prosperity on a wider stage. Its European partners were themselves caught up in the same Middle Eastern problems. The economic crisis arising from the Arab oil embargo struck just as the EC was readjusting to the needs of its new members, most notably Britain. There was a marked absence of community spirit as members sought to safeguard their own oil supplies and this cast doubt on the development of a coordinated political role for the EC in foreign affairs, re-emphasizing the predominant role of the United States in the defence of western Europe. A sharp deterioration in US–Soviet relations and the perception of an increase in Soviet military expenditure created a renewed atmosphere of Cold War, and a strain on both the American budget and on relations between the United States and its European allies whom it continued to see as shirking their responsibilities in paying the economic cost of defence. The Americans could no longer subordinate their economic policy to the policy of a Cold War requirement for European cooperation and the economic challenge of the EC, itself a politically and ideologically desirable phenomenon in Cold War terms, could no longer be ignored. In Secretary of the Treasury, John Collin's graphic 1971 phrase, the Americans had 'to screw the Europeans before they screw us' (Smith, 1992, p. 110).

This unpromising situation was hardly improved when the boundaries of popular culture and politics were merged as Ronald Reagan, the 'B' film hero, became president in 1980, and revived the platitudes of the Cold War at the point at which the certainties of European security arrangements were being undermined. Europeans were alarmed to hear Eugene Rostow, Reagan's nominee as chief arms control planner, declare 'We are living in a pre-war and not a post-war world' (Barnett, 1984, p. 413). Yet the 1980s saw a remarkable transformation. Reagan, who had portrayed the Soviet Union as 'the evil empire' and who had markedly increased the stakes in armaments spending, was seen walking hand-in-hand with Mikhail Gorbachev (Soviet General Secretary since 1985) in Red Square, whilst the Soviet perception of the American president changed from 'Rambo to Mister Rogers' (Lundestad, 1992, p.247). The Cold War was over and the impending collapse of the Soviet Union left little doubt as to who had won. Yet even success had its complexities. In military and political terms at least, the states of Europe had desired an American presence because of their fear of the Soviets. Now this had greatly diminished, perhaps even disappeared, and this encouraged a trend apparent since the 1960s.

> The Europeans still wanted a strong American presence, but they
> wanted fewer strings attached to that presence and also a much larger
> European influence than in the early years of the Atlantic alliance.
>
> *(Lundestad, 1992, p. 253)*

President Ronald Reagan – rewriting the script (credit: Camera Press, London).

International developments

During the 1970s the main issues affecting the relationship between the United States and western Europe were substantially those of the previous two decades – the nuclear balance of power, the relationship with the Soviet Union and economic affairs. The period of American predominance was at an end and, at a time of common economic difficulties, the United States wished its European partners to assume a greater share of the financial burden of defence. Aware that the Europeans felt neglected by the American concentration on South-East Asia, Henry Kissinger, the American Secretary of State had declared 1973 'The Year of Europe', but events in the Middle East forced him to retitle it, 'The Year of Opec' (Smith, 1992, p. 110). The oil crisis of October 1973 created a period of economic stagnation and rising inflation until the end of the decade. Economic diplomacy dominated the relationship between the United States and Europe, with four summits culminating in the Bonn meeting of 1978. The results of these meetings have been described as 'quite meaningless', but they did witness attempts by the United States to encourage other economies to stimulate international trade for its own needs. This was in marked contrast to events in the late-1940s and demonstrated the relative weakening of the American position. Whereas in 1945 the United

155

States produced almost half of the world's manufactures, by 1960 this had declined to 30 per cent and by 1992 to 23 per cent (Gatzke, 1980, pp. 232–7; Lundestad, 1992, p. 251).

Questions about the nuclear deterrent and *détente* were addressed through attempts to construct a more stable relationship between the western alliance and the Soviet Union through the medium of continuing Strategic Arms Limitation Talks (SALT) and the Mutual and Balanced Force Reductions (MBFR) negotiations. Arising from the Conference on European Security and Cooperation (CESC), held in Helsinki in 1975, the issue of human rights complicated these discussions and threatened to bring the *realpolitik* of 'peaceful co-existence' into conflict with the ideology of individual freedom, a cause close to the heart of President Carter. It also added a further dimension to the debate about the definition of Europe, which under CESC terms appeared to stretch from Vancouver to Vladivostock. Carter's main thrust in foreign policy was directed to extra-European issues. Although he played a major role in bringing Egypt and Israel together in the Camp David Accords (September 1978), the prestige of both the United States and its president suffered from failure of its policy in Nicaragua, Iran and the seizure of American hostages. The Soviet invasion of Afghanistan in December 1979 led the president to revert to a Cold War rhetoric reminiscent of the 1950s. Withdrawing the American team from the Moscow Olympics of 1980, he referred to the prestige that Hitler had gained from the Berlin Olympiade of 1936, thus reiterating the view expressed in the 1940s that there was little difference between the totalitarian outlook of National Socialism and Soviet Communism (Melanson, 1991, pp. 110–11).

The suppression of the Polish Solidarity movement in the following year seemed to confirm the image of a malevolent Soviet Union presented by the new President Ronald Reagan, who capitalized on Carter's apparent ineptitude and vacillation during the election campaign of 1979. The west Europeans did not perceive so clearly the revival of a Soviet threat and were disconcerted by Reagan's simplistic rhetoric. The Soviet intention to target SS-20 intermediate range missiles on western Europe did strengthen the NATO alliance once again, though the American decision to station its own intermediate range missiles in Europe in 1983 and the subsequent 1987 decision to trade their removal for the Soviet withdrawal of its weapons, emphasized that the Europeans had had little influence on the decisions. This in turn encouraged moves, not surprisingly led by France, towards considering security outwith the Atlantic framework and the development of a west European defence strategy against the moment when the Americans decided to withdraw. The main vehicle for this was the Western European Union (WEU), founded in 1954 when the Brussels Treaty was enlarged, but whose main function to date had been to provide a forum for coordinating the activities of Britain and the Six before British entry into the EC. Reactivated in 1984 WEU, in parallel with extended Franco-German defence collaboration, challenged, though inconclusively, the patterns that had become traditional since 1945.

Notwithstanding this European initiative the key decision by Reagan in 1983 to initiate the Strategic Defence Initiative (SDI), popularly known as 'Star Wars', was the most important factor in future developments in Europe. Attempts by the Soviet Union to match American resources and technology placed a critical strain on a political and economic system already stretched to maintain its superpower status. Indeed 1980s Central Intelligence Agency (CIA) estimates that the Soviet Union, with an economy half the size of that of the United States, was spending 50 per cent more in real terms on defence, may well have been underestimates (Reynolds, 1992, p. 228). It also placed an enormous burden upon the American economy and under Reagan the United States moved within four years from being the world's greatest creditor to becoming the world's greatest debtor (Lundestad, 1992, p. 251). America's partners in western Europe viewed these developments with mixed feelings. SDI appeared to offer opportunities to capitalize on American investment in new technology and research, however, it threatened to destabilize both the existing nuclear balance and the structure of the international economy. The strongest supporter within Europe for a continuing American involvement was the British Prime Minister, Margaret Thatcher, who shared both Reagan's rhetorical and economic outlook. Their mutual admiration and shared perceptions in the 1980s tended to isolate Britain from its European partners, reviving memories of the 'special relationship' between London and Washington, encouraged by support and cooperation during the Falklands War of 1982. Shrewd observers, however, suggested that the real United States/European axis ran through Washington and Bonn (Rummel and Schmidt, 1990, pp. 266–70).

Margaret Thatcher – the iron lady reforging Atlantic links (credit: Camera Press, London).

Economic and cultural developments

From the mid-1970s the United States and western Europe were becoming 'post-industrial' and 'information' societies. These are simplified expressions for fundamental changes in industrial activity linked to the expansion of global communication networks and computer systems. The 'fordism' that characterized American industrial production with an emphasis on large runs of standardized goods, mass consumption and management of demand by the state was replaced by an emphasis on decentralization of production, with specialized products for segmented markets, and the state allowing 'market forces' to regulate supply and demand. At the same time the growth of communication systems has encouraged the globalization of production and the capability of opening up world markets. West European economies, which were still dominated by American investment in the late-1960s, increasingly became part of a multinational economic network. Indeed Jean-Pierre Lehmann suggests that it is the *défi japonais* that Europe faces in the 1990s and the twenty-first century (Lehmann, 1992, pp. 37–53).

Traditional mass-production industries declined as new capital-intensive technological products were marketed internationally in an aggressive fashion, particularly by those who had absorbed the main aspects of Americanization in the post-war period, the Japanese and the Germans. The result in many west European countries was the growth of a large 'service sector', encouraged by some governments, notably the Thatcher administration in the United Kingdom, as a solution to the problems of large-scale unemployment. By 1981 in Italy 50 per cent of the workforce were in service sector occupations (Forgacs, 1990, p. 171). The proliferation of new technologies, particularly VCRs, cable and satellite systems and the possibility of a tariff-free single market in Europe in 1993 produced new opportunities for the cultural industries. Increasingly these were multinationals concerned with selling both hardware, and cultural products into the global market, of which individual European states were only a small part. Deregulation and privatization in western Europe allowed Italian and German entrepreneurs, for instance Berlusconi and Bertelsmann, to concentrate ownership of television, satellite and publishing enterprises as bases for European and international expansion.

The experience of the United States has thus been replicated in Europe. The 'framework for diversity' has led to a uniformity of product and outlook. A multiplicity of channels requires cheap programming, and the United States with its large domestic market can provide a range of 'products' to fill the time spaces, while delivering specific audiences for advertisers. This might be regarded as the ultimate 'success' of American culture, in that it is the construction of an homogenized cultural experience, offered to multinational populations and linking together a whole range of cultural industries and products, thus apparently confirming George Ball's 1968 boast that:

> The fact that Ho Chi Minh smokes Salems rather than Gauloises, or that Middle Eastern potentates sip Coca-Cola rather than ginger beer, may be a fatuous measure of American prestige. But sometimes even the trivial cultural nationalism of cigarettes and soda pop and comic strips is a ritual representation of a deeper reality: the passion of non-western

leaders for power and modernity and their psychological association of those qualities with all things American.

(Ball, 1968, p. 16)

Mickey Mouse and friends – American culture or Disney culture? (credit: Camera Press, London)

Yet this oversimplifies a much more complex process. The opening of the EuroDisney theme park on the outskirts of Paris in 1992 is the most obvious example of the diversification of an entertainment organization into the total leisure market, a development first established successfully in the United States and now capitalizing on the whole European market. However, what is being marketed is not American culture, but Disney culture. It has no specific national base, but is tailored for specific markets and aims to shape the tastes of future consumers. Mickey Mouse and Coca-Cola are now marketed internationally but the American origins, while still clear, are masked by an attempt to provide a more general cultural significance – the transforming power of Disney magic and the underlying message of friendship in Coke.

The development in the 1970s and 1980s that best represents the extension of American 'culture' to Europe is the success of fast-food outlets and particularly the pioneer in the 1970s Macdonald's. This was the first American retail organization, apart from oil companies, to extend its operations to Europe and essentially change the cultural habits of whole populations since 'quick-service food was uniquely American'. It was also 'exporting what has become the centrepiece of American industry – the service sector' (Love, 1988, p. 418). Macdonald's was the epitome of the 'post-industrial' society and developed the forms of expansion originated by Coca-Cola: the local franchise and encouragement of local entrepreneurs, thus avoiding the 'distasteful image of a huge American multinational corporation with designs on the global market' (Love, 1988, p. 433). There were still problems of marketing in Germany and France where food had strong cultural symbolism but the emphasis was on the indigenous participation in the preparation of the products. The European experience was shared by most countries outside the Soviet bloc and by the mid-1980s Yugoslavia was seen as the easiest point of entry to countries further east. The opening of a Macdonald's restaurant in Moscow in 1990 had little effect on Soviet eating habits but signalled a further and significant step in the winning of the Cold War, at least in the publicity it engendered in the West.

Conclusion

This victory in the Cold War came as something of a surprise. Economic hard times tested the trading relationships between the United States and the EC and, as America felt the strain of economic recession, an increasing number of questions began to appear as to the wisdom of its commitment to the defence of a western Europe which seemed reluctant to assume what Americans perceived as a fair share of the burden. American self-confidence, slowly recovering after the shock of defeat in Vietnam, was dealt another hard blow by Watergate and the scandal of President Nixon's enforced resignation. Americans were prepared to believe that the days of United States hegemony were limited and Paul Kennedy's analysis of the rise and decline of great powers became a best-seller as they sought to discover the signs presaging their own decline (Kennedy, 1988). Yet it was the Soviet Union rather than the United States that cracked and the new era of *Glasnost* and *Perestroika* brought the possibility of an undivided Europe, with all the opportunities and hazards that that entailed. As in 1919 or in 1945 the mid-1980s saw

Europe and the United States faced with a series of problems and choices that combined to enforce a radical reappraisal of issues that seemed to have been set in an unbreakable mould.

After the Cold War: the future of the Atlantic Partnership?

In political terms Mrs Thatcher's Chicago speech in June 1991 was redolent of the debates that have dominated the last forty-six years: the definition of the relationship between the United States and Europe; the definition of Europe in such a context (with Thatcher coming close to a reassertion of the Kennedy version); and the position of Britain, geographically and politically nearly, but not quite, European with strong political, cultural and economic links with the United States. Many in Britain still wish that there was a Churchillian choice between Europe and the deep blue sea. For Americans that choice has reasserted itself for the first time in two generations and troop reductions in Europe mean that the boys are indeed coming home, though rather later than expected. The demolition of the Berlin Wall and the reunification of Germany together with the changing relationships between the superpowers mean that the definition of America's relationship with Europe must remain, at least in part, open-ended, particularly in a period when problems have re-emerged in areas of Europe more familiar as sources of tension to Bismarck or Bethman Hollweg than to most post-war decision-makers.

President Bush, in his State of the Union speech in January 1992, hailed the end of the Cold War as the success of American ideals based upon the morality of liberal individualism and capitalism. These were the ideals that the United States had defended in western Europe since 1945 and that their European allies had appeared to accept. However, this essay has argued that the process has been more one of negotiation and adjustment rather than the imposition and acceptance of American values. The experience of modernization in western Europe has certainly involved an acceptance of American methods and ideological outlooks, but in turn the Americans themselves have been affected by their involvement over forty years in the reconstruction and development of western Europe. The dissolution of the Soviet Empire and indeed the Soviet Union itself, will pose further questions about the ability of such ideals to consolidate and stabilize areas of Europe that have not had direct experience of and exposure to Americanization. Geir Lundestad suggests that 'The need for America's strategic deterrence will decline, the American troop commitment will be cut at least in half, a two thirds reduction is probably more likely'. It also poses a problem for the future development of the European Community which was formed, at least in part, at the American behest and as a response to the threat from the Soviet Union. Despite achieving a 51.9 per cent share of world manufacturing exports between 1984 and 1987 'The European Community has not even reached the level of integration found in the Acts of Confederation of 1776–77' whilst the Danish rejection of the Maastricht Treaty may prevent early progress towards greater political unity (Lundestad, 1992, pp. 252–3; Sharp, 1992, pp. 17–35).

The overall question is 'What is Europe'? This essay has suggested that there is no simple answer. The definition depends upon the perceptions of individuals, organizations and societies attempting to grapple with the problems of reconstruction, modernization and a rapidly evolving international environment. In the period after 1945 the United States was bound to be a major influence in the reconstruction of European society, but its active involvement in the defence and economic rebuilding of western Europe secured for itself a predominant role in the definition of what would be understood by 'Europe'. Nonetheless, the definitions that have evolved have demonstrated that the relationship between the United States and Europe has been both dynamic and involved mutual readjustments. In the 1990s that process will continue in an international environment that has changed. Lord Ismay's definition of the original function of NATO ('to keep the Americans in, the Germans down and the Russians out') will require reappraisal. The question for the future is the particular character of the United States' participation in the development of a new Europe.

References

AMBROSE, STEPHEN (1971) *Rise to Globalism: American Foreign Policy, 1938–1970*, Harmondsworth, Penguin.

BALL, GEORGE (1968) *The Discipline of Power*, London, Bodley head.

BARNETT, R. J. (1984) *Allies: America, Europe, Japan since the War*, London, Jonathan Cape.

BELOFF, MAX (1963) *The United States and the Unity of Europe*, London, Faber.

BULLOCK, ALAN (1983) *Ernest Bevin Foreign Secretary 1945–1951*, London, Norton.

DE GRAZIA, VICTORIA (1991) *The Culture of Consent*, Cambridge, Cambridge University Press.

EDWARDS, JILL (1990) 'Roger Makin: "Mr Atom"' in ZAMETICA, JOHN (ed.) *British Officials and British Foreign Policy, 1945–1949*, Leicester, Leicester University Press, pp.8–38.

ELSASSER, THOMAS (1975) 'Two decades in another country: Hollywood and the cinephiles' in BIGSBY, C. W. E. (ed.) *Superculture: American popular culture and Europe*, London, Elek, pp. 199–216.

ELLWOOD, DAVID (1985) 'From 're-education' to the selling of the Marshall Plan in Italy' in PRONAY, N. and WILSON, K. (eds) *The Political Re-education of Germany and her Allies after World War II*, London, Croom Helm, pp. 219–402.

FEIS, HERBERT (1957) *Churchill, Roosevelt, Stalin: the war they waged and the peace they sought*, Princeton, Princeton University Press.

FORGACS, DAVID (1990) *Italian Culture in the Industrial Era 1880–1980*, Manchester, Manchester University Press.

GATZKE, HANS W. (1980) *Germany and the United States: a 'Special Relationship'?*, Harvard.

GROSSER, A. (1980) *The Western Alliance: European-American relations since 1945*, trans. M. Shaw, New York.

GUBACK, THOMAS (1986) 'Shaping the film business in post-war Germany: the role of the US film industry and the US state' in KERR, PAUL (ed.) *The Hollywood Film Industry,*London, Routledge, Kegan, Paul/BFI, pp. 245–75.

KENNEDY, PAUL (1988) *The Rise and Fall of the Great Powers: economic change and military conflict from 1500 to 2000*, London, Fontana.

KEYNES, J. M. (1919) *The Economic Consequences of the Peace*, New York, Macmillan.

KUISEL, RICHARD F. (1991) 'Coca-Cola and the Cold War: the French face Americanisation, 1948–1953', *French Historical Studies*, Spring, pp. 96–116.

LEHMANN, JEAN-PIERRE (1992) 'France, Japan, Europe, and industrial competition: the automotive case', *International Affairs*, **68**, January, pp. 37–53.

LOTH, WILFRIED (1988) The *Division of the World 1945–1951*, London, Routledge.

LOVE, JOHN F. (1988) *Macdonald's: behind the arches*, London.

LUNDESTAD, GEIR (1984) 'Empire by invitation: the United States and Western Europe', *Newsletter of the Society of Historians of American Foreign Relations*, 15, September, pp. 1–21.

LUNDESTAD, GEIR (1992) 'The end of the Cold War, the new role for Europe and the decline of the United States', *Diplomatic History*, **16**, Spring, pp. 247–55.

MAYNE, RICHARD (1970) *The Recovery of Europe: from devastation to unity*, London, Weidenfeld & Nicolson.

MEE JNR, CHARLES L. (1984) *The Marshall Plan*, New York, Simon & Schuster.

MELANSON, RICHARD A. (1991) *Reconstructing Consensus: American foreign policy since the Vietnam war*, New York, St Martins Press.

MILWARD, ALAN (1989) 'The Marshall Plan – America, Britain, and the reconstruction of Western-Europe, 1947–1952', *Diplomatic History*, **13**(2), pp. 231–253.

MONNET, JEAN (1978) *Memoirs*, translated by Richard Mayne, London.

MORGAN, ROGER (1972) *West European Politics Since 1945: the shaping of the European Community*, London, Batsford.

OVENDALE, RITCHIE (ed.) (1984) *The Foreign Policy of the British Labour Governments 1945–1951*, Leicester, Leicester University Press.

REYNOLDS, DAVID (1992) 'Beyond bipolarity in space and time', *Diplomatic History*, **16**, Spring, pp. 225–33.

ROBERTS, FRANK (1984) 'Ernest Bevin as Foreign Secretary' in OVENDALE, RITCHIE (ed.) *The Foreign Policy of the British Labour Governments 1945–1951*, Leicester, Leicester University Press, pp. 21–42,

RUMMEL, REINHARDT and SCHMIDT, PETER (1990) 'The Changing Security Framework' in WALLACE, WILLIAM (ed.) *The Dynamics of European Integration*, London, Pinter, pp. 261–75.

SERVAN-SCHREIBER, JEAN-JACQUES (1969) *The American Challenge*, Harmondsworth, Penguin, originally published as *Le Défi americain* (1967).

SHARP, MARGARET (1992) 'Tides of change: the world economy and Europe in the 1990s', *International Affairs*, **68**, Spring, pp. 17–35.

SORLIN, PIERRE (1991) *European Cinemas, European Societies 1939–1990*, London, Routledge.

SMITH, ANTHONY (1973) *The Shadow in the Cave: the broadcaster, the audience and the state,* London, Allen & Unwin.

SMITH, MICHAEL (1992) '"The devil you know": the United States and a changing European Community', *International Affairs*, **68**, January, pp. 103–20.

SPANIER, JOHN (4th edition, 1971) *American Foreign Policy since World War II*, London, Nelson.

TUNSTALL, JEREMY (1977) *The Media are American*, London, Constable.

URWIN, DEREK (4th edition, 1989) *Western Europe since 1945*, London, Longman.

US GENERAL ACCOUNTING OFFICE (1989) *Military Presence: United States Personnel in NATO Europe*, October.

WILLETT, RALPH (1989) *The Americanization of Germany, 1945–1949*, London, Routledge.

WARNER, GEOFFREY (1984) 'The Labour governments and the unity of Western Europe' in OVENDALE, RITCHIE (ed.) *The Foreign Policy of the British Labour Governments 1945–1951*, Leicester, Leicester University Press, pp. 61–82.

WATT, D. C. (1984) *Succeeding John Bull: America in Britain's place 1900–1975*, Cambridge, Cambridge University Press.

ZAMETICA, JOHN (1990) 'Three letters to Bevin: Frank Roberts at the Moscow Embassy, 1945–46' in ZAMETICA, JOHN (ed.) *British Officials and British Foreign Policy, 1945–1949*, Leicester, Leicester University Press, p.39–97.

Essay 4
Europe in the global economy

Prepared for the Course Team by Grahame Thompson
Senior Lecturer in Economics, The Open University

Introduction

What place does Europe occupy in the international economic order? While this might seem to be a straightforward question, to answer it properly means addressing a set of preliminary questions about which there is considerable debate, ambiguity and even controversy. Over what time period are we to judge the importance of Europe? With which other parts of the globe do we compare Europe? Indeed, what is meant by the term 'Europe' anyway? Furthermore, the economic order can be measured in relation to a number of different dimensions. Is it wise to address just the

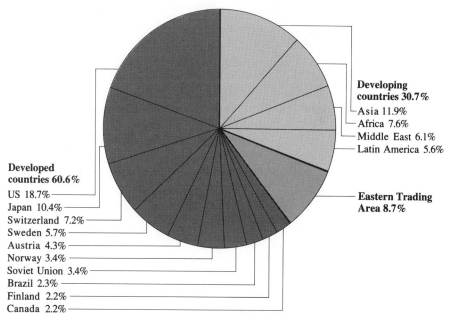

Figure 1   EC trading partners.

Source: Eurostat, *External Trade Statistical Yearbook* and monthly statistics, *Financial Times*, 17 April 1991.

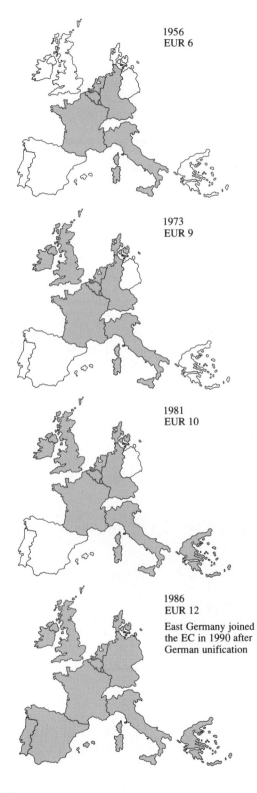

1956
EUR 6

1973
EUR 9

1981
EUR 10

1986
EUR 12

East Germany joined
the EC in 1990 after
German unification

*Figure 2   The Europe of
the European Community.*

economic position of Europe without, at the same time, looking at its political or cultural roles and at how these roles might connect to the economic realm?

These and other questions form the basis of the analysis in this essay. One way of showing the importance of Europe can be seen in Figure 1. The data in this figure reflect a measure of European trade in the global context; they show the share of the European Community's (EC) merchandise imports originating from various countries or regions in 1989. Broadly speaking, the 'Developed countries' account for 60 per cent of these imports, the 'Developing countries' 30 per cent, and the 'Eastern Trading Area' the other 10 per cent (approximately). For the purposes of Figure 1, Europe comprises the twelve member states of the European Economic Community (EEC) in 1989. However, a number of other European countries, in a geographical sense, are separately accounted for as either members of the 'Developed countries' group or as part of the 'Eastern Trading Area'. Thus one of the main problems to be encountered in the analysis that follows is exactly where to draw the boundaries around Europe as an economic entity. And this problem is not solved by simply appealing to the EC as a representation of the geographical centre of the European economy. Figure 2 demonstrates that the EC has changed its geographical boundaries over the years, and it could enlarge them again very soon as is indicated in Figure 3.

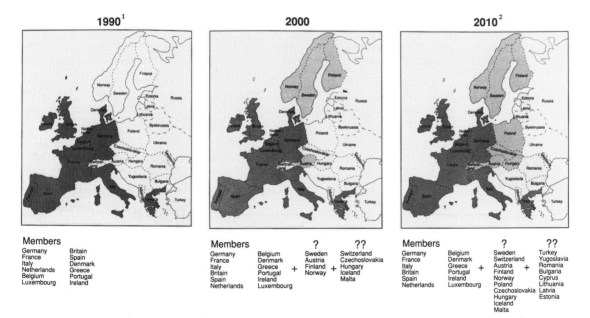

Figure 3   The expanding European Community.

[1]   *Between 1970 and 1990 the European Community's membership doubled, its area and population nearly doubled and its gross domestic product more than doubled.*

[2]   *Between 1990 and 2010 the membership of the European Community may double again; but if all ten of the most likely new members join, this will increase the Community's total population by less than one third, and its gross domestic product by less than half the increase expected in the economies of the existing members.*

Source: *Britain in 2010: the PSI Report*, 1991, London, Policy Studies Institute.

In the next section the changing conceptions of Europe as an economic centre (and its accompanying character as a political centre) are discussed as a prelude to a more thorough analysis of its place in the wider international environment. The theme of this section will be the multidimensional character of 'economic Europe' – particularly its political establishment and regulation, and the geographical extent and embrace of these defining features.

What is the European economic space?

Is the contemporary Europe to which we refer the same as the Europe described by our predecessors 30, 60, let alone 100 years ago? Clearly, the characteristic features shaping the *European economic space* (as I shall call it) in various historical periods are themselves likely to be diverse and contingent. We need to think these through against the changing background of what have been momentous world-wide transformations, as well as against those changes that impinge more exclusively and directly on the European economic space itself.

There are two possible routes to follow in an analysis of the European economic space (hereafter the EES). The first is to take an overtly *institutional* focus. Using this route we trace the evolution of those institutional mechanisms in which the idea of Europe as an economic unit figured directly, or was implicated by dint of geo-political presence. The other route is to look at the characteristic *patterns of economic interaction* which the European states, or the private economic actors residing within them, developed between themselves. The first route relies upon a more 'political' approach. It involves charting the definition and redefinition of those typical, Europe-wide consultative, regulatory and administrative mechanisms and associated practices which implicate some notion of Europe in their operations. The second route is, perhaps, a more obviously 'economic' approach. It implies an analysis of the progressive development and reconstruction of market mechanisms to trace growing patterns of trade, investment, production, and technological and other economic relationships between the countries of Europe.

Now, while these look to be different and separate approaches, a moment's reflection reveals that they represent only a difference in emphasis. At least, that is what we shall argue. As the essay unfolds these two focuses will be progressively run together until we deploy both approaches in combination. However, it is still useful to begin our analysis with them as separate perspectives.

The institutional matrix of economic Europe

Taking a broadly defined 'western Europe' first, this is largely how the EES has come to be known over the 50 years since the end of the Second World War. In this period the EES was pitched against a, perhaps, even less clearly demarcated 'eastern Europe', but more of this later. In an economic sense, western

Europe included those sixteen liberal-market economies that originally set up the Organization of European Economic Cooperation (OEEC) in 1948, and subsequently expanded to include, first, the Federal Republic of Germany, then Finland and Spain, to make up the present European nations in the Organization of Economic Cooperation and Development (OECD); *or* it could be traced to the ten signatories of the statute setting up the Council of Europe (COE) in 1949, which itself expanded to include 23 members over 40 years later. The OECD has retained an explicitly 'economics' brief – to foster the development of liberal-market economic relations between its members. It does this as a consultative and information-gathering organization, carrying out economic assessments of individual countries, dealing with issues of common economic interest and disseminating the results. On the other hand, the COE/Western European Union (WEU) represented the political side of pan-(western) European cooperation in the post-war era, though the reality has not matched the political aspiration for much of this period.

In addition to these essentially cooperative and consultative institutional mechanisms, post-war western Europe also saw the emergence of a set of more integrationist and coordinatory organizational formations. Even while still in exile in London, the governments of Belgium, the Netherlands and Luxembourg decided in 1944 to set up a customs union to begin on 1 January 1948 and be known as Benelux.[1] This developed into an early prototype for the wider economic unions that were to follow and, by the late 1950s, had achieved the elimination of all remaining trade barriers, the free movement of capital and labour, and an important agricultural accord between the countries involved. In March 1948, France and Italy also set up a customs union (Francital) which embodied similar provisions and which, by the middle 1950s, had achieved much the same result (though not on agricultural activities).

Probably still more important in retrospect was the foundation of the European Coal and Steel Community (ECSC) by the Treaty of Paris in 1951 (which became operational the following year). Involving France, West Germany, Italy and the Benelux countries, this community eliminated tariff and quantitative restrictions (including subsidies) between its members on trade relating to coal and steel. (The UK did not join, even though it had participated in the negotiations to set up ECSC.) The ECSC had a considerable symbolic effect on subsequent integrationist tendencies within western Europe though, as will be discussed later, its immediate effects upon the coal and steel sectors within the community members themselves were limited.

Rudimentary though they were, the early economic cooperative and coordinatory relations fostered by these institutions (and other important organizations that will be discussed more fully in a moment) culminated during the second half of this century in the development of the EEC of the six, expanding to the EC of the twelve by 1986 (see Figure 2), and the European Free Trade Area (EFTA), which originally comprised nine member states but dropped to six when the UK, Denmark and Portugal left to join the EC.

---

[1]   A customs union between just Belgium and Luxembourg, the BLUE, had been in operation since 1921.

Broadly speaking, these developments represent the main institutional contours of the western European economic space since the Second World War. In a later section, the evolution and importance of the EEC/EC will be discussed more fully. But it is worth reiterating that this economic space, formed in the main over the past 50 years, is not the only way of looking at the western European economy in an historical sense.

The integrating, institutionalized economic space of the post-war period had a certain geographical continuity and logic; it was centred on the industrial heartland of northern Europe, bounded by the Saar and Ruhr, and stretched southwards to northern Italy. In addition, for much of the pre-1914 period Germany occupied a pivotal position within central Europe, producing the manufactured goods which were exchanged for agricultural produce from eastern and other central-European countries. How different from the previous 'European' economic spaces of the Mediterranean basin in Antiquity, or the North Sea and Atlantic Ocean maritime countries of the sixteenth and seventeenth centuries (England, the Netherlands, Spain, Portugal and France). As has already been discussed in other essays, these earlier periods of European pre-eminence established their own typical regimes of economic relationships in which, in a sense, the EES was extended to areas and regions far beyond the borders of continental Europe itself. In a way then, the EES has, for much of its history, not been confined to just the countries of Europe. In many ways it has had a global presence. This global presence, especially in its contemporary form, is analysed in the next section of this essay.

Indeed, the period since the Second World War has seen one further way in which the European economic space could be constituted, at least in part. This involves the role of the United States of America in particular, and the institutional matrix it was instrumental in developing and supporting after 1945. The term 'western Europe' as an economic concept owes much to the US and to US-sponsored developmental agencies, particularly those established immediately after the war. This broader Europe was originally defined by the United Nations' plan for post-war reconstruction, but the intensification of the 'Cold War' during the late 1940s left it moribund. The work of the US-sponsored UN Economic Commission for Europe would have included 'eastern Europe' and the Soviet Union in the reconstruction, but required that those benefiting from assistance should agree to promote a system of liberalized multilateral free trade as they recovered, something to which the USSR could not agree. Thus, although the eastern European countries were offered Marshall Aid (as it came to be known), it was more or less vetoed by the USSR.

Instead, the main institutional instrument of US-led reconstruction efforts centred upon those sixteen countries that set up the OEEC in 1948 to administer the European wing of the Marshall Plan (named after the American Secretary of State in the 1940s, General George Marshall, who was responsible for administering the programme). By most accounts the Marshall Plan was a great success.[2] Originally intended to operate for only four years (from 1947 to 1951), it eventually involved

[2]   There remains some controversy here. For a recent, positive assessment see Hogan (1989); for a more sceptical view see Milward (1984).

US$3 billion of official (World Bank) loans and US$17 billion of direct US government gifts (in total, reaching some 3 per cent of US Gross Domestic Product in 1948 and 1949), and continued, in its second phase, to well after the Korean War which ended in 1953. The Marshall Plan contributed significantly to a modernization of European infrastructure and the reconstruction of its productive industries, but it also enabled rearmament to take place. It provided for the 'dollar shortage' at a vulnerable time for Europe, helping the OECD countries to finance their severe balance of payments deficits. In addition, the Plan, particularly in its second phase, envisaged increasing intra-European cooperation as quota and tariff barriers to trade were lifted. In this, the immediate outcome was less successful.

It is clear, then, that US concern about European economic reconstruction and integration was set very much within the principles of its wider strategy of containment. The policy was driven by the Cold War and a hostile attitude towards the Soviet Union's presumed expansionary intentions in Europe (and elsewhere). But there was another, if secondary, driving force, involving relationships *within* western Europe, between France and Germany in particular. It was expected that the form of economic and political reconstruction in Europe after the war would solve once and for all the 'German problem' – it would lock (West) Germany into a system of liberal market relationships *and* into a system of constitutional arrangements with its neighbours that would prevent a repeat of the inter-war experience in continental central Europe. This is a theme we shall return to later in this essay.

If the western European economic space was constituted by a number of different determinations and overlapping institutional frameworks, then defining the eastern European economic space turns out to be nearly as problematical. As a response to the rejection of the US initiatives to eastern Europe in the context of the Marshall Plan, the Soviet Union set up its own reconstruction package – the Cominform and the Molotov Plan (1947). This was later extended to form the Council of Mutual Economic Aid (CMEA or Comecon), which was set up in Moscow in 1949. Comecon became the premier instrument for the construction of an integrated economic system amongst the centrally planned economies (CPEs) under Soviet tutelage.

After Stalin's death Comecon developed as a mechanism for national and sectoral economic specialization amongst its members (a kind of socialist international division of labour), though the extent of intra-Comecon trade remained relatively small as the basic autarkic national development strategies of the socialist countries failed to break down fully. However, in certain key sectors a *de facto* country specialization did emerge (for example, in bus and coach production, which was almost exclusively centred on Hungary). For some countries this proved a major weakness as the eastern economic bloc began to disintegrate in the late 1980s/early 1990s, something that we shall return to in a later section.

To sum up this section, we have seen how an EES is by no means an easy thing to define in a consistently institutional sense. It has been the subject of a number of determinations and transformations. A complex and overlapping framework emerges, especially for western Europe. In addition, 'Europe' as an economic object should not necessarily be confused with the geographical limits of what is normally understood as Europe. (For instance, Iceland, Greenland and the Faroe Islands have associated status as members of EFTA; the US/Canada operated as an adjunct of Europe immediately after the war; and the 68 African and Pacific states signing the Lomé Convention have a privileged associate status with respect to the EC.) What is more, 'eastern Europe' presents us with another set of problems of definition, the characteristic limits of which are equally ambiguous. (During the 1950s, Mongolia, the People's Republic of China, North Korea and North Vietnam became associate members of Comecon – Mongolia, Cuba and Vietnam later became full members.) Where exactly does Europe end in the east and Asia begin? Is Turkey a part of Europe? Bearing these points in mind we can now move on to review the pattern of actual economic interactions that have characterized the institutional spaces of Europe since the end of the Second World War.

Patterns of European economic interactions

In an influential – if slightly 'revisionist' (at least, in Anglo-Saxon intellectual circles) – analysis of the reasons for the post-Second World War 'long boom' in economic activity, Matthews (1968) argued that it was less the result of the (publicly inspired) Keynesian demand management of the European and American economies, and more the result of the (privately inspired) dramatic increase in investment and trade between the countries of the 'West'. We shall concentrate on the importance of trade and investment in this section.

The crucial impediment to the rapid re-establishment of international trade between the main capitalist countries after the Second World War was the 'dollar shortage', particularly amongst the countries of Europe. In one way or another this was solved by the Marshall Plan, with its associated aid and loan arrangements, and the inauguration of the European Payments Union (EPU). The EPU acted to conserve the available dollar and other official reserve holdings used by the European countries in making international payments between themselves; this enabled the most effective use to be made of them in financing the trade and balance of payments of the participants with the outside world.

With the easing of the immediate crisis of the dollar shortage, it was the devaluations in 1949 that set the European countries on the route to dramatic increases in international trade. This massive realignment of 26, mainly European, currencies against the dollar (by around 30 per cent) secured a competitive advantage for Europe *vis-à-vis* the US that lasted until the early 1970s. The European economies were effectively transformed into export-orientated economies almost overnight.

The historical record of European economic growth, compared with that of the US and Japan, is shown in Table 1. The period of rapid growth to the early 1970s is clear. From the middle of the 1970s the growth rate fell. Note that over the entire period Europe had a marginally better growth record than the US, but a much poorer record than Japan.

The second part of Table 1 contains information on the investment records of OECD Europe, the US and Japan. In terms of gross capital formation, Europe achieved a better result than the US, and a quite consistent one too, but again it compares unfavourably with the Japanese record. This striking difference is confirmed if we look at just investment in machinery and equipment, the basis of investment in the traded goods sector. Perhaps one of the main reasons for the poorer European (and, to an even greater extent, US) performance in all categories of investment is that savings are low in these two economies. A dramatic collapse in the levels of savings in the US economy during the 1980s is evident from the table, the full consequences of which we shall discuss later. The remarkably high levels of savings in Japan, and their relative robustness over this period, is also something we shall take up later. The record of OECD Europe on savings falls somewhere between the two.

The final part of Table 1 gives one indicator of the trade position of Europe compared with the US and Japan. Over the period as a whole the position of Europe has been more or less neutral in terms of the balance of trade. The US, by contrast, fell into a negative balance on its trade account after 1974, while Japan strengthened its positive position in the 1980s.

Table 1 Comparative European growth, investment and trade record, 1960 to 1988

	1960–67	1968–73	1974–79	1980–88	1960–88
Real GDP growth (yearly % changes):					
OECD Europe	4.7	4.9	2.6	2.2	3.5
US	4.5	3.2	2.4	2.8	3.3
Japan	10.2	8.7	3.6	4.1	6.5
Gross capital formation (as % of GDP):					
OECD Europe	22.9	23.5	22.4	20.3	22.1
US	18.0	18.4	18.7	17.8	18.2
Japan	31.0	34.6	31.8	29.2	31.4
Investment in machinery and equipment (as % of GDP):					
OECD Europe	9.2	9.0	8.9	8.6	8.9
US	6.7	7.3	8.0	7.9	7.4
Japan	n/a	14.4	10.8	10.5	12.3
Net savings (as % of GDP):					
OECD Europe	15.3	15.9	11.9	9.1	12.6
US	9.8	9.2	7.7	3.6	7.3
Japan	21.2	25.1	20.2	17.8	20.7
Trade balances (as % of GDP):					
OECD Europe	–0.1	0.3	–0.5	0.4	0.0
US	0.7	0.1	–0.4	–2.0	–0.5
Japan	0.2	1.5	0.4	2.0	1.1

n/a Not available

Note: Figures for EC rather than OECD Europe do not differ significantly, except in the case of trade balances where the EC does marginally better.

Source: compiled from *OECD Historical Statistics 1960–1988*, 1990, Paris, OECD.

The investment relationships *between* the European OECD countries are shown for a more recent period in Table 2. The comparison here is between individual OECD countries which, as a whole, account for the vast bulk of direct foreign investment in the world. What is significant about this data is the continued dominance of the UK economy in terms of the proportion of OECD direct investment it either attracts or originates. The UK economy is a highly penetrated one as far as international investment flows are concerned. This makes the economy particularly vulnerable to the decisions of international investors, whether made at home or abroad. Within the rest of Europe, the Netherlands has also traditionally been heavily involved with international direct investment. Despite its size and importance, the West German economy was, in relative terms, less involved with international direct investment up to the middle of the 1980s, particularly as a destination for inward investment.

Table 2   Inward and outward European investment amongst the OECD countries, 1971 to 1989

Outward direct investment flows from selected European countries as a percentage of investment by the OECD countries

	1971–80	1981	1982	1983	1984	1985	1986	1989
France	4.6	9.3	13.2	6.6	5.5	3.7	5.3	18.1
West Germany	7.7	8.2	12.0	10.7	11.4	7.9	9.7	14.1
Italy	1.2	2.8	4.4	7.2	5.2	3.0	2.8	2.0
Netherlands	9.2	9.5	14.3	12.7	13.3	5.2	4.5	11.1
Switzerland	n/a	n/a	n/a	n/a	3.0	7.6	1.5	6.9
UK	18.0	24.2	30.1	27.5	21.1	18.7	17.9	35.3

International direct investment flows to selected European countries as a percentage of the inward investment received by the OECD countries

	1971–80	1981	1982	1983	1984	1985	1986	1989
France	9.0	5.9	5.2	5.2	6.2	6.2	5.8	9.5
West Germany	7.4	0.8	2.7	5.7	2.1	2.0	2.9	6.7
Italy	3.0	2.8	2.1	3.8	3.6	2.8	−0.4	2.5
Netherlands	5.8	4.3	3.8	4.5	4.9	3.2	4.4	6.3
Switzerland	n/a	n/a	n/a	0.9	1.5	3.0	3.0	1.9
UK	21.6	14.4	17.6	16.3	−0.7	16.0	16.8	28.7

Source: *International Direct Investment and the New Economic Environment*, 1989, Paris, OECD, Tables 15 and 16; and *Industrial Policy in OECD Countries: Annual Review 1991*, 1991, Paris, OECD, Tables 24 and 25.

The traditionally dominant post-war economy as far as direct investment is concerned has been the US. Its position *vis-à-vis* a number of other important OECD economies is shown in Table 3. Clearly, between 1971 and 1980, and 1981 and 1989, the US experienced a dramatic reversal in its fortunes. It turned from being the most important source of such funds to being a major recipient. The rise in the importance of Japan as a direct investor abroad is signalled by these data, as is the confirmation of the UK as a significant player, particularly in its remarkable position as a continued source of overseas investment. These data reinforce the comment made earlier about the UK economy being a highly internationally inter-dependent one on the investment front.

Table 3 Cumulative outward and inward direct investment flows as a percentage of total flows, 1971 to 1980 and 1981 to 1989

	1971–80	1981–89
Outward flows		
US	44.4	19.1
Japan	6.0	18.8
France	4.6	8.0
West Germany	7.7	8.6
UK	18.2	22.6
Inward flows		
US	30.0	53.8
Japan	0.8	0.3
France	9.0	6.0
West Germany	7.4	2.6
UK	21.6	15.6

Source: compiled from *OECD Historical Statistics 1960–1988*, 1990, Paris, OECD.

Returning to the question of the US, the data in Table 3 showed it becoming a major net importer of direct investment. From Table 4 it can be seen that Europe is the most important source of that investment in the US – accounting for nearly 66 per cent of the total in 1989. The most important single country source outside of Europe was Japan with 17.4 per cent. As we have already seen, Japan became a significant player in direct investment relationships during the 1970s.

Table 4 Stock of foreign investment in the US by country of origin (percentage of total), 1989

	1989		1989
Europe	65.5	Canada	7.9
France	4.1	Japan	17.4
West Germany	7.1	Latin America	5.1
Netherlands	15.1	Middle-East	1.6
UK	29.8	Rest of the world	2.7
Switzerland	4.8		

Source: *OECD Industrial Policy in OECD Countries: Annual Review 1991*, 1991, Paris, OECD, Table 26.

The overall position of Japan can be seen from Table 5. It confirms the dramatic entry of that country into the international investment environment, particularly as an investor abroad. While Europe is still a net recipient of Japanese investment, its relative importance as a cumulative investor in Japan has increased since 1975.

Table 5   Direct investment in and by Japan (US$ billion)

	1975	1980	1985	1986
Total Japanese outward investment	9.7	17.6	38.6	51.1
Japanese investment in US	2.5	5.3	12.2	n/a
Japanese investment in Europe	1.6	2.8	5.7	n/a
Total investment in Japan	1.5	3.0	6.4	7.4
US investment in Japan	0.9	1.6	2.7	n/a
European investment in Japan	0.3	0.9	1.2	n/a
Cumulative Investment in Japan (% of total):				
US	66	54	48	49
Europe	21	23	24	27
Others	19	23	28	24

n/a   Not available

Source: *International Direct Investment and the New Economic Environment*, 1989, Paris, OECD, compiled from Tables 12, 13, 14 and 15.

One of the implications of this statistical review is that the advanced industrial countries are becoming increasingly interdependent in terms of direct investment holdings. The data in Table 6 indicate the extent of this interdependence. As a percentage of national assets or wealth, foreign direct investment (FDI) was most significant in the UK, followed by the US, West Germany and, lastly, Japan. Clearly, however, in the late 1970s the proportion of national assets or wealth held by foreign investors was still quite small in all these countries. Even ten years later this situation is unlikely to have altered appreciably.

Table 6   Foreign direct investment, national assets and national wealth of the US, Japan, UK and the Federal Republic of Germany, late 1970s

Country	Stock of FDI	National assets	National wealth	Stock of FDI Percentage of national assets	Stock of FDI Percentage of national wealth
US, 1978 (billions of dollars)	146.0	17,887	9,104	0.82	1.60
Japan, 1977 (trillions of yen)	2.9	1,792	894	0.16	0.32
UK, 1977 (billions of pounds)	20.1	1,328	617	1.51	3.26
Federal Republic of Germany, 1977 (billions of Dm)	51.6	10,172	5,534	0.51	0.93

Source: 'The Process of Transnationalization and Transnational Mergers', *UNCTC Current Studies*, No. 8, Series A, February 1989, New York, United Nations, Table I.16, p. 22.

One obvious omission from the data presented so far has been the 'rest of the world'. But the main point to note here is that these other countries are relatively unimportant as either sources of direct investment or as destinations for it. In fact in the 1980s the less developed countries (LDCs) became a *less* important destination for investments from more developed countries (MDCs). There was a dramatic fall in total private resource flows to the developing countries in the period from 1980 to 1986, from US$66 billion to US$26 billion. But the decline in investment in the LDCs has not affected them all to the same degree. Direct investment tends to go to relatively few countries, only eighteen of them receiving 86 per cent of the total between 1980 and 1986. These are the ones with extensive factor endowments: well provided with natural resources, at the centre of vast regional or national markets, and in possession of a skilled and low-cost labour force. The period of particularly favourable growth trends in the LDCs themselves ended with the world recession of the early 1980s. This coincided with the rise of the 'Third World debt problem', which compounded the reluctance of the MDC firms to invest there. In addition, the MDCs have redirected much of their investment effort towards the newly industrializing countries (NICs), in which new liberal regimes for investment arose in the 1980s. Thus the Asian NICs (Hong Kong, Indonesia, Korea, Singapore, Taiwan, Thailand and the Philippines) increased their share of the total advanced country direct investment to LDCs from 21.5 per cent from 1967 to 1980 to 30 per cent from 1981 to 1986.

As well as direct investment – which, broadly speaking, encompasses investment for productive purposes – the international economy is characterized by large-scale capital and bank borrowing to finance balance of payments and public expenditures. This international borrowing is shown in Table 7. Note that in 1990, 90 per cent of total capital market borrowing was within the OECD area, with a similar percentage for just external medium-term bank loans.

Table 7   Borrowing on international capital markets, 1986 to 1990

Borrowing on international capital markets (in 1,000 millions of US dollars)

	1986	1987	1988	1989	1990
World total	388.1	392.9	453.5	466.5	425.3
Japan	47.1	55.2	61.0	107.0	60.9
UK	30.0	50.4	77.9	46.5	52.1
US	72.1	66.2	61.3	66.7	43.7
Italy	15.9	16.1	14.8	21.2	31.1
France	25.8	18.8	28.6	24.5	26.0
Canada	25.8	13.9	24.3	21.4	22.0
Australia	24.5	18.9	21.0	28.5	18.1
West Germany	15.1	11.9	13.6	15.6	15.1
Percentage of world total					
OECD area	90.9	89.1	91.2	91.4	89.1
Developing countries	5.0	6.7	5.0	4.6	5.4
Eastern Europe	1.0	0.9	1.0	1.0	1.1
Others	3.1	3.3	2.8	3.0	4.4

Table 7   Borrowing on international capital markets, 1986 to 1990 - continued

Medium-term external bank loans (in 1,000 millions of US dollars)

Borrowers	1987	1988	1989	1990
OECD area	66.8	103.8	99.8	98.3
LDCs	20.1	15.5	16.2	16.1
non-OPEC	17.9	14.2	11.9	10.2
OPEC	2.2	1.3	4.3	5.9
Eastern Europe	2.9	2.7	2.4	3.0
International development institutions	1.6	2.5	2.6	0.4
Others	0.3	1.0	0.1	0.4
Total	91.7	125.5	121.1	118.2

Source: *Atlantic Outlook: US Perspectives on the Global Economy*, No. 4, May 1991, p. 6.

So much for investment. We can now move on to look more closely at trade.

We can begin with the distribution of EC trade in a global context as shown in Table 8. This table compares the position in 1958 with that in 1990. The remarkable feature of these data is the overwhelming significance of 'western Europe' in world trade: it accounted for 73 per cent of exports and 70 per cent of imports in 1990. If the old, centrally planned economies are added to this total (the vast bulk of trade for this group being conducted by the European CPEs plus the USSR), then the importance of 'Europe' becomes even greater. The other big trading group is the LDCs, but their significance has declined over the period.

Table 8   The structure of EC trade by country and region, 1958 compared with 1990

	Exports (%)		Imports (%)	
	1958	1990	1958	1990
Intra-EC trade	37.2	61.0	35.2	58.8
Other European OECD countries	13.7	12.0	10.1	10.9
Total: 'western Europe'	50.9	73.0	45.3	69.7
Centrally planned economies	4.3	2.8	3.8	3.7
Total: 'western Europe' plus CPEs	55.2	75.8	49.1	73.4
US	7.9	7.1	11.4	7.6
Japan	0.6	2.1	0.7	4.1
LDCs	27.4	12.5	29.5	12.8
Rest of the world and unspecified	8.9	2.5	9.3	2.1
World total	100.0	100.0	100.0	100.0
(World total excluding EC)	62.8	36.9	64.8	40.5

Source: *European Economy: Annual Report 1991–92*, Brussels, Commission for the European Communities, calculated from Tables 44 and 45, p. 257.

Another major point to emerge from this table is that not only is western Europe the main contemporary player, but it was also the most significant in 1958. For all practical intents and purposes, 'international trade' can be considered as intra-advanced industrial country trade. The intra-EC trade alone accounted for 60 per cent of the world total in 1989. Interestingly, tracing this further back in time shows that, in the inter-war period, intra-European trade (defined as trade between Belgium, France, Germany, Italy, the Netherlands and the UK) was, even then, as much as 70 per cent of Europe's foreign trade, although it then declined immediately after the Second World War (Milward, 1985).

Concentrating on the eastern European economies for a moment, it has already been mentioned that these economies were not well integrated into the global economic mechanism in terms of trade, and not as well integrated as a group as the western European economies had been (see Drabek and Greenaway, 1984). As Table 9 demonstrates, in its comparison of 1970 with 1989, the proportion of the eastern European economies' intra-country trade had actually *declined*. Instead, they had increased their trade with the 'West' and with the 'Other' category. A similar result emerges if we look at just the Soviet Union's trade.

Table 9   Structure of the trade of Eastern Europe and the Soviet Union, 1970 compared with 1989

	Exports (%)		Imports (%)	
	1970	1989	1970	1989
Eastern Europe's trade with:				
ECE East[1]	63.7	50.6	63.2	49.9
ECE West[2]	26.7	37.8	28.8	39.1
Other	9.6	11.6	8.0	11.0
Total	100.0	100.0	100.0	100.0
Soviet Union's trade with:				
ECE East	52.8	46.5	56.5	48.8
ECE West	21.7	27.0	25.7	31.0
Other	25.5	26.5	17.7	20.2
Total	100.0	100.0	100.0	100.0
EE and SU trade with:				
ECE East	59.2	48.3	60.7	49.2
ECE West	24.6	31.6	27.6	34.3
Other	16.2	20.1	11.8	16.5
Total	100.0	100.0	100.0	100.0

Notes:

1 European Commission for Europe East: Bulgaria, Czechoslovakia, German Democratic Republic, Hungary, Poland and Romania.

2 European Commission for Europe West: western market economies plus Japan.

Source: *Economic Survey of Europe in 1989–90*, New York, United Nations, calculated from Appendix Tables C.4 and C.5, pp. 409 and 410.

Returning to the Western countries, the trends in trade flows here since the 1960s have been towards ever greater integration between the economics involved. As a proportion of GDP, trade increased from between 15 per cent and 25 per cent in 1960 to between 40 per cent and 55 per cent in 1990 for the main European economies. The average external trade for EC countries was just over 46 per cent in 1990. It was during the middle of the 1970s that the most significant boost to foreign trade occurred for these countries.

However, an important point to note, in contrast to the situation amongst the EC countries, has been the much lower and steadier level of trade penetration in the US and Japan. As a percentage of GDP this was only 10 per cent and 18 per cent for the US and Japan respectively in the 1960s, rising to a figure of 17 per cent for the US in 1990 and remaining much the same for Japan at 18 per cent (see Figure 4).

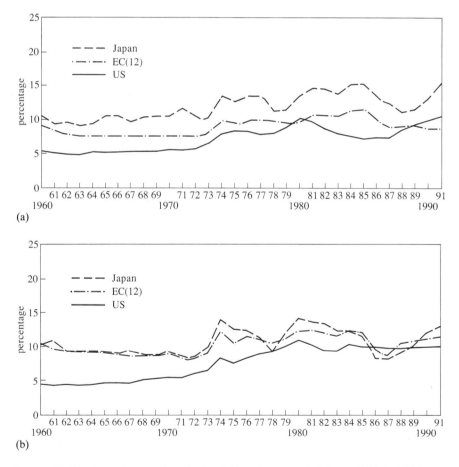

Figure 4   The importance of trade for different economic blocs, 1960 to 1990.
(a)   Exports of goods and services at current prices (as a percentage of GDP).
(b)   Imports of goods and services at current prices (as a percentage of GDP).
Source: *OECD Economic Outlook*, 1991, Paris, OECD.

Again, it was during the 1970s that trade penetration really hit the US economy, nearly doubling over the decade as a proportion of GDP.

Another important point to emerge from Figure 4, however, is the remarkable similarity in trade to GDP ratios if the three main economic blocs are considered together. Thus the extra-Community trade of the EC as a whole was 18.6 per cent in 1990, very close to the US and Japanese levels.

In a later section we shall return to the possible significance of this symmetry in the context of Europe's evolving place in the management of the emerging global economy.

In the context of that later discussion it will be useful at this stage to refer to Figure 5 which shows the trade balances of the major economies since the early 1980s. We have already drawn attention to this aspect of economic activity in Table 1. It is clear from Figure 5 that the US and, to a lesser extent, the UK have gone into a 'structural' deficit on their trade accounts, while Japan and West Germany remain in a 'structural' surplus. (France, Italy and Canada are close to a balance.) The question this poses is: For how long will this seeming 'structural' imbalance last and what have been, and continue to be, its consequences? As Figure 5 shows, the trends in recent years could be leading towards a righting of this imbalance.

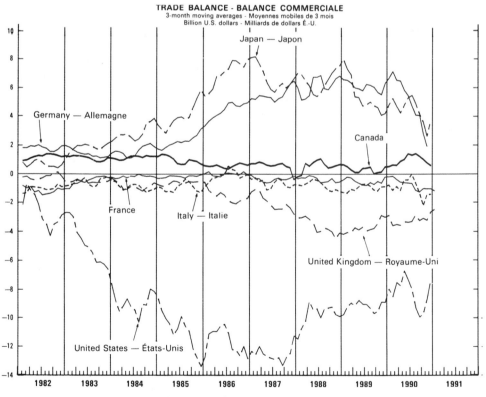

Figure 5   Foreign trade, seasonally adjusted.

Source: *OECD Main Economic Indicators*, April 1991, p. 24.

For the final set of comments in this section we shall refer to Tables 10 and 11. These tables show the 'consequences' of the kinds of general trends indicated by the statistical analysis conducted in this section. Table 10 reports the levels of investment income and non-factor services income of the three main contemporary international economic actors (with separate data for West Germany). The two main manufacturing trading nations, West Germany and Japan, show relatively high levels of investment income and low levels of service income, while the reverse is the case for the EC as a whole and for the US in particular. Thus, although it is often thought that the advanced industrial economies are becoming 'post-industrial' and increasingly reliant upon services to generate their income, this is not the case for *all* economies of this type. The 'bottom line' on economic activity, so to speak, is indicated in Table 11, which shows the European proportion of total world GDP. This was 40 per cent of the total in 1987, compared with 26 per cent for the US and 14 per cent for Japan. Thus just these three countries together accounted for a staggering 80 per cent of world GDP in 1987.

Table 10   Investment income and non-factor services income by country group (US$ billion), 1989

	Investment income	Non-factor services income
EC	−1.2	29.9
(West Germany)	11.8	−15.0
US	−0.9[1]	20.5
Japan	23.4	−39.0

Note:

1   US 1988, 1.6

Source: *Economic Outlook*, December 1990, Paris, OECD, derived from Tables 78 and 80.

Table 11   Europe's place in global GDP, 1987

	US$ millions, 1987	% of total	US$ *per capita* GDP	Multiple of world total *per capita* GDP
Total world GDP	17,265,070		3,434	1.0
Europe total	6,816,850	40.0	8,781	2.6
EEC	4,310,080	25.0	13,328	3.9
Eastern Europe	1,350,936	8.0	3,403	1.0
US	4,472,910	26.0	18,374	5.4
Japan	2,373,707	14.0	19,471	5.7
	Bangladesh		180	0.05
	Cambodia		81	0.02
	Zaire		61	0.02

Source: *UN Statistical Abstract of National Accounts*, 1990, New York, United Nations, derived from various tables.

In the second part of Table 11 these figures are converted into GDP totals *per capita*. Europe as a whole had 2.6 times the world average *per capita* GDP. For just the EC the figure was 3.9 times the average. (However, note the figures for the US and Japan!) As a comparison with these figures the table also reports the *per capita* GDP of three of the poorest countries on the globe. For Bangladesh, Cambodia and Zaire the average income *per capita* was, respectively, 0.05, 0.02 and 0.02 of the world average. This should remain with you as a sobering thought as this essay continues with a discussion of the role of the evolving Europe in the international economy.

The international economic order and Europe's place within it

We have seen in the previous section that Europe is increasingly playing a key role in the operation of the global economy. It could develop this central role further if the moves towards economic and monetary union of the member states of the EC accelerate in the 1990s. But to analyse the nature and consequences of these developments requires a step back from the immediate empirical reality of European economic interactions. In this section we shall try to focus on the more general nature of the trends and movements within the world economic order. We shall attempt this here as a prelude to a detailed discussion of the present position of the EC and its likely future trajectory in later sections.

When looking at the realm of international economic and political relations it is useful to think of the global order as having moved through a number of different phases or stages. In this section I shall concentrate upon *three* of these phases, which I shall call the *internationalized economy,* the *world-wide economy* and, finally, the *globalizing economy.*[3] As we shall see, each of these phases in the international economic order has displayed a specific set of characteristics which have different implications for the states of Europe. On the basis of these characteristics, and their combined and complex nature in the contemporary era, we shall be better able to think imaginatively about the present character of the European economic space and about the possibilities for its future evolution.

One final preliminary point is in order. The terms 'internationalized economy', 'world-wide economy' and 'globalizing economy' now begin to take on specific meanings which are different from the more general uses of these terms in the context of international economic relations, and different from the way they have been used until now in this essay. Thus we must define a particular set of concepts that can be deployed in the later analysis of 'Europe's place in the global economy'.

The early origins of 'international economic relations' can be traced to the emergence of what anthropologists have called 'long-distance trade' between the

---

[3] These terms are drawn from Thompson (1992).

societies of pre-history. This enduring system of exchange continues in many parts of the world even today, if in a modified form. Comprising mainly the exchange of luxury and utility goods that typify a craft-based production, this kind of trade represents the precursor of the more organized trade between genuine nation states that began in earnest in the fourteenth and fifteenth centuries, and centred on the expansion of European influence around the globe. The features of such a pre-fourteenth century *internationalized economy* thus involved occasional economic interactions, conducted on an essentially *bilateral* basis, between economies whose main business was still heavily orientated to the domestic sector. International activity involved only a very small section of the population and a fraction of its economic output. For these reasons the societies involved remained *highly autonomous* in their international economic relations.

Around the fourteenth century, however, a different stage in international economic relations began to emerge. This eventually matured into what might be termed a *world-wide economy*. Such an economy was typified by a series of more systematic international interactions between economies, with the emergence of a pattern of enduring trade and investment relations that focused attention at a world level. A division of labour between the different economies arose under these circumstances, some tending to produce raw materials and agricultural products, say, while others specialized in the production of manufactured goods. In addition, as such a system matured, financial relationships progressively displaced trading relationships from the centre stage of economic interactions, and sources of investment became the poles around which the system revolved.

What would particularly come to mark this idea of a world-wide economy was the gradual drawing together of an increasing number of countries into a set of enduring *multilateral* international economic relationships involving the division of labour at the world level, as described in a previous section. Under these circumstances a *systematic interdependence* between the different national economies and different types of economic agent arose, creating new problems of coordination.

This period of history also saw the development of what subsequently came to be known as the *multinational corporation* (MNC). Earlier versions of the MNC, straddling the transition period from the internationalized economic order to the world-wide economy, were the great European-based imperial trading partnerships and companies that have been described in other essays (see Essay 1). The distinctive feature of the MNCs, however, was that, while they operated in a number of different countries, they continued to have a clear 'home-base' to their operations and were centred in one particular country. The home-base country served as the organizing centre for the MNC's operations and they were normally required to meet the regulatory obligations set by the government of the home-base country.

Perhaps we can now discern a further stage in this evolution of international relations, typical of certain tendencies observed in the contemporary world. This might be termed the *globalizing economy* to indicate its difference from the world-wide economy just outlined. To some extent a globalizing economy implies the dissolution of the features of the world-wide economy at the same time as it transforms them.

If the world-wide economy is an economy typified by a *widening* of the range of countries and other agents involved in international economic relations, then the globalizing economy could be characterized as a *deepening* of these interactions. The globalizing economy represents a qualitative change rather than a quantitative one. Furthermore, the analytical focus shifts to the idea of the 'global economy' as an all-encompassing characteristic structure which exists 'independently of', or 'in addition to', the purely national economies. Thus the global economy would encompass an economy whose principles of operation might *supplant* those of national economies and undermine the division of labour into which they had fallen. We would then be dealing not just with a number of interacting individual national economies or economic agents – whose fundamental attachment was still towards their domestic environments, even though they were, at the same time, being drawn into a widening set of international economic interactions – but rather with a different entity altogether: the global economy. It is the global economy that increasingly defines and structures the individual economies that form it, not the other way around. With a world-wide economy we still have the national economies as dominant. With the globalizing economy it is the global economy itself that dominates the national economies existing within it. Once again, this poses a new set of problems for the continued regulation and coordination of economic activity.

The characteristic international economic organizational unit in this kind of an economy would no longer be the MNC of the world-wide economy but the *transnational corporation* (TNC). With this organizational form the home-base aspect tends to become significantly less important. A TNC represents the epitome of 'global capital': its base of operation would be the global arena rather than one

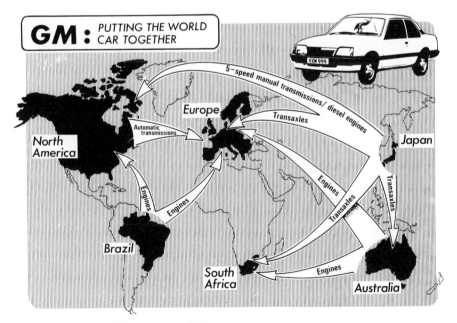

Figure 6   General Motors as a TNC?
Source: *Financial Times*, 26 August 1981.

particular country or even a small group of countries; it would probably source and manufacture in a wide variety of locations across the globe and have a global view of its market, without being committed to any single centre of operation. The developmental planning, manufacturing and marketing processes would form an integrated and interdependent whole in the global context. In addition, as a result of these features of its operation, it would escape easy regulation by a national authority. Thus instead of 'international relations' being typical of cross-border economic interaction, we would now be in an era of 'transnational relations', articulating an economy that no longer directly conforms to a national remit.

Each of these forms of international economy thus displays its own typical and characteristic combination of economic autonomy and interdependency. An important factor in the history of this development has been the increasing role of markets in breaking down the barriers to interdependency. A wide range of economic agents come into play here which cut across the divisions involved in nation to nation relationships. This creates the potential for tensions between the sovereignty of the nation state on the one hand and the activity of private economic agents, who need not respect that sovereignty, on the other. It is in this context that the moves towards new forms of economic cooperation and coordination between the countries within Europe can be productively assessed.

Drawing on the analysis in this section and the data presented in the previous one, we can sum up the idea of a 'globalizing economy' under the following four features:

1   The internationalization of financial markets, in particular the integration of trading on currency and equity markets.

2   The increasing volume of trade in manufactured goods, between the advanced industrial countries in particular – most markets for major industrial products are now international and the major economies both import and export significant volumes of such goods.

3   The development of transnational production organizations which operate in so many different countries that they cease to have a clear home base.

4   The formation of supra-national trading and economic blocs, something explicitly developed later in this essay.

So much for our definition of a globalizing economy. However, we should not think that the three stages previously outlined (the internationalized economy, the world-wide economy and the globalizing economy) are necessarily mutually exclusive. Just as we could think of the world-wide economy as *enfolding* that of the internationalized economy, without completely destroying it, so we might think of the globalizing economy as enfolding the world-wide economy in its turn. Thus the features of all three forms of international economy could continue to inform the analysis of contemporary international economic relations. We can find 'traces' of all three forms within the complex articulation of the contemporary global economy.

Indeed, it is just this complex combination that needs to be unravelled in the light of current European trends and their impact on the global economic order. The period since the Second World War can provide a highly productive illustrative history of the transitional features typifying the movement from the pre-war world-wide economy to the globalizing one of today, *or so it might seem*. Part of the analysis that follows will be an examination of just this proposition.

At the pinnacle of the world-wide economic order stood the Gold Standard (GS) regime of international economic regulation, with the City of London and the UK economy at its centre. *Pax Britannica*, in which European countries other than the UK played a subsidiary part, relied upon the 'automatic' operation of the GS to effect the necessary internal and external adjustments in the level of economic activity. Whether the *actual* GS operated in quite the automatic manner that economists like to think is another matter, but it did rely upon a hegemonic power that was able to police the system and impose sanctions on recalcitrant participants.

However, as the UK's waning hegemony began its rapid decline after the First World War, a period of inter-war instability set in in international economic relations, which was only resolved by the emergence of a new hegemonic power and *Pax Americana* after 1945. Box 1 details the differences between the Gold Standard of *Pax Britannica* and the post-war Bretton Woods system of *Pax Americana*. The box also details the post-1972 floating rate regime associated with the demise of America as a hegemonic power.

But this passage *within* the embedded structure of the world-wide economy, from one hegemonic power to another, is in danger of masking an important change in its character. The hegemonic stability in international economic relations organized by Britain via the pre-First World War GS regime was essentially a *unilateral* one. The UK acted very much in isolation from any other organized centre of power, and although it was forced to 'cooperate' with other countries in Europe (and beyond) at times to maintain the GS mechanism, it did this rather on its own terms and subject to its own dictates. The post-Second World War Bretton Woods system, by contrast, was a hegemonic one in which the US faced an alternative centre of organized power, and a situation that increasingly – and quite rapidly after its inception – placed the US in need of 'mutual cooperation' from those under its dominance, even in strict economic terms. The US was never in a position to act in a totally unilateral way as the UK had done. It was constrained by the existence of the Soviet Union on the one hand, and by the necessity to *organize* the support of the European nations on the other (rather than rely upon their passive acceptance of its action). Even in the negotiations to establish the Bretton Woods system the US was forced to compromise on its preferred position on a number of important matters (Gardner, 1956; Eichengreen, 1987; Thompson, 1990). The Bretton Woods regime (which, for the purposes of this exposition, includes the World Bank and the GATT system of trade negotiations) is thus better understood as a form of *multilateralism*; a kind of hegemonic multilateralism rather than the 'purer' form of hegemonic unilateralism experienced under the *Pax Britannica* period of the world-wide economy. The Bretton Woods system thus lived up to its name as a period of multilateral 'liberal' trade and other economic interactions, evolving within a system of (semi)-fixed exchange rates. The question is: What has happened to this system since the collapse of that (semi)-fixed exchange rate regime in the early 1970s? (See Figure 7.)

Box 1 International exchange rate mechanisms

The Gold Standard. Under this system all participating countries fix the price of their currencies, once and for all, in terms of gold. Thus there is no international adjustment in the value of their currencies. All the adjustments are in terms of domestic price movements. As and when a balance of payments problem arises, the country with a deficit must ensure that its domestic prices fall, and the country with a surplus must ensure that its domestic prices rise. In fact, with the assumption of a full flexible price system, the market will ensure that this adjustment takes place automatically, via movements in gold between countries and the domestic price adjustments based upon these movements. Thus there is no need for governments to intervene in the process of adjustment. However, in practice the GS did not work as implied by this abstract model. The problem was the assumption of domestic wage and price flexibility. This was hardly ever automatically secured. Rather it required domestic government policy (expenditure – reducing policies) to effect the flexibility and secure the necessary domestic adjustments.

The Bretton Woods system. This system can be described as a paper-dollar system as each participating country fixes the value of its (paper) currency in terms of the dollar. Only the dollar is designated in terms of a fixed value with respect to gold. The system involves an explicit rejection of the market determination of exchange rates, and of the process of (domestic) adjustments if balance of payment difficulties emerge. Governments intervene both to set their currency's value *vis-à-vis* the dollar in the first place, and to 'manage' their domestic price systems so as to produce desired internal adjustments. In addition, when an agreed 'structural disequilibrium balance of payments' was seen to emerge for any single country, it was allowed to refix its exchange rate *vis-à-vis* the dollar. (Thus, strictly speaking, the Bretton Woods system was a *semi-fixed* exchange rate regime rather than a truly fixed one.) Without the option of a revaluation, however, the normal process of adjustment took the form of managing internal demand and internal prices to effect the required restoration of the balance of payments on the current account, while various capital controls took care of the capital account.

The post-1972 floating rate period. Between 1972 and the early 1980s the major currencies floated against each other. Thus there was a combination of internal (domestic) and external (international) adjustments. In particular, a change in the exchange rate for a currency *vis-à-vis* all other currencies would effect a domestic adjustment. It would alter the domestic price regime inasmuch as the prices of internationally traded goods would be changed automatically under these circumstances. Given an open economy, that is, an economy with no formal capital-impeding or trade-impeding controls, any temporary balance of payments problems could be financed until the (international) price system operated (via changes in exchange rates) to force the desired domestic adjustment in inflation, bringing the domestic and the international price system into a new 'automatic' equilibrium.

The immediate aftermath of the collapse of the Bretton Woods exchange rate mechanism resulted in a short period of totally floating rates (see Figure 7 and Box 1). But in 1979 the European Monetary System (EMS) was established by the EC to provide a 'regime of stability' in exchange rates between the European member countries. (It originally operated without the participation of the UK, which decided not to join the exchange rate mechanism (ERM) in 1979. The UK joined in October 1990, but was

Exchange rates of major currencies against the dollar

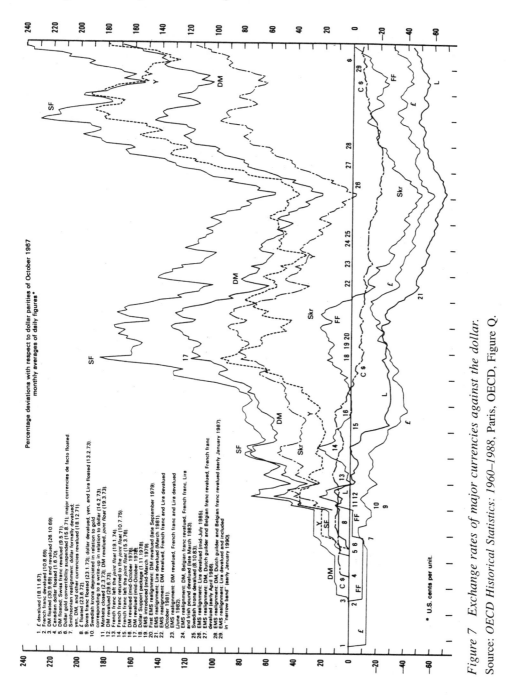

Figure 7   Exchange rates of major currencies against the dollar.

Source: *OECD Historical Statistics: 1960–1988,* Paris, OECD, Figure Q.

forced out two years later in the autumn of 1992.) A more general retreat from a totally free floating system emerged in the middle 1980s as the advanced industrialized countries of the G-10, G-7, and most importantly G-5, set up a series of regular meetings from which a new system of 'international economic coordination' developed, centred on exchange rate stabilization (Artis and Ostry, 1986; Funabashi, 1988). However, whilst a modified 'multilateralism' on exchange rate matters would still seem to be *just* in place via these mechanisms, the multilateral *trading* system came under increasing pressures in the 1980s, culminating in the faltering of the Uruguay Round of GATT negotiations in early 1991 and their subsequent half-hearted resolution in 1992.[4] Thus the post-war multilateral system of international economic relations under US leadership could be, at least in part, in serious decline, or will be so modified that it ceases to be an effective regulatory mechanism at all.

In its wake, we are not seeing so much the emergence of a totally globalized economy as the emergence of a newly *regionalizing world economy.* If a strict multilateralism, in its post-war sense, is dead (or perhaps still dying) then it is a regionalized *trilateralism* that could replace it. This trilateralism is made up of the US and its North American trading partners, the EC and its immediate associate and candidate members, and a trading and investment system based upon Japan and the NICs of the Pacific Rim. There are other small trading groups on the fringes of this system – the 'Cairns Group' of agricultural producers, for instance, and of course that heterogeneous group of Third World Countries (TWCs) that have tried so hard, but so far in vain, to establish a 'new international economic order'. But for all practical intents and purposes it is the 'Big Three' that dominate the world trading and investment system, and will continue to do so for the foreseeable future.

It is the formation of this 'triad power' system and its possible consequences, particularly for Europe, that I shall analyse in the rest of this essay. In the next section I shall look specifically at the European dimension, but to end this section the roles of the US and Japan will be integrated further into the analysis as they are indicative of the more general trends.

In the face of its relative loss of direct economic strength and the emergence of alternative centres of economic power, the US has been pursuing a *dual* strategy in international economic relations (Schott, 1989). On the one hand it has tried to re-assert its influence over the multilateral trading framework and rekindle some momentum for this by pressing for the Uruguay Round of GATT trade talks, which began in 1988. The US was instrumental in initiating these negotiations, in part to head off domestic pressure for outright protectionism. On the other hand, and at the same time, it has been conducting a series of *bilateral* trade negotiations with

---

[4]   These talks had on their agenda intellectual property rights, investment issues, and most controversial of all, agricultural trade. It was agricultural trade that was mainly responsible for stalling the talks in 1990. The US was pressing for the elimination of European agricultural subsidies (the dismantling of the Common Agricultural Policy) and open access to the Japanese domestic rice market. Neither the Europeans nor the Japanese were prepared to agree to these American demands. The talks were re-started in 1991 and an interim agreement finalized in 1992. At the time of writing, however, the final outcome remains uncertain.

favoured countries to secure free-trade deals to the advantage of the US. The most important of these deals are the ones signed with Canada in 1987 and the one being negotiated with Mexico in 1991–92 (Thompson, 1991).

These bilateral deals are designed as a kind of an 'insurance policy' should the remains of the post-war multilateral system completely break up under the pressures of triad power and the world retreat into a highly protectionist environment. Under these circumstances, the US would have secured a truly continental-wide free trade area in North America, at very little cost to itself and without all the difficulties of institution building that has beset the EC in its attempt to go beyond what the US has now achieved – which is essentially a large customs union. This dual strategy – multilateralism and bilateralism – may prove effective in bolstering the US position in the longer run, but that remains to be seen.

The position of Japan and the Pacific Rim countries, on the other hand, looks to be the more precarious one. To some extent the idea that they are forming a regional economic block with Japan as the dominant partner remains fanciful, though the degree of interpenetration between them is growing rapidly. However, this is far less advanced, and less part of a conscious policy, than with the US position just outlined, let alone that of the EC. Japan itself is pursuing a range of policies in an attempt to keep its options open. One of these is to diversify its highly domestically concentrated manufacturing base by investing in the US and EC. In this way it hopes to circumvent any direct protectionist discrimination against its goods within Europe and the US that could develop in the wake of the break up of American-led multilateralism. If this were to happen, and the EC and the US became more discriminatory and protectionist – which remains a real possibility – it would be the Japanese economy that would stand to lose the most. This is an economy highly dependent upon both the import of raw materials and energy products and the export of manufactures and semi-manufactures for its prosperity. If any of these were disrupted by a move towards overt protectionism on the part of inward-looking trading blocks, the Japanese economy could take a rapid and potentially catastrophic nose-dive into deep depression (with all the attendant risks of domestic instability and unrest that this would produce). The Japanese economy is thus the most vulnerable to widespread discrimination in trade matters because it is peculiarly dependent upon international trade for its prosperity (despite the fact that, in aggregate terms, it shows a no higher trade to GDP ratio than the EC or US – see Figure 4), and because it has little prospects of quickly finding other foreign markets or of switching to domestic markets.

It is against this emerging background that we can assess the particular position faced by the European nations. Where exactly does Europe fit into the newly evolving 'regionalized' global economy? What are the likely consequences of such a regionalized configuration on the 'governance' of the global order? Where does all this leave the idea of a globalizing economy as described in earlier sections? It is these questions that are addressed in the following final two main sections of this essay. I shall begin this assessment with a more detailed analysis of the evolving European order in the next section. The impact of the tendencies described in the essay more generally are taken up in the section after next.

The evolving European economic order

The development of the European political and economic order has traditionally been thought about as either the result of some 'grand design' on the part of a set of visionary political leaders, bureaucrats, key country groupings and so on, or as an evolving response to a series of essentially *ad hoc* and incremental problems that have produced particular, if often highly innovative, institutional developments. Has the 'dynamic' of European integration been a 'planned' one or a 'spontaneous' one? Has it been the subject of detailed advanced preparation with the long-term goal of a unitary state or federal Europe always in mind, or has it been the result of stumbling along with no particular destination in sight? (Wallace, 1990).

Although by now a rather tired debate, this characteristic way of posing the question of European integration helps capture one essential and important feature; it enables us to reintroduce an assessment of the relative strengths of the 'market mechanism' and the 'political calculations' of those involved in building a united Europe. This will take us back to a further discussion of, first, the ECSC in the 1950s and, then, the evolving EEC that was built upon it.

As we have seen, the European economies emerged from the Second World War in a battered state and were initially dependent upon the US for capital goods, financial assistance and markets. The productive potential of the economies was not completely devastated however. Perhaps surprisingly, significant amounts of private capital remained intact, it having been the social and economic infrastructure, often publicly owned, that suffered the most damage. The problem was to modernize and reconstruct the productive base that remained as quickly as possible. The question was: 'How could this be done?'

The immediate post-war period was one in which a number of reports and 'plans' were suggested for the future of Europe, plans associated with those now famous historical names of European integration: the Marshall Plan, the Schuman Plan, the Monnet Plan, the Tinbergen Report, and more besides.[5] A technicist ideology pervaded both the conduct of the war and its aftermath in terms of 'planning' for the future. Any problem was amenable to a rational and technical solution – even the evolution of social and economic relationships.

The Schuman Plan for a European Coal and Steel Community (ECSC) was one successful manifestation of this trend. Along with the Monnet Plan for the restructuring and modernization of the French economy, it captured the mood of the times.[6] To a large extent these twin plans developed in tandem and became the

[5]   See Milward (1984), Chapter XII for a discussion of all these reports and plans. In the early 1950s, they included the *Mayer Plan* (1952) for a European army, the *Beyer Plan* (1955) for economic unification, and the *Spaak Report* (1956) on a common European nuclear energy programme. Later versions of the same trend included the *Werner Report* (1970) on economic and monetary union, and the *Delors Report* (1989) on a similar theme.

[6]   A more Anglo-Saxon inflection of this trend is associated with the Keynesian policy programme of macro-economic demand management.

prototypes for the formation of the EEC in 1957. Tinbergen later added some intellectual refinement with his distinction between 'negative integration' and 'positive policy integration', referring respectively to the removal of barriers and obstacles to integration on the one hand, and the development of common new policies on the other (Tinbergen, 1954).

The ECSC, which was set up in April 1951 and became operational in July of the following year, was both an economic and a political organization. In this way it exactly prefigured most subsequent European institutional developments. On the economic front it was designed to promote free trade and a rationalization of the coal and steel sector, and so secure a regular supply of these vital materials for economic growth. On the political front it was designed to 'settle' the long-running dispute between France and West Germany over the territory of the Saar and the Ruhr and the natural resources located therein. It is probably difficult for us today to fully appreciate how important this issue was in the immediate aftermath of the war.

The important feature of the ECSC from the point of view of subsequent developments was that it established an executive High Authority to manage community relations – the first supranational unit in the post-war history of European integration, and one with its own budget. This became a prototype for the much more ambitious Commission for the European Communities set up in the context of the Treaty of Rome establishing the EEC in 1957.[7]

It was the exclusive sectoral focus of the ECSC that was partly responsible for its relative lack of success in achieving its immediate economic aims. The coal and steel industries could not be 'managed' independently from the rest of the European economy. The EEC was designed to remedy this defect by creating an organization with an economy-wide focus. The history of the EEC is well known and there is no need to recount it in detail here.[8] The EEC has always been more than a pure customs union, though this was its first and foremost function. The Treaty provided a framework for the formation of an evolving Community, and this is probably the best way of viewing its development. An important event in this history was the signing of the Single European Act in February 1986 (coming into force in July 1987). The Single European Act introduced some modifications to the Community's decision-making processes. In particular, it opened the way for (qualified) majority voting on certain matters where strict unanimity had

---

[7]   The Treaty of Rome established: (a) the Commission, which could formulate initiatives for European integration and monitor the way the objectives of the Treaty were being implemented; (b) the Council of Ministers which had final decision-making authority; (c) the Court of Justice which deals with legal issues associated with the Treaty and its implementation; and finally (d) the European Parliament which has remained advisory rather than legislative. This set of arrangements may be dramatically modified or completely revised as a result of the inter-governmental conference (IGC) on political union which completed its work in late 1991 and the subsequent Maastricht Treaty signed in February 1992.

[8]   For a good, recent British description of the EC and other European institutional arrangements, see Nicoll and Salmon (1990).

previously been required. This produced the possibility of novel country coalitions forming in the Council of Ministers. From the point of view of economic relations, the most important outcome of the Act was the move towards the Single Market in 1992.

The original 1957 treaty establishing the Community had signalled the emergence of a customs union in which all tariff barriers between the members would be eliminated and a common trade barrier regime erected around the Community as a whole. This was substantially realized by 1968. The Community then went on to form the European Monetary System (EMS) in 1979, which has worked to link the member currencies together (around the German Deutschmark) and reduce exchange rate fluctuations. It also provides a mechanism to cushion the Community currencies against the vagrancies of the wider international financial system – in particular, to provide stability *vis-à-vis* the US dollar.

The aim of the Single Market programme is to build on this stability by tackling *non-tariff* barriers to trade. However, this is essentially a *purgative* programme – a case of what Tinbergen called 'negative integration' (Tinbergen, 1954). The idea is to cleanse the system of its impurities – impurities being seen as anything that presents an obstacle to the full rigours of market operation. Thus the accompanying EC competition policy has as its main and overriding objective the removal of all the 'inefficiencies' in the operation of the European Economic Space (EES) so that the market can properly dispense its benign virtues 'automatically' and with as little regulation as possible. That, at least, is the declared, almost rhetorical, intention.

But, as in any economic situation, the building of a single market requires the establishment of a new institutional structure to manage those economic relations so fostered, and this remains the cause of some major disputes between the EC members as the drive towards economic and monetary union gathers momentum. It was the objective of the Maastricht Summit in December 1991 to consolidate this institution-building process by initiating definite moves towards closer political union. The outcome of this meeting remains ambiguous; the scepticism of the British and Danish voters and authorities in particular over further serious political union may have undermined the whole process and stalled its momentum.

One preliminary point to recall is that the EC is already very well integrated economically, as the statistics presented in the previous section testify. There is thus a question mark over whether there are many additional benefits to be gained from the Single Market programme, and whether those benefits are as extensive as suggested by the Commission.[9] Be that as it may, there are also some other significant developments that could interrupt the smooth transition to a fully integrated market within the EC. These concern the possibilities of membership expansion as the eastern European economics queue up for admission alongside the Scandinavian countries, Austria (and possibly Switzerland), and Turkey. Already the absorption of (East) Germany into the EC has had a significant effect on the (West) German economy – in 1991, it went into deficit on its trade account, confounding all the

---

[9]   The key Commission documents justifying the moves towards economic and monetary union are *European Economy* (1988) and *European Economy* (1990). For a critique of the former see Thompson (1991).

statistical evidence on the German economy contained in the previous section. In addition, inflationary worries re-emerged in the united Germany as the government's budget deficit soared in response to the social and economic readjustment costs associated with the transformation of the newly absorbed eastern part of the economy. It is unlikely that these costs will decline rapidly for a number of years, and they may even increase in the immediate future. The pivotal role the German economy occupies within the EC implies that these problems are likely to affect all the member countries in one way or another. We shall return to this below.

Mention of the role of the German economy within Europe prompts a further discussion of the political forces that have driven the moves towards greater integration since the Second World War. Chief amongst these must be Christian Democracy, a widespread European political movement (though one conspicuous by its absence in the UK), and one that has drawn its greatest strength from the West German Christian Democratic Union (CDU) Party. The CDU – in conjunction with the Christian Social Union (CSU) and, at times, in coalition with the German Liberal Party (FDP) – provided the crucial political impetus for what was initially seen very much as a western European integrative solution to the problems besetting the continent. In particular, its hostility to the Soviet Union and the Eastern Bloc focused the party's political attention on the integration of Germany into a strong economic and political mechanism founded on liberal market principles. But this did not take the form of the unregulated *laissez-faire* favoured by conservative forces in the UK. Rather it took the form of constructing a consensual and democratic distributive coalition around the notion of the social market economy. Similar consensual coalitions developed elsewhere, particularly in the Netherlands. (Christian Democracy is a strong political force in the Netherlands and also in Italy.)

In addition, the CDU continually outflanked the Social Democratic Party (the SPD) on foreign policy. The SPD initially took a more conciliatory and accommodating stance to the East (see Figure 8) and, when in office itself, tended to adopt the CDU's position on European integration. The most recent example of the CDU outflanking the SPD was during the tumultuous year of 1990, when it effectively reversed its position on the East, threw caution to the winds by whole-heartedly embracing the East Germans, and reaped the reward of a stunning all-German election victory under the leadership of Chancellor Kohl. The East was, as a result, fully *politically* absorbed into the EC very rapidly. Finally, it is Christian Democracy that has provided the key term under which much of the discussions of wider European political union proceeded within the IGC in 1991. 'Subsidiarity' – a concept with a range of interpretations, but defined as the principle that things should only be done at a higher level when they cannot be done at a lower one, and which looks destined to dominate the discussion of the form of any political institution building in the years to come – was first systematically enunciated by Pope Pius XI in his 1931 Encyclical Letter, *Quadragesimo Anno*.

If one looks for a parallel political movement in the other great integrationist power of Europe, France, it can probably be found in the form of 'Gaullism'. This mirrors in many ways the Christian Democratic tradition in terms of its emphasis on a European solution to Europe's problems. But the emphasis here is different.

Gaullism pressed more for an *exclusively* European focus, and was hostile to the US in particular and to those powers like the UK that stressed the virtues of an 'Atlanticist' alliance. The German Christian Democrats, by contrast, were never that hostile to the US presence in Europe nor to a continuation of close economic and political ties between the US and Europe. If the German Christian Democrats

Figure 8   German campaign poster. The poster reads: 'All Marxist roads lead to Moscow. For that reason, [vote] CDU.'

(Source: Bildarchiv Preussischer Kulturbesitz, Berlin.)

represent the pragmatic face of European integration, then the Gaullist tradition represents the more dogmatic face of the same movement. Both have shared similar objectives in Europe, though the French, in both their domestic and their external policies, have tended to support rather more programmatic schemes for European integration and domestic economic progress.

The final topic in this section concerns the issue raised earlier of the expansion of the European Economic Space. If the EC is to advance it will have both to *deepen* and to *widen* its institutional base. If it does not succeed in deepening its institutional base, the Community is in danger of slipping back into something approaching an elaborate customs union which will increasingly come under the dominance of the German economy. The EC could emerge as little different from the North American Free Trade area being constructed by the US in the early 1990s. This implies that it would not be in a position to provide the means by which new members could be equitably admitted into the Community, particularly those on its eastern flank. It could simply become an increasingly inward looking 'exclusive club'.

Of those countries queuing up to gain admittance, the likes of Sweden, Finland and Austria (with Norway to follow?) would present little problem in terms of ease of accommodation. They already have advanced economic status and their consensual political approach, with its semi-corporatist features, would only add to the existing decision-making structure in a positive manner. On the other hand, the countries of middle and eastern Europe present significant difficulties. They have neither the economic base nor the political traditions necessary to fit easily into the existing EC structures. Thus there needs to be some mechanism that could ease these countries into full membership without it undermining the existing EC framework, itself built up so carefully over the last 30 years.

Perhaps a new 'Marshall Plan' for eastern Europe would fit the bill? To create one would require a major political commitment on the part of the Community, and would be costly. It would have to be installed in an environment in which there was no perceived threat to the very existence of the contemporary European power structure, as there was in the late 1940s. In addition, the original Marshall Plan involved outright grants (not loans) to Europe of US$17 billion – comprising 3 per cent of US GDP in the late 1940s. In terms of today's money it is estimated this would amount to nearly US$100 billion (Economic Commission for Europe, 1990, p. 13 – rounded up to take account of differences in base Marshall Aid figures). The existing European Bank of Reconstruction and Development, created in 1991, had only approximately US$12.3 million paid in capital and was to operate on strictly commercial lines, with high returns expected from its investments in eastern European ventures. Also, as Table 12 confirms, the levels of contemporary government assistance are minimal compared to the original Marshall Aid.

What, then, might it take to propel the EC into a serious response to the need to create a 'ladder' for entry into the Community from the east? One possible condition could be a full-scale collapse of the ex-Soviet Union economies. If this happened, there would be little incentive for the newly established and unstable

Table 12 A comparison of official assistance from governments

	1978–80 average	1988	1989
1 Norway	0.90	1.13	1.04
2 Sweden	0.85	0.86	0.97
3 Denmark	0.72	0.89	0.94
3 Netherlands	0.90	0.98	0.94
5 France	0.60	0.72	0.78
10 West Germany	0.42	0.39	0.41
13 UK	0.43	0.32	0.31
16 US	0.24	0.21	0.15

Source: World Bank.

national entities created in the wake of the Soviet sphere to prevent a mass migration westwards, something the old Soviet authorities were keen to avoid. Indeed, there might be incentives for those new national authorities to encourage this migration. With any mass migration, the EC might have an incentive to establish a 'buffer zone' in eastern Europe, and this could be a spur to the granting of massive aid to those economies. Without assistance from the G7 or EC countries the prospects for the eastern economies look bleak.

Europe and the management of the global economy

Another issue for which the deepening of the European institutional mechanisms could prove to be crucial involves the management of the newly evolving regionalized–global economy, a point that has already been introduced briefly. In particular, it concerns the establishment of effective European-wide economic management mechanisms to carry through the programme of monetary and economic union. The form this union might take, and the institutions devised to foster it, were the subject of intense debate in the early 1990s. Of particular importance in this respect would be the characteristics of monetary union and the role of the European Central Bank.

Broadly speaking, two types of bank were being proposed in the early 1990s. For want of a better terminology these can be classified as a 'political' bank and an 'independent' bank. For the purposes of this exposition I shall slightly exaggerate the characteristics of each of these positions, and the differences between them, to try to bring out more clearly the nature of the debate.

The political bank was favoured by the French in particular, but also by certain elements in the UK position (which was rather hostile to the whole notion of monetary union, however). Such a political bank would act directly in the name of the countries of the EC. It would be directed, for instance, by a board made up of representatives of all the countries of the union and would be made politically accountable to those representatives or their governments. By contrast, the independent bank, which was favoured by the Germans in particular and which was modelled on the *Bundesbank*, would act quite independently of political pressure in the way it undertook monetary policy. Thus with this idea of a Central Bank there would be less direct political control and accountability.

The differences in these two conceptions were thought to result in different outcomes for inflation. Those arguing for the independent bank saw the control of inflation as the top priority. From this position the political bank option was thought to be more likely to be 'soft' on inflation, as the bank would yield to premature political pressures to reflate and so on. However, the argument from those supporting the political bank was that there were other, quite legitimate, objectives to which monetary policy should be sensitive, the levels of employment for instance, and an institution as important as a European Central Bank must be subject to political accountability in some way. Although nuanced in various ways, these points constituted the main contours of the debate about the form of the Central Bank in the early 1990s. The outcome of this debate, as it emerged at the Maastricht Summit in December 1991, was a compromise between the two conceptions, though from the draft statutes of the Central Bank embodied in the Treaty it looked as though the independence option had gained the upper hand.

Behind these manoeuvres on the nature of the Central Bank lay deep differences associated with the pace and character of wider monetary union. The Delors Report (Committee for the Study of Economic and Monetary Union, 1989) had suggested a three stage process for moving towards full monetary union. The first stage involved all the member countries joining the ERM and adhering to a narrow band of exchange rate variation. The second stage involved the gradual establishment of some kind of central banking mechanism and a movement towards closer financial and monetary cooperation by the individual national authorities. The third stage would involve the establishment of an irrevocably fixed system of exchange rates between the participant countries, the introduction of a single currency within the Community, monetary policy conducted by the central banking system (implying a single European interest rate, or spectrum of interest rates), and most probably the introduction of a highly coordinated, or even a single, fiscal policy as well. In effect this final stage would mean that individual governments would no longer have control over their monetary (or fiscal) policy. The Maastricht agreement set 1997 as the target date for the introduction of a Central Bank and monetary union – the UK could join later if it so wished.

In the light of this schedule – however long it might take to implement – the decision has to be made about the form of the single currency. A number of proposals have emerged and it has proved an area of bitter controversy. The disputes have centred on whether there should be one currency 'imposed' on Europe, or whether there should be 'competing curren*cies*', the final decision as to which one of these would become the dominant, or only, currency for Europe being left to the market and time to decide. All these proposals have invoked the European Currency Unit (ECU) as the currency option, but in a number of different versions:

1 *The official 'basket' ECU*, made up of a weighted average of all the Community currencies and subject to fluctuations in value on the basis of fluctuations in the values of its constituent currencies. The official ECU is one mainly used as a means of account between the member countries.

2 *The 'private' ECU*, used as a means of international finance by companies and governments. (The UK government even issued Treasury Bills denominated in ECUs – see Figure 9.)

3 *The 'hard' ECU*, originally proposed by the UK government to become a competing currency with other existing European currencies, the value of which could not be devalued because of the way the institution issuing hard ECUs – a European Monetary Fund (not a central bank) – was to be constrained to force the re-purchase of its backing currencies at a given stable rate against the ECU or some other non-devaluing currency.

4 *The 'harder' ECU*, the compromise currency emerging from the IGC on monetary union, proposed by Germany and Spain, which would eventually replace all other currencies but which, in the meantime, would be 'hardened' by being more closely linked to the DM. This final option seems the one most likely to be developed in the run-up to monetary union in 1997, if it actually takes place then.

The Maastricht Summit may mark a watershed in these negotiations. A rather complex compromise outcome emerged from the meeting. At best it might be seen as the emergence of a 'two-speed' (and possibly 'two-tiered') Europe, with the UK opting for non-participation in the immediate development of European Monetary Union (EMU) and the so called 'Social Europe' while the other eleven EC members (plus new entrants) proceed more speedily towards further economic and political integration.

The social dimension to future European integration proved a particularly difficult stumbling block to unanimous agreement at Maastricht. Eventually the UK completely opted out of this section of the Treaty. What are the implications of this?

In the first place, the UK authorities clearly see a different future for Europe from that envisaged by the other member states. In a period of traumatic economic dislocation the EC has become a very attractive destination for economic migrants. The provisions of the 'Social Europe' part of the Treaty try to put a floor under the EC labour market through the introduction of minimum guaranteed working conditions and minimum wages. Without these there is a strong possibility that the European economy will be tempted down the route of low wages, low productivity and low value-added production. Without a floor under the labour market, wages and working conditions are liable to be continually 'rendered down' in the name of increased competitiveness, particularly as lower-skilled migrants enter from the east and south. This was something that the UK authorities deliberately urged, as they had already followed a similar policy on the domestic front. The other members of the Community see the future in terms of high productivity and high value-added production – which implies a high-wage economy.

TENDER NOTICE

UK GOVERNMENT ECU TREASURY BILLS

For tender on 14 May 1991

1. The Bank of England announces the issue by Her Majesty's Treasury of ECU 1,000 million nominal of UK Government ECU Treasury Bills, for tender on a bid-yield basis on Tuesday, 14 May 1991. An additional ECU 50 million nominal of Bills will be allotted directly to the Bank of England.

2. The ECU 1,000 million of Bills to be issued by tender will be dated 16 May 1991 and will be in the following maturities:

ECU 300 million for maturity on 13 June 1991
ECU 300 million for maturity on 15 August 1991*
ECU 400 million for maturity on 14 November 1991

3. All tenders must be made on the printed application forms available on request from the Bank of England.Completed application forms must be lodged, by hand, at the Bank of England, Securities Office, Threadneedle Street, London not later than 10.30 a.m., London time, on Tuesday, 14 May 1991. Payment for Bills allotted will be due on Thursday, 16 May 1991.

4. Each tender at each yield for each maturity must be made on a separate application form for a minimum of ECU 500,000 nominal. Tenders above this minimum must be in multiples of ECU 100,000 nominal.

5. Tenders must be made on a yield basis (calculated on the basis of the actual number of days to maturity and a year of 360 days) rounded to two decimal places. Each application form must state the maturity date of the Bills for which application is made, the yield bid and the amount tendered for.

6. Notification will be despatched on the day of the tender to applicants whose tenders have been accepted in whole or in part. For applicants who have requested credit of Bills in global form to their account with Euro-clear or CEDEL, Bills will be credited in the relevant systems against payment. For applicants who have requested definitive Bills, Bills will be available for collection at the Securities Office of the Bank of England after 1.30 p.m. on Thursday, 16 May 1991 provided cleared funds have been credited to the Bank of England's ECU Treasury Bills Account No. 59005516 with Lloyds Bank Plc, International Banking Division, PO Box 19, Hays Lane House, 1 Hays Lane, London SE1 2HA. Definitive Bills will be available in amounts of ECU 10,000, ECU 50,000, ECU 100,000, ECU 500,000, ECU 1,000,000, ECU 5,000,000 and ECU 10,000,000 nominal.

7. Her Majesty's Treasury reserve the right to reject any or part of any tender.

8. The arrangements for the tender are set out in more detail in the Information Memorandum on the UK Government ECU Treasury Bill programme issued by the Bank of England on behalf of Her Majesty's Treasury on 28 March 1989, and in supplements to the Information Memorandum. All tenders will be subject to the provisions of that Information Memorandum (as supplemented).

9. The ECU 50 million of Bills to be allotted directly to the Bank of England will be for maturity on 14 November 1991. These Bills may be made available through sale and repurchase transactions to the market makers listed in the Information Memorandum (as supplemented) in order to facilitate settlement.

10. Copies of the Information Memorandum (and supplements to it) may be obtained at the Bank of England. UK Government ECU Treasury Bills are issued under the Treasury Bills Act 1877, the National Loans Act 1968 and the Treasury Bills Regulations 1968 as amended.

* Participants are reminded that the 15 August Bill will be repaid at par on 16 August 1991, in accordance with the provisions of the Information Memorandum, since 15 August 1991 is an ECU non-clearing day (Assumption Day).

Bank of England
7 May 1991

Figure 9 Tender notice – UK Government ECU Treasury Bills.
Source: *Financial Times*, 7 May 1991.

But a possibly more important consequence of the fracturing of the unity of the EC at the Maastricht Summit, and in the period of its immediate aftermath, was that further serious European political unity could be stifled in the longer run. A clear political momentum had been built up behind further political integration before the summit, and this could have been dissipated and dissolved by its outcome and subsequent events. In the absence of any political integration to 'govern' and regulate the Common Market, a neo-liberal, *laissez-faire* outcome seems more likely in the long run, with all its attendant inequalities and uncertainties.

What these events have probably hastened, if they prove to have no other long-term effects, is a real move towards a 'two-tiered' Europe. The inner core of Germany, France, Benelux and Holland (possibly along with Denmark, Austria and Switzerland) could more easily move to monetary union around the DM, while the rest tagged along very much behind in a rag-bag, second-tier formation. However, this rather pessimistic scenario for political integration is not clear cut. It is too early yet to judge the final outcome.

A partial break-up of the ERM? The events of September 1992

Many of the post-Maastricht tensions to which I have already alluded became manifest from the middle of 1992. First, the Danish electorate voted by a narrow margin against the Treaty on 2 June 1992; then the Irish voted for the Treaty. This was followed by a very narrow vote in favour of the Treaty by the French in their referendum of 20 September 1992. In the run up to these political events acute stresses appeared in the money and capital markets. In early September 1992 the weakest currency aligned to the DM, the Italian lira, came under fire and was devalued by 7 per cent within the ERM. This failed to ease the pressures, however, and attention switched to sterling. On Wednesday 16 September 1992, after massive intervention to try to prop up the pound, UK interests rates were raised by 5 per cent (to 15 per cent), and the pound then floated free of the ERM, along with the lira. Subsequently, on the same day, UK interest rates were brought down to their previous level (10 per cent) and, the next day, reduced by a further 1 per cent. A month later the pound had been devalued by nearly 15 per cent against its previous DM central rate. After the French referendum a speculative attack against the French franc developed but was beaten off with the sustained assistance of the German *Bundesbank*.

The British government was the loudest in its complaints. It condemned the ERM mechanism in general and the *Bundesbank* and 'speculators' in particular. But this condemnation presumed that its long-term economic strategy at the time was both correct and viable. The difficulty with this argument arises over the original 1990 valuation of the pound within the ERM mechanism. The British government insisted that its currency was not over-valued and thus not vulnerable in relation to the 'fundamentals' of the economy. But most commentators, including the German authorities, recognized that the conditions for the maintenance of the then exchange rate at DM2.95 to the pound were just not there if any sustained pressure were tobe mounted against sterling. The British joined the ERM in October

1990 at what officials involved then recognized as a very ambitious rate. It did not consult with its partners on either the timing of its entry or the rate at which it should enter, presenting them with a *fait accompli* by letting them know only an hour before what it intended to do. The government failed to look to the conditions in the real economy where the most serious recession since the 1930s had taken hold and where the balance of trade continued to deteriorate. The government failed to raise enough taxes to keeps its budget deficit within acceptable bounds, and it failed to raise interest rates at the appropriate time. For all these reasons the *Bundesbank* was reluctant to support the pound indefinitely and unconditionally when the pressure mounted.

The *Bundesbank* clearly acted differently in the case of the French franc. But there were good reasons for this. It was a genuinely speculative attack from the start. The 'fundamentals' of the French economy were basically sound at the time: it had lower inflation than Germany and similar interest rate levels and, although in recession, was not in such deep, long-term difficulties as the British economy. The French had also displayed a 'co-operative' attitude towards Europe in general and the ERM in particular. If the franc had been devalued, or forced out of the ERM altogether, the Germans realized that the Maastricht Treaty was truly dead.

The three blocs considered

It is still worth considering how a post-1992 Single European economy might be managed. The core states, whatever their composition, could eventually inherit a single market, with a single economic policy-making body, managing a single currency, the ECU. How would an economic entity like this one fit into the overall global framework? To answer this we need to return to the idea of a tripartite world order, the most likely outcome from the present trends in global economic developments.

Clearly the most important issue to initially emerge in this situation would be the management of the ECU exchange rate.[10] The creation of a single European economic space (EES) would introduce a new major player into the global currency markets. Given that this new player represented an attractive and stable currency base, the likelihood would be for an increase in the demand for ECU-denominated assets. This particularly would be the case if, at the same time, the US and Japan were seen to be weakened by these developments. Other things being equal, this would force up the ECU exchange rate. What is more, this might be happening at just the time there was added interest in making real direct investment in Europe to take advantage of developments associated with the single market. This would also add to the demand for ECU notes.

Two consequences could follow from this (likely) scenario. In the first place, Europe would become uncompetitive because of its over-valued exchange rate.

---

[10]   Some of the issues discussed in the following sections are broached in *European Economy* (1990).

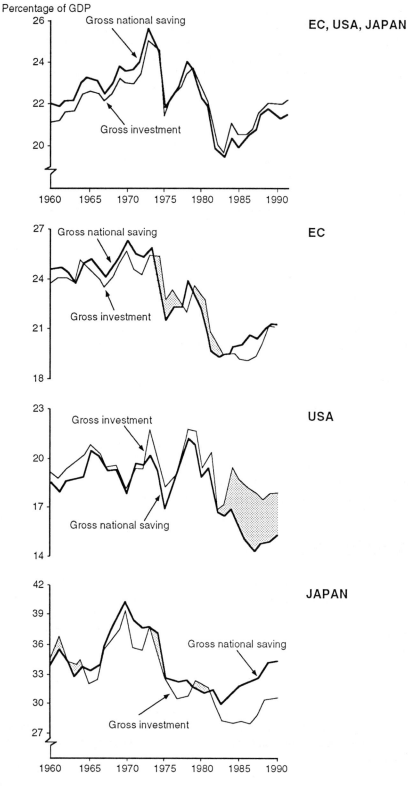

Figure 10 Evolution of saving and investment rates in the EC, US and Japan, 1960 to 1990.

Source: derived from European Commission Services and OECD Financial Accounts.

This could have detrimental implications in the long term for its economic health (remember the parallel US position after the war). Secondly, the increased demand for the ECU could produce domestic (European) inflation as the money supply expanded to accommodate the increase in ECU demand. If the ECU interest rate were raised to try to control this situation, the European economy could be further disadvantaged. These are the kinds of issues that could initially confront the new managers of the EES.

But what about the general possibilities of coordinating economic activity between the big three blocs: Europe, the US/North America and Japan? Here we can refer to some of the data contained in the previous sections, and to Figure 10, which shows the financial balances between the big three. I used this figure for the purposes of illustration only, since the actual situation in the late 1990s is unlikely to match this exactly, but it indicates the possibilities in the run up to full economic union.

What is striking about this figure is the symmetry between the three blocs. While the EC is in rough balance between savings and investment, the imbalance between savings and investment in the US is more or less completely offset by the reverse balance in Japan. What is more, it has already been pointed out that the trade to GDP ratios of the three were also rather similar (Figure 4). Perhaps, then, these underlying symmetries might make the coordination and management of the global economy *easier* if Europe itself were to coordinate further during the 1990s. With the European economy emerging as a single managed entity in relation to the US and Japan, and the symmetries outlined above in place, there is an added incentive to coordinate between the three parties themselves. They are caught in a relationship from which it would be dangerous for any party to withdraw unilaterally. In addition, gaining agreement between just three players is likely to be easier than between the existing G5 or G7 players.

Thus the final point in this section is to indicate that 'trilateralism' could produce better results than either G5/G7 'multilateralism' has, or (a protectionist) 'unilateralism' would, in terms of international economic policy coordination. The move to EMU could help secure this beneficial result.

Conclusions

It would be difficult to discuss the place of Europe in the global economy without, first, elaborating the nature of the global economy of which Europe is a part. Thus one of the objectives of this essay has been to see how we can understand the changing nature of the international economy and Europe's relationship to it. It has been argued that the period since the beginning of this century has seen a movement from a *world-wide economy* of individual nations existing and operating in much their own right to one characterized as a *globalizing economy*. Here the interdependencies between the national economies have increased to such an extent that a new entity seems to be evolving – a truly global economy – which increasingly operates independently of the individual national economies and serves to limit and, possibly ultimately, control those economies.

Against this backdrop of the evolving international economy, I have focused on the particular place occupied by Europe. It was the difficulty of providing a consistent definition of '*the* European economy' that first organized the discussion. The founding and evolution of those mechanisms of European integration arising since the Second World War served to provide a way of posing the issue of a truly European economy around institutional developments on the one hand and market-driven interactions involving trade and investment on the other. Whilst at the beginning of our period there existed a clear alternative centre of political, military and economic power, organized around the Soviet Union, this had totally collapsed by 1990 and the Soviet Union itself a year later.

These momentous events have, at the time of preparing this essay, had no clear impact on exactly what course the newly-constituted European economic space will take in the future. Indeed, they are combined with an internal debate within the European Community and its immediate candidate members as to the future course of political and economic union that is potentially almost as momentous as the events taking place to the east. Europe is in the middle of one of those historic periods of transformation that few could have envisaged even in the mid-1980s.

But whilst great uncertainties remain with respect to the immediate future, let alone the long-term future, certain trends from the past look likely to continue in one form or another. It is these trends that we have focused upon and analysed in this essay. For the foreseeable future it will be the German economy that is likely to dominate in Europe, even an extended Europe. In addition, there is unlikely to be an interruption in the growth of interdependencies between either the national economies of Europe or between Europe itself and other centres of economic power. Within this complex structure, Europe as a whole looks set to play an increasingly important role. Whether Europe is politically equipped to play the role marked out for it in terms of its economic integration remains another uncertainty. But towards the end of this essay it was suggested that there is at least a possibility that managing the global economy could become easier if European economic and political integration occurs.

Appendix 1: Glossary of abbreviations

CAP	Common Agricultural Policy
CDU	Christian Democratic Union
CMEA	Council of Mutual Economic Aid
COE	Council of Europe
Comecon	See CMEA
CPEs	centrally planned economies
CSU	Christian Social Union
ECSC	European Coal and Steel Community
ECU	European Currency Unit
EEA	European Economic Area
EEC/EC	European Economic Community/European Community
EES	'European economic space'
EFTA	European Free Trade Area
EMS	European Monetary System
EPU	European Payments Union
ERM	Exchange Rate Mechanism
EU	European Union
FDI	Foreign direct investment
FDP	German Liberal Party
G5	group of five most important economies
G7	group of seven most important economies
G10	group of ten most important economies
GATT	General Agreement on Tariffs and Trade
GDP	gross domestic product
GS	the Gold Standard
IG	inter-governmental conference
LDCs	less developed countries
MDCs	more developed countries
MNC	multinational corporation
NICs	newly industrializing countries
OECD	Organization of Economic Cooperation and Development

OEEC	Organization of European Economic Cooperation
SPD	German Social Democratic Party
TRIMS	Trade-related investment measures
TNC	transnational corporation
TWC	Third-World country
UK	United Kingdom
US	United States of America
USSR	Union of Soviet Socialist Republics
WEU	Western Europe Union

Appendix 2: *World economic groupings*

OECD + EC		G5 + G7		OPEC	Former CMEA	EFTA
Belgium	Australia	US	Italy	Algeria	Bulgaria	Austria
Denmark	Austria	Japan	Canada	Ecuador	Cuba	Finland
France	Canada	Germany		Gabon	Czechoslovakia	Iceland
Germany	Finland	France		Indonesia	East Germany	Norway
Greece	Iceland	UK		Iran	Hungary	Sweden
Ireland	Japan			Iraq	Mongolia	Switzerland
Italy	New Zealand			Kuwait	Poland	
Luxembourg	Norway			Libya	Romania	
Netherlands	Sweden			Nigeria	USSR	
Portugal	Switzerland			Qatar	Vietnam	
Spain	Turkey			Saudi Arabia		
UK	US			United Arab Emirates		
				Venezuela		

References

ARTIS, M. and OSTRY, S. (1986) *International Policy Coordination*, Chatham House Papers no. 30, London, Royal Institute for International Affairs.

COMMITTEE FOR THE STUDY OF ECONOMIC AND MONETARY UNION (1989) *Report on Economic and Monetary Union in the European Community*, Luxembourg, Office for Official Publications of the European Communities.

DRABEK, Z. and GREENAWAY, D. (1984) 'Economic integration and intra-industry trade: the EEC and CMEA compared', *Kyklos*, **37**, pp. 444–69.

ECONOMIC COMMISSION FOR EUROPE (1990) *Economic Survey of Europe in 1989–1990*, New York, United Nations.

EICHENGREEN, G. (1987) 'Hegemonic stability theories of the International Monetary System', Discussion Paper No. 193, July, London, Centre for Economic Policy Research.

EUROPEAN ECONOMY (1988) *The Economics of 1992*, No. 35, March.

EUROPEAN ECONOMY (1990) *One Market, One Money*, No. 44, October.

FUNABASHI, Y. (1988) *Managing the Dollar: from the Plaza to Louvre*, Washington DC, Institute for International Economics.

GARDNER, R. N. (1956) *Sterling-Dollar Diplomacy in Current Perspective*, New York, Columbia University Press.

HOGAN, M. J. (1989) *The Marshall Plan*, Cambridge, CUP.

MATTHEWS, R. C. O. (1968) 'Why has Britain had full employment since the War?', *Economic Journal*, **78**, pp. 556–69.

MILWARD, A. S. (1984) *The Reconstruction of Western Europe 1945–1950*, London, Methuen.

NICOLL, W. and SALMON, T. C. (1990) *Understanding the European Communities*, London, Phillip Allen.

SCHOTT, J. J. (1989) 'More Free Trade Areas?', *Policy Analyses in International Economics*, No. 27, Washington DC, Institute for International Economics.

THOMPSON, G. F. (1990) 'Monetary policy and international finance', in HINDESS, B. (ed.) *Reactions to the Right*, Routledge, London.

THOMPSON, G. F. (1991) 'The role of economies of scale in justifying free trade; the US–Canada Free Trade Agreement and Europe 1992 Programme compared', *International Review of Applied Economics*, **5** (1), pp. 47–76.

THOMPSON, G. F. (1992) 'Economic autonomy and the Advanced Industrial State' in LEWIS, P. and MCGREW, A. (eds) *Globalization and the Modern Nation State*, Cambridge, Polity Press.

TINBERGEN, J. (1954) *International Economic Integration*, Amsterdam, North Holland.

WALLACE, W. (1990) *The Transformation of Western Europe*, London, Pinter and the Royal Institute for International Affairs.

Postscript, April 1994

When this volume of essays went to press in early 1993, there was considerable uncertainty – reflected in the Introduction – about the direction of development in the European Community and in Europe's trading relations with the rest of the world: the Maastricht Treaty on European Union had not then been ratified, and the Uruguay Round of the GATT negotiations was in deadlock over EC agricultural exports to the USA and American 'cultural' imports into Europe. Uncertainty was also evident in relations with the states of eastern and south-eastern Europe due to the inability of the EC to formulate a common policy towards the escalating civil war in the former Yugoslavia, and the deepening political crisis in Russia. The completion in October 1993 of the ratification of the Maastricht Treaty has, in a legalistic sense at least, resolved the uncertainty about the European Union. The treaty formally entered into effect on 1 November 1993, though fundamental doubts remain about the Union's future course. Similarly, the successful conclusion of the Uruguay Round of the GATT talks has dispelled forebodings about a wave of retaliatory protectionism in the world's trading blocs and a collapse of world trade. We cannot, unfortunately, be so sanguine about international relations between the western and eastern parts of Europe, principally because there seems little or no prospect of a general cessation of hostilities in the Balkans where NATO air strikes have failed to curb Bosnian Serb aggression against the designated 'safe haven' of Gorazde and the use of air power has led to a deterioration of relations between Russia and the western Allies. Russia's own on-going domestic political crisis has interacted with the Balkans' conflagration because the Serb cause has been championed by the extreme nationalists led by Vladimir Zhirinovsky. Though President Boris Yeltsin has indicated a desire to co-operate with the West in settling the Balkans' crisis, his ability to contain the nationalist right is one of those imponderable questions which make European international relations exceptionally unsettled and unpredictable. It seems fair to add that the EU states' commitment to a common foreign policy under the Maastricht Treaty has not disguised major internal differences on how to resolve the Balkan crisis. So, in contrast to the confidence expressed around 1989 that a 'new Europe' would emerge from the convergence of democratic revolution in the east and economic integration in the west, uncertainty about the continent's future handicaps contemporary analysis.

Grahame Thompson writes: The points made in Essay 4 *Europe in the global economy* with respect to the enlargement of the European Union (see Figure 3, page 167) are pertinent to current debates about the nature of the Union. Figure 3 relates to the 'fateful' decision on whether to *widen* the Union and/or to *deepen* it. Broadly speaking, the 'wideners' have seen this as an anti-federalist strategy – expanding the Union would keep its political deepening in check, while the 'deepeners' have seen the necessity of underpinning the economic development and integration of the EU with appropriate political institutions adequate to 'govern' the emerging European economy. At present the 'wideners' seem to be in the ascendancy. First, on 17 March 1993 six EFTA countries (excluding Switzerland) and the 12 EC countries signed a protocol to the agreement establishing a free trade zone, the European Economic Area (EEA) – Switzerland has observer status and Liechtenstein will be applying to join after it has renegotiated its bilateral trade agreement with Switzerland. Secondly, four of the five EFTA countries (Austria, Finland, Norway and Sweden, but not Iceland) are involved in negotiations for full EU membership, with a target date of accession in January 1995). However, these negotiations gave rise to a characteristic dispute within the Union, involving its decision-making procedures after any enlargement; the issue of the 'blocking minority' of votes in the Council of Ministers. An interesting point about this was the attitude of the UK government (and to a lesser extent of Spain, which wished to protect its agricultural interests and was more pragmatic on the general issue of EU political integration). The UK was the strongest advocate of enlargement, though it was instrumental in delaying the advent of the agreement by insisting on preserving its 'blocking' position in the Council of Ministers' decision-making structure. Thus the UK government looked at these matters in a negative light – how could it hold up or prevent things happening – rather than in the positive light that pervaded the original formation of the Community – how can the governments advance their *common* interests. The ambivalent attitude of the UK towards the Community/Union lives on.

The UK still remains formally committed to further enlargement, however, as part of its particular 'view' of the Europe of the future. This view perceives Europe mainly as an enlarged 'free-trade' area (rather like that being constructed by the USA in North America) with few common economic governance mechanisms, and certainly no formal political institutions of a state-like nature for Europe as a whole. But any enlargement to include the eastern European states would, under present conditions, generate enormous *economic* problems, not least for those countries themselves. Their economies remain internationally highly uncompetitive, a situation likely to continue for another decade or two at least. Therefore, subjecting them to the same competitive conditions as prevail in and between the existing EU countries could undermine their economic transformation even more rapidly and thoroughly.

This is not to suggest that the plight of these countries should be ignored, however, but it is to suggest that a different approach to their situation is called for. The only way to secure the proper and feasible economic (let alone political) conditions for their successful entry to the EU is paradoxically for there to be a political deepening of the EU first, it might be argued. Such a political deepening would ensure the economic capacity of the Union to provide proper support and resources for a successful restructuring of the eastern economies. The economic fate of the existing EU is thus crucially dependent upon what happens on its borders to the east. Broadly speaking, while the existing EU countries have 'excess economic capacity' (20 million unemployed, underutilized capital equipment, no robust sustainable economic upturn in sight, etc.) the eastern economies have 'excess demands' (the need for an expansion of their consumption possibilities and an enhancement of their living standards). The problem is to marry these two – for the west to provide the credit so that the east can buy from it. Both parts of

Europe could thus gain from such a policy (it could be a positive-sum game). There is a strong argument, then, that the economic future for Europe as a whole is vitally dependent upon the character of the developing relationship between its western and eastern parts.

This relationship needs to be set in the context of a wider evolving global economic order of which Europe is a part. One thing looks certain: there will be no global 'meltdown' of the multilateral trading and investment system for the foreseeable future. On this issue, the analysis of the relationship of 'mutual dependence' between the three main economic blocks, as expounded in Essay 4, still stands. What is clear, however, is that the central axis around which that evolving relationship is structured is changing. Broadly speaking, the post-war internationalisation of economic relationships was driven by the dramatic increase in world trade – which expanded at a much faster rate than did world output. But since the early 1980s, this expansion of world trade has been eclipsed by the expansion of foreign direct investment (FDI). It is the expansion of FDI that is now driving the global economy, as marketing, sourcing and production internationally integrate as never before. It was this transition that partly stalled the Uruguay Round of the GATT talks. The GATT mechanism was successfully developed to 'govern' the expansion of trade. But the Uruguay Round attached to these trade talks issues involving specific investment relationships ('trade' in services, which involves investment since few services can be internationally traded; trade-related investment measures (TRIMs); and trade-related intellectual property rights, crucially involving the outputs from research and development investment expenditure). The fact that this Round was finally completed indicates the still strong commitment to the idea of an open, multilateral international trading and investment regime. However, it stores up problems for the future in that the basic problem of investment rather than trade now driving international integration has not been properly posed let alone solved. Perhaps the GATT mechanism has come to an end as the main institutionalized arena for negotiations about the governance of international economic relationships (in fact the GATT is to be replaced by the World Trade Organization), but the point remains.

Seventy-five percent of FDI is conducted between just the three main economic blocs: North America, Japan and the EEA. These blocs also account for a similar percentage of world trade, although they only contain 14% of the world population. There are thus enormous inequalities in the distribution of international economic activity and the international distribution of income. In fact the distribution of income has become more unequal since 1970 rather than less. Quite how long such an inequitable position can be sustained is debatable, particularly as the global order continues to 'integrate' even further and more transparently. And here is the nub. The global economic order, just like the European one, is poised between strong centrifugal and strong centripetal forces. Which will dominate, only time will tell.

Paul Lewis writes: Developments in Russia during the second half of 1993 and the first months of 1994 proved to be no less dramatic than those of the preceding years. They provided ample evidence that no solution to the fundamental questions of the direction of change in post-communist Russia had yet been reached and that major issues effecting Russia's relationship with Europe remained largely unresolved. President Boris Yeltsin's victory in the referendum of April 1993 secured him a new mandate to proceed with the reform process. However this gave him only a brief respite and a limited period of freedom from the pressures of political opposition, popular dissatisfaction with consequences of socio-economic change and the continuing dismantling of the Soviet system. Yeltsin's call for new parliamentary elections to sustain the reform movement and enhance its effectiveness indeed provided the grounds for intensified opposition from opponents associated with pro-communist and nationalist forces. These components now saw that their opportunity to block reforms and work at undermining the president's position was likely to be short-lived. The opposition grew significantly stronger as Vice-President Aleksandr Rutskoi joined forces with Ruslan Khasbulatov, chairman of the Supreme Soviet (or parliament), to press the anti-reform case. The question of who would succeed Yeltsin as Russian president was also clearly at issue and liable to rapidly move up the agenda if reports of Yeltsin's health problems proved correct or if a presidential election was called to accompany those for the parliament. The situation grew tense when on 21 September, the president issued a decree dissolving the Supreme Soviet in anticipation of December elections and provided for a three-month period of presidential rule before they would be held. The measure was promptly rejected by the Supreme Soviet itself, which proceeded to vote Yeltsin out of office and install Rutskoi as acting president in his place. While Yeltsin backed the reform process and was broadly associated with the democracy movement, it was nevertheless the case that his action violated an article of the Russian Constitution which denied him the use of power to dissolve 'legally elected bodies of state power'.

The question at issue was not only one of forces committed to democracy opposing those blocking it, but also concerned the nature of the democratic process and the institutional form it might take – whether, essentially, it should primarily take a presidential or parliamentary form. This issue was closely linked with the thorny question of Russia's federal structure and the relationship of the centre to the 89 constituent parts of the Federation. A further consideration was the degree of economic and administrative decentralization that was needed to sustain the relatively free play of economic forces and help create an effective market economy. A set of complex and extremely difficult problems was therefore involved and no immediate solution was likely to be identified, when a significant portion of the Supreme Soviet dug its heels in and refused to leave the parliament building. On 3 October Yeltsin imposed a state of emergency and, after Rutskoi had retaliated by encouraging armed demonstrators to attack the Mayor of Moscow's office and the television centre, proceeded to give the orders for parliament to be bombarded into submission. It is thought that as many as 200 people were killed in the hostilities. Yeltsin thus survived the confrontation but incurred a significant debt to the army and appeared more vulnerable in political terms.

The results of the December parliamentary elections were also something of a shock. Although the democratic, pro-reform Russia's Choice party had been identified as the likely victor, it trailed behind the so-called Liberal Democratic Party of Russia of ultra-nationalist Vladimir Zhirinovsky in the first results to be released (those relating to party-list votes rather than those cast in single-member constituencies). Russia's Choice, however, emerged as the largest party when the combined results were announced, but anti-reform forces nevertheless held dominance in the State *Duma* (as the new parliament was now called). The reformist orientation of the Russian government was also diluted by the resignations of Russia's Choice leader Yegor Gaidar and finance minister Boris Fedorov.

The move away from the market emphasis in economic policy and the problematic development of Russian political democracy was accompanied by or, more accurately, followed by a changing orientation in Russia's foreign policy and its attitude to the West. During a visit to the United States in August 1993 Prime Minister Viktor Chernomyrdin stressed that Russia was more in need of access to western markets than of its aid, and drew attention to Russia's desire to be recognized once more as a world power. In January 1994 he dismissed a number of western economic advisers and stated that Russia was no longer prepared to apply a purely western model of economic development. The new approach in foreign policy had other dimensions. One of the first decisions taken by the new State *Duma* was to pass a motion condemning western pressure on Serbia during the current Balkan crisis. This was soon followed by Russia's diplomatic *coup* in securing Serbian compliance with UN/NATO demands concerning the lifting of the siege of Sarajevo. But this also assured Russia a major part in the emerging possibility of a solution to the Bosnian crisis and thus, once more, securing a significant role in the Balkans as a traditional locus of Russian interest.

All this underscored a major shift in the emerging foreign policy of the new Russia. Two major tendencies could be detected in this field following the collapse of the Soviet Union, although these strains can be traced far back into pre-Soviet Russian history. They may be distinguished as the liberal and national-patriotic approaches, also readily identifiable with conflicts between Atlanticist and Eurasian conceptions of Russia's role. The liberal view was clearly dominant in the first post-communist year 1992 and it was characterized as being profoundly internationalist and democratic, even being described as a 'romantic period of foreign policy until it was overwhelmed by western indifference and Eurasian conflicts' (Sakwa, 1993, p. 300). For a variety of reasons, attitudes in this area changed during 1993. Russia's weakened international position, its worsening economic situation and the hesitant process of democratization encouraged a resurgence of conservatism and elements of pan-Slavism (the doctrine of the common fate and interests of Slavic peoples), which recalled political currents that had developed in the nineteenth century.

This change in attitudes, however, also had more immediate causes. The rapid diminution in Soviet international power and loss of global reach soon encouraged a sharper focus on Russia's relations with her European neighbours. Yeltsin's first international visits after being elected chairman of the Russian Supreme Soviet were to Strasbourg and Paris in April 1991, where he suggested that Russia could play a unique bridging role between Europe and Asia. In the European parliament he also affirmed Russia's commitment to a full return to the sphere of European civilization. But the United States nevertheless remained a major, if not the primary, focus of international attention in terms of its role in financial exchanges and overwhelming pre-eminence in the sphere of nuclear weapons. In some ways, then, the reinforcement of Russian–European relations was little more than a stepping stone to a reconsolidation of the relationship with the major western power.

The evident failure of European institutions to devise a solution to the worsening Yugoslav crisis and the growing involvement of NATO in working out some practical response to the problems in the region was a further inducement for Russia to direct more attention to the former superpower adversary. The appearance of formally independent post-Soviet states like the Ukraine and Belarus also created a new 'eastern Europe' that served to separate Russia not only from direct contact with former Soviet client states but even more from the established states of western Europe. Several different factors therefore entered into the rapidly changing domestic and international status of contemporary (early 1994) Russia.

An interesting contrast can be drawn between Yeltsin's 1991 view of Russia as a potential bridge between Europe and Asia and that expressed by Foreign Minister Andrei Kozyrev in early 1993 concerning the proposal to incorporate former Soviet client states in eastern Europe into NATO: in this respect, he suggested, it was they who should be left as bridges linking the east and west of the continent (and thus should remain outside NATO). The critical gulf that needed to be bridged, it appeared, was again moving westward and relations between Europe and Russia were by no means as unproblematic as had appeared at the demise of Soviet communism.

Acknowledgements

Grateful acknowledgement is made to the following sources for permission to reproduce material in this book:

Essay 1: Figure: (p. 65) OECD (1965) *Review*, Organization for Economic Cooperation and Development.

Essay 2: Map: 'The expansion of Muscovy': Grey, I. (1973) *Ivan III and the Unification of Russia*, courtesy of Penguin Books.

Essay 4: Figures: Figure 3: PSI (1991) *Britain in 2010: the PSI Report 1991*, Policy Studies Institute; Figure 5: OECD (1991) *Main Economic Indicators*, Organization for Economic Cooperation and Development; Figure 6: GM: 'Putting the world car together', *Financial Times*, 26 August 1981; Figure 7: OECD (1990) *Historical Statistics 1960–1988*; Organization for Economic Cooperation and Development; Figure 9: 'Tender notice for UK Government ECU treasury bills', 7 May 1991, courtesy of the Bank of England.

Tables: Tables 1, 3: adapted from OECD (1990) *Historical Statistics 1960–1988*, Organization for Economic Cooperation and Development; Tables 2, 5: adapted from OECD (1989) *International Direct Investment and the New Economic Environment*, Organization for Economic Cooperation and Development; Table 4: OECD (1991) *OECD Industrial Policy in OECD countries: Annual Review 1991*, Organization for Economic Cooperation and Development; Table 7: *Atlantic Outlook: US Perspectives on the Global Economy*, No. 4, May 1991.

The work of the Humanities Programme Committee of the EADTU has been carried out with the support of the Commission of the European Community within the frameworks of the ERASMUS Programme and the Jean Monnet Project.

Notes on contributors

Bernard Waites

Bernard Waites has worked for The Open University since 1972 and contributed widely to courses on British and European history, as well as the history of science and technology and popular culture. His doctoral dissertation on the effects of the First World War on English class structure was published as *A Class Society at War* (1987) and he is currently working on a study of Europe and the Third World.

Paul Lewis

Paul Lewis took a first degree in Russian studies at the University of Birmingham and studied for his Ph.D. in Poznan, Warsaw and Birmingham. He is a senior lecturer in government at The Open University and has worked on a variety of social science and interdisciplinary courses, including *Soviet Politics, Global Politics* and *Understanding Modern Societies*. He has studied various aspects of east European and communist politics and is currently completing a history entitled *Central Europe since 1945*.

Alan Sharp

Alan Sharp (born 1943) is a senior lecturer in history at the University of Ulster, Coleraine. He teaches European and international history and has published various articles and *The Versailles Settlement: peacemaking in Paris 1919* (1991).

Ken Ward

Ken Ward (born 1943) studied history at the University of Durham and is senior lecturer in history at the University of Ulster, Coleraine. He teaches modern and contemporary international and European history, popular culture and courses on the development of the mass media. In this field he has published *Mass Communication and the Modern World* (1989).

Grahame Thompson

Grahame Thompson (born 1945) studied economics at the Universities of Leicester and Birmingham. He is currently a senior lecturer in economics at The Open University. His latest books are *The Political Economy of the New Right* (1990 and 1993), *Markets, Hierarchies and Networks* (ed.) (1992), and *The Economic Emergence of a New Europe? The Political Economy of Cooperation and Competition in the 1990s* (1993). He is currently preparing a book entitled *Globalization in Question*.

Index to Book 4